Local Governance in England and France

Local Governance in England and France addresses issues at the cutting edge of comparative politics and public policy. The book is based on extensive research and interviews – over 300 in total – with local decision-makers in two pairs of cities in England and France: Leeds and Lille; Southampton and Rennes. This book will be an invaluable resource for students and professionals alike.

Local Governance in England and France provides a rigorous checklist of institutional and policy reforms in two countries since the early 1980s. Throughout, it demonstrates how comparable, but not identical, trends have restructured the different systems of local government in each country. The authors contend that there has been a transformation in traditional local governance in Britain and France, which has been particularly marked since the 1980s: old systems of policy-making have changed; new actors participate in local decision-making; accountability mechanisms have been contested and fresh challenges have emerged.

Key questions are posed about the changing role of the state, about the difficulties of policy co-ordination in a fragmented institutional context, and about the relationship between governance, networks, and political and democratic accountability. This book will be of great interest to the professional research community, and practitioners in Britain, France and beyond, as well as to students of comparative politics, European public policy, British/French politics, European studies, public management and local government studies.

Alistair Cole is Professorial Research Fellow at Cardiff University. His many publications include *Franco-German Relations, French Politics and Society* and *François Mitterrand: A Study in Political Leadership*. **Peter John** is Anniversary Reader in Politics, Birkbeck College, University of London. He chaired the Political Studies Association Research Sub-Committee, 1999–2000, and has worked with the Economic and Social Research Council as an adviser. He is the author of *Analysing Public Policy*.

Routledge studies in governance and public policy

Local Governance in England and France

Alistair Cole and Peter John

Routledge
Taylor & Francis Group

LONDON AND NEW YORK

First published 2001
by Routledge
2 Park Square, Milton Park,
Abingdon, Oxon, OX14 4RN

Simultaneously published in the USA and Canada
by Routledge
270 Madison Ave, New York NY 10016

Routledge is an imprint of the Taylor and Francis Group

Transferred to Digital Printing 2005

© 2001 Alistair Cole and Peter John

Typeset in Baskerville by
The Running Head Limited, Cambridge

British Library Cataloguing in Publication Data
A catalogue record for this book is available from the British Library

Library of Congress Cataloging in Publication Data
Cole, Alistair, 1959–
    Local governance in England and France/Alistair Cole and Peter John.
    p. cm.
    Includes bibliographical references and index.
    1. Local government—England. 2. Local government—France. 3. Leeds
(England)—Politics and government. 4. Lille (France)—Politics and government. 5.
Southampton (England)—Politics and government. 6. Rennes (France)—Politics and
government. I. John, Peter, 1960– II. Title.

JS3111.C56 2001
320.8′0942—dc21   00–068998

ISBN 0–415–23942–7

Contents

Preface

Local Governance in England and France is the final output of a long-running comparative research project which started life with the title 'Local policy networks and intergovernmental co-ordination in Britain and France', financed as part of UK Economic and Social Research Council's local governance programme (grant L311253047). We thank the ESRC for its support and the programme director, Gerry Stoker, for his encouragement at all stages. Alistair Cole is also grateful to the Leverhulme foundation (grant Rf+G/10711) and to the Nuffield foundation (grant SGS/LB/0278) for subsequent grants to investigate related projects. The support of these funding agencies was absolutely critical; this type of empirical work can only be undertaken with the support of the research councils and charities. We thank them.

At the core of the book lie over 300 semi-structured, face-to-face interviews with decision-makers in two pairs of cities in England and France: Leeds and Lille, Southampton and Rennes. The interviewees are far too numerous to list here but we thank each and everyone of them. Most of the interviews (303) were carried out in 1994–6, with some follow-ups (15) in 1999–2000. They lasted about one hour and we taped and transcribed them. We retained a copy of each interview for our reference as we guaranteed interviewees their anonymity.

We would like to thank all of the institutions and individuals that co-operated in the project. In England, we are indebted to individuals in the following organisations: Leeds, Southampton, Eastleigh, Fareham, Hampshire and New Forest Councils; Leeds, Southampton and Fareham Chambers of Commerce and Industry; numerous private companies and partnerships in Leeds, Southampton and Hampshire; Hampshire and Leeds Training and Enterprise Councils; the Transport and General Workers' Union; Leeds and Southampton universities; schools in Leeds and Hampshire; the Government Office for Yorkshire and Humberside; and the Government Office for the South East.

In the case of the French fieldwork, we would like to thank the following organisations which granted interviews and were very generous with their time: Academic Inspectorate, Nord Department; Academic Inspectorate, Ille-et-Vilaine Department; Academy of Lille (Rectorate); Academy of Rennes (Rectorate); Agency for the Promotion of Lille Metropole (APIM); Bonduelle, SA; Bréquigny school, Rennes; Brittany Building Federation; Brittany Economic and Social

Council; Brittany Economic Cell (CEB); Brittany Regional Council; Brittany Regional Prefecture; Catholic Teaching Federation, Ille-et-Vilaine (DDEC); Chateaubriand school, Rennes; Communes of Acigné, Cesson-Sevigné, Fâches-Thumesnil, la Chapelle des Fougeretz, Lambersart, Lille, Rennes, Roubaix, Saint Grégoire, St Jacques, Tourcoing, Wasquehal and Wavrin; CREAT'IV; Crédit Agricole; Education Ministry, Paris; Maison des Professions, Lille; Euralille mixed economy society; Eurasanté; Fénélon school, Lille; French Democratic Labour Confederation (CFDT); French Society of Financial Analysts (SFAF); Lille General Labour Confederation (CGT); Hautes-Ourmes school, Rennes; ID 35; Ille-et-Vilaine Departmental Council; Ille-et-Vilaine Employers' Union (UPIV); Ille-et-Vilaine Prefecture; Industry ministry (DRIRE), Douai, Rennes; Lille-Roubaix-Tourcoing Chamber of Commerce; Lille Place Financière; Lille Urban Community; Lille Metropole Urban Development Agency (ADUML); National Parents' Federation (FCPE); Nord Prefecture; Nord Departmental Council; Nord/Pas-de-Calais Développement; Nord/Pas-de-Calais Regional Council; Nord/Pas-de-Calais Regional Prefecture; Office of Edmond Hervé, mayor of Rennes; Office of Pierre Mauroy, mayor of Lille; Ouest Standard Télématiques, Rennes; Ouest-Atlantique, Rennes; Pasteur school, Lille; Regional Development society (SDR), Brittany; Regional Development Society (SDR), Nord/Pas-de-Calais; Regional Economic and Social Committee, Lille; Rennes Chamber of Commerce; Rennes Urban Development Agency (AUDIAR); Rennes Urban District; Rennes-Atalante; Research and Technology ministry (DRRT), Rennes; Secondary School Teachers' Union (SNES), Lille; SEMAEB, Rennes; Senate; Society of French stock markets (SBF, Lille); Unified Trade Union Association (FSU). We also extend our warm thanks to the Centre for Administrative and Political Research in Rennes and the Centre for Administrative, Political and Social Research in Lille; the collaboration of these two French partners was central to the success of the project.

There are many individuals to whom we owe a debt of gratitude in both countries. In England, we thank Michael Goldsmith, Dilys Hill, John Stewart and David Wilson for their encouragement and ideas; we are grateful to Mike Campbell and Adam Tickell for their introductions to Leeds; we thank Alan Whitehead for sharing his invaluable knowledge of Southampton, as well as opening many doors for us, and we express our gratitude to the numerous interviewees who took time to answer carefully our questions. In France, we extend our thanks to Michèle Breuillard, Jacques Coillet, Joseph Fontaine, Patrick Le Galès, Gérard Marcou, Erik Neveu, Bernard Toulemonde, Jean-Louis Thiebault and Antoine Vion, as well as the officials, politicians, businesspeople, educational and civil society actors who gave up their precious time for interviews.

Local governance in England and France is a comparative study. Throughout the book, we demonstrate how comparable (but not identical) trends have restructured the different systems of local government in each country. Old systems of making policy have changed. New actors participate in local decision-making and the roles of familiar decision-makers have been transformed. Established routines of making policy have been disrupted. Fresh challenges have emerged.

Accountability mechanisms have been contested. We investigate different aspects of these changes from a comparative angle in each of the chapters.

After setting out the theoretical debates concerning the new local governance (chapter 1), the book compares changing patterns of governance across the three dimensions of country, policy sector and city. In our country comparison chapters (2 and 3), we demonstrate how similar (but not identical) internal and external pressures have reshaped central–local relations and patterns of local public management in England and France. Our policy sector chapters (4 and 5) focus the analysis more sharply on two contrasting issue-areas in public policy: economic development and education. While economic development highlights many features of the new governance in England and France (partnerships, new forms of contractual relationship and the problems of policy co-ordination), the education systems of both countries resisted attempts at externally driven change for a long time. Through our detailed investigation, we find the emergence of new ideas, actors and structures in education in England and (to a lesser extent) France.

The local context is our third unit of analysis, along with national institutions and policy sectors. Chapters 6 and 7 investigate how these changes have been experienced on the ground through detailed case studies of local policy management in Leeds, Southampton, Lille and Rennes. Chapter 8 draws together the various strands and themes running throughout *Local Governance in England and France*. We conclude that there is no 'one-size fits all' description of governance; it is influenced by national contexts, policy sectors and local environments. While local governance can imply an opening up of politics, it also raises serious problems of political accountability that policy-makers in England and France must address.

1 The age of governance

The subject of this book is local governance. While traditional local government took place in a set of well-defined local political and administrative institutions, governance occurs in a more fragmented organisational context and incorporates a wider group of decision-makers than hitherto. Wider policy networks, stronger public–private partnerships, more complex policy problems, a move away from hierarchical patterns of public sector organisation and Europeanised public policy-making characterise the new governance. We claim that such a pattern now describes local politics and decision-making in both England and France, the countries we study in this book. Both systems have lost some of their hierarchical and closed character and have moved towards a more flexible and networked pattern of politics.

The reasons for changes in the pattern of governing localities include the pressures of greater economic competition, both national and international; the transfer of policies across nations; the rapidity of changes in ideas and economies; the growing incentives for central governments to improve the delivery of public services; reforms of the institutions of local government; and the profound changes in political behaviour that have occurred within localities. These changes are cross-national in the sense that they affect local administration and politics across economically advanced democracies, including England and France. Our research maps how rapid institutional, economic and policy changes have reshaped local political systems. We argue that local and central government decision-makers have had to cope with greater problems of co-ordinating policy. Traditional methods of municipal management, such as political clientelism and tight party control, have become less effective in the new governing environment. Contemporary political leaders must build broad networks of new and old decision-makers; they must respond to the challenges of economic restructuring; and they need to adapt to the varied initiatives that come from national governments and the European Union.

At the same time as there are cross-national trends, much depends on the contexts in which they take place. Though we observe much that is similar in England and France, the two countries have very different starting points – and this influences how policy networks form and what implications we draw for democratic practice. Moreover, the practice of policy-making varies according to the task at hand; in this book we consider the contrasting examples of economic development and secondary education. Most of all, each locality has its own political culture and tradition that affects the practice of politics and mediates whatever national or cross-national influences take place. While cities and localities are changing, they approach the new politics in manners consistent with their own political traditions.

We return to these themes at various points during the book. This first chapter sets the scene. We first review traditional perceptions of local government in England and France and consider whether the approach of governance is useful in understanding changing patterns of local policy-making in the two countries. We investigate the forces behind the emergence of governance and give a working definition of the concept. We address the issue of the effectiveness of public decisions and discuss the dilemmas of political accountability and leadership that arise from our empirical investigation. The chapter finally sets out the comparative method underpinning the study, which is based upon the relative importance of political institutions, policy sectors and cities.

Local government in England and France: a most different comparison?

There is a long tradition of Anglo-French comparison. England and France are shaped by highly distinctive historical and institutional legacies. Whether defined in terms of legal frameworks (common versus Roman law), state traditions (the dual polity against the indivisible Republic) or political culture (representative versus directive democracy), England and France have represented contrasting liberal democratic poles. They have traditionally both been 'exporting' nations. Each has cultivated its political model and has been reluctant to accept innovations coming from elsewhere, especially from its cross-channel neighbour. Throughout the nineteenth century there was open political competition between the institutional models of English parliamentary sovereignty and French republicanism. There is also an older tradition of exchange and emulation; in the eighteenth-century Enlightenment, Montesquieu and Voltaire looked to England as the model of a limited and balanced parliamentary regime.

In certain respects, the Anglo-French case is an exemplar of the most different comparison (Przeworski and Teune 1982; Dogan and Kazancigil 1997). Not only do Anglo-French contrasts stand out as a theme of academic commentary in the last three decades; the two countries form part of a more general framework for comparing sub-central governments across Europe. Differences in institutions, legal frameworks and political cultures underpin the comparison of English and French local politics (Lagroye and Wright 1979; Ashford 1982). Writers such as Page (1991) and Sharpe (1993), while applying the necessary qualifications and recognising the diversity of nation-states, contrast local government systems across Europe. They distinguish countries with Napoleonic traditions like France, Spain and Italy, with their strong states and weak local governments, from the functionally stronger local governments in states like Sweden and England (Page and

Goldsmith 1987; Page 1991; Sharpe 1993). On the other hand, the 'most different' properties of the Anglo-French comparison are balanced by countervailing forces. The United Kingdom and France have generally been considered as unitary (or 'union') states with coherent doctrines of undivided political sovereignty that break with the federal political tradition. They are countries of comparable economic and demographic importance with strong senses of their respective historical legacies and distinctive French and English traditions.

In the sphere of sub-national politics and administration, however, distinctive French and English state traditions bestowed varying levels of discretion upon local governments (Wunder 1995). While local government was functionally stronger in the English case than in the Napoleonic French model, it was less well linked into central government networks. In England, the corollary of local autonomy was a separation between the spheres of local and central administration. This was well captured in Bulpitt's metaphor of the 'dual polity' (see chapter 2) where politicians in the UK centre and the periphery co-existed in two separate policy spheres, at least up until the 1960s (Bulpitt 1983). In the French case, the counterpart to weak and divided local authorities was a pattern of strong peripheral linkage to central government. The practice of multiple office-holding (*cumul des mandats*) lay at the core of this system. In order to defend the interests of their localities in the central decisions over the distribution of resources, ambitious politicians accumulated several local offices (such as mayor or president of a departmental council) with national elective mandates (usually those of deputy or senator). This interconnection has been interpreted as producing an adaptable, negotiated system in which policies were implemented flexibly because of the strong ties between central and local governments.

These contrasting models of French and English sub-national politics and administration are set out in detail in chapters 2 and 3. The thesis of French and English local divergence was pushed furthest by Ashford (1982) who contrasted centralist and inflexible traditions of policy-making in England (dogmatism) with a flexible and negotiated style in France (pragmatism). Ashford's thesis was that, in spite of all the authority delegated to sub-national authorities, the English state was locked into a rigid system of central control: it pushed through dogmatic solutions because it did not have much contact with and distrusted local government; in contrast, the practice of French central–local relations, revolving around the *cumul des mandats*, was based on the political representation of local interests in central government and resulted in more pragmatic solutions. Ashford's controversial thesis focused attention on the different state traditions operating in each country. In the UK, in keeping with its ideology of the limited state, the formal apparatus of the centre was kept small, while service delivery functions were offloaded onto local government or other public bodies. Local authorities administered vast tracts of the post-1945 welfare state. Their primary concern with service delivery partly explains the functional specialisation of English local authorities and the high degree of autonomy acquired by professionals in their policy communities. In France, the state took on a more direct and directive role; in England, local government administered vast tracts of the post-1945 welfare state. The primary concern with service delivery partly explains the functional specialisation of English local authorities and the high degree of autonomy acquired by professionals in their policy communities. Unlike in England, the French welfare state was administered directly by government departments (for example, in education or social welfare) or nationally organised partnership agencies (for example, in social security and housing), with local authorities reduced to a minor service delivery function. Each system had its costs and benefits. The English system prided itself on the efficient and professional delivery of services and clear lines of accountability. But it tended to be rather rigid in its approach and to lack sensitivity to political contexts of the centre and the periphery. The French, in contrast, represented local interests more flexibly, but local services were delivered with minimal concern for democratic accountability.

In so far as they represent distinctive traditions within the EU, Anglo-French comparisons make sense; good Anglo-French comparisons allow for the examination of similar policy challenges in specific policy contexts. When common trends appear in the case of France and England, it is likely they will have a more general validity across EU states. In the main body of the chapter we argue that comparable (but not identical) trends have restructured the different systems of local government in each country. Old systems of making policy have changed. New actors participate in local decision-making and the roles of familiar decision-makers have been transformed. Established routines of making policy have been disrupted. Fresh challenges have emerged. Accountability mechanisms have been contested. We set out these changes in the following chapters. But first we need to develop a working definition of governance.

Varieties of governance

The research questions developed throughout this chapter are broadly derived from a decade of academic debates over 'governance' (see summary in Pierre 2000). Political science theory has grappled with the circularity, indeterminacy and ambiguity of the concept. Rhodes (1996, 1997) proposes six separate interpretations of governance. The use of governance ranges from a loose metaphor to a causal explanatory model. Theorists typically understand governance as wider than 'government', often as a useful descriptor for the compound of diverse internal and external pressures that have reshaped traditional patterns of public administration in western liberal democracies since the early 1980s (Kohler-Koch and Eising 1999). Many proponents of governance argue that the wider structural context of government has changed under the impact of global economic pressures, regional integration in supranational organisations, such as the European Union, and the increased incidence of transnational policy exchanges (Mayntz 1993; Cerny 1997; Andrew and Goldsmith 1998; John 2001). Internally focused explanations place greater emphasis on endogenous changes, which have produced more interdependent actors, leading to 'overcrowded policy making' (Richardson and Jordan 1979), the rise of meso-level government (Sharpe 1993;

Rhodes 1996, 1997), a decentralisation and fragmentation of the state (Keating and Loughlin 1997), and a greater involvement of private actors in public policy-making processes (Bennett 1990; Stoker 1991).

Governance is highly abstract and elusive. The definition provided by Mayntz (1993) is a useful benchmark. She draws a distinction between governing and governance. The process of governing involves goal-directed interventions on behalf of the public authorities; the metaphor of 'steering' refers to 'the ability of political authorities to mould their social environments' (Mayntz 1993: 11). Governing through steering described the traditional practice of government; in recent decades, however, western societies have been confronted with new problems of ungovernability, defined as a weakening capacity to steer social development. Of the many causes of ungovernability (social, political and economic) the most important concerns the governmental system. The state is no longer able to steer society by proposing solutions to the problems it has identified. Modern states need to lower expectations of public policy action and develop new policy instruments. Governance is thus rooted in the weakening of older forms of regulation. In one colourful formulation, the nation-state has been 'hollowed out' as the principal locus of social and economic regulation (Jessop 1998, 2000), challenged by global market forces, new supranational institutional forms and the consequences of past state failure.

Governance is not synonymous with ungovernability, however. The new governance is based on new types of 'goal-directed interventions' on behalf of the public authorities, whose competencies are increasingly dissipated across several interdependent levels (local, regional, central, European) and which recognise the need to develop new forms of policy co-ordination. These new 'goal-directed interventions' break with traditional hierarchical forms of state control. They are directed towards mobilising policy networks, building inter-institutional (and public–private) partnerships and creating organisational incentives to achieve rational policy outcomes. Governance is reflexive (Rhodes 1997; Ascher 1998). Its rationality is based on dialogue, exchange and long-term commitment. In one version, governance consists in 'instituting negotiation around a long-term consensual project as the basis for both positive and negative co-ordination among interdependent actors' (Jessop 2000: 16). As a generic concept, governance is best understood as a new form of regulation of an increasingly complex, indeterminate and multi-layered polity.

Governance also refers to new patterns of state–society interactions, hence the particular importance placed on policy networks and new coalitions of actors. Marin and Mayntz (1991: 19) affirm that 'policy networks are "new" phenomena; they are linked to structural changes in society and the polity'. Policy networks, they argue, represent new forms of policy-making to deal with the complexity of modern governance. Fragmentation has increased pressures for coalition formation to implement policy. Policy actors are dependent on each other; they need to pool resources (knowledge, finance) to resolve complex, dynamic and diversified problems. In this 'differentiated polity' (Rhodes 1986) co-ordination occurs through bargaining, rather than hierarchical control (van Waarden 1992).

The governance concept has gradually gained ground in the study of sub-national politics and administration (Andrew and Goldsmith 1998; Pratchett 2000; Stoker 2000). In France and England and elsewhere there have been profound changes in the external and internal environments within which local authorities and other public and private bodies operate. External pressures on localities have become more pronounced since the late 1970s and provide a plausible context for policy change. These are considered immediately below. The internal changes within localities and within the organisations of local government itself have also been important in both countries. As it is the internal changes that directly lead towards local governance, they are the main focus of this book.

Governance and externally driven change

Certain observers contend that governance has come about primarily because the wider structural context of government has been affected by new international economic pressures and transnational policy exchanges (Mayntz 1993; Cerny 1997; Goldsmith 1997). For Goldsmith (1997) 'globalisation', Europeanisation and ideological change are the pressures that have underpinned the move from local government to local governance over the last twenty years. External changes have affected the operation of localities in various ways. Localities have had to respond to the direct and indirect consequences of 'internationalisation'. They have had to react to the growth of transnational policy-making in bodies such as the European Union. They have been encouraged to exchange ideas and build networks across nations.

'Internationalisation' has affected local as well as national governments. We prefer the term internationalisation to that of globalisation: internationalisation describes the growing competition in international markets and the greater mobility of capital, without implying either that nation states are withering away or that the main centres of power are becoming global (Hirst and Thompson 1999). The economic integration of Europe, competition from new regional centres of economic activity and changes in the concentration of multinational firms have all had an impact upon localities. Increased economic interdependence has led to growing competition between cities (Harding 1998); in a fast-changing economic climate, cities and localities have become aware that new policies need to be adopted if they are to survive economically. Because the type of economic activity which is easiest to cultivate is (or was) on offer to most cities – growth in the service and financial sectors – cities are in competition with each other, both within nations and between them. Business interests are in a power-ful position to determine business location decisions. Economic interdependence has arguably made economic management at the level of the nation-state much more difficult, but it can favour sub-regional cohesion. Cities can influence investment decisions by deliberate strategic actions (Harding 1998). There is, it is argued, a direct link between external challenges and the internal quality of local governing coalitions. Hence the move to urban regimes, the long-term public–private governing coalitions that involve shared visions and values amongst political and economic decision-makers, and a commitment to economic growth (Stone 1989).

Internationalisation has increased pressures for labour market deregulation and for improved training and education provision. It has encouraged national and local governments to offer incentives for inward investment. In a more economically interdependent and integrated environment, national governments are less able to use traditional economic policy instruments, such as Keynesian demand management and full employment policies. International constraints encourage governments to adopt supply-side policies and to impose budgetary restraints, privatisation and the retrenchment of the welfare state. This has implications for centre–periphery relations as national governments tend to favour economic development objectives over traditional welfare concerns.

Transnational policy-making in political institutions, such as the European Union, also appears to reduce the salience of national governing processes and thus of traditional central–local government relationships. European-wide ideas and international policy exchanges have had a more general impact upon local political systems. In England and France, local governments have recognised the developing importance of the European Union: there is a growing awareness of new sources of policy funding and a recognition that local policies need to be specifically tailored to meet European policy objectives to obtain public funding (John 2001). Localities seek to build their international political contacts in order to access funding and investment. The European Union, with its own agenda for harmonisation, also seeks to influence local policy-making and inter-country co-operation through sponsoring transnational networks. Cities compete fiercely for the limited resources available.

The increased incidence of international policy transfers is a further feature of governance. The European Union and the internationalised economy have encouraged policy-makers to exchange ideas across nations. In part this practice occurs through international networks of decision-makers, sometimes sponsored by the European Union. It also happens directly through national government policies and EU directives and from the international aspirations of local politicians and contacts between cities. City policy-makers are searching for new policies; European companies and consultants diffuse fresh ideas. There is a limited stock of new ideas upon which policy-makers can draw when addressing similar problems such as attracting inward investment, improving local training and employment opportunities, and ameliorating educational provision.

Is there a trend to the convergence of public policies? There are certainly comparable trends across European countries. In so far as it has been used to signify the overarching transformation of west European societies, (meta-)governance has sometimes been used as synonymous with policy convergence. States have accepted limits to their sovereignty, in the higher interest of peace, stability and economic gain. Under the impact of Europeanisation and the challenges of the international political economy, European states have voluntarily pooled sovereignty in international organisations and increasingly converged their rules and institutions to conform to a common standard (Mény 1993b). New institutionalist analysis contributes important insights. Ideas of best practice and a desire to imitate the most successful can produce a form of institutional isomorphism, whereby states import those non-native organisational models perceived to be the most effective (Powell and DiMaggio 1991). The importance of bench-marking and ideas of best practice – propagated by the EU, as well as national governments – have gradually filtered down to the sub-national level.

Common pressures do not necessarily imply convergent responses. The counter-argument to policy convergence is that old-established states such as France and Britain will reaffirm their nationally distinctive policy practices and referential frameworks when confronted with similar pressures for change (Kitschelt 1999). By extension, new local and regional forms of governance – however significant – are pre-shaped by pre-existing patterns of national dis-tinctiveness, whether these are understood in terms of state traditions (Loughlin and Keating 1997; Dyson 1980), policy styles (Richardson 1982) or the nebulous concept of political culture (Eatwell 1996). There are strong pressures for trans-national convergence, but also lasting forms of national specificity, derived from distinctive historical legacies and the persistence of laws, institutions, cultures and languages. Subsequent chapters will examine these contrasting approaches.

Governance and domestic policy change

While externally driven changes provide a plausible context for policy change, internal changes lead more directly to local governance. They include pressures for decentralisation, the greater involvement of private actors in public policy-making processes, the reshaping of local politics, demands to reform the quality of service delivery and organisational reforms.

The pressure for decentralisation

Changes in advanced liberal democracies have produced more participants in the policy-making process; this has overcrowded the state level and has created a governing crisis. As the state is less able to steer social development, so it attempts to lower the expectations from public policy programmes, to offload functions and to develop alternative instruments to deliver services (Mayntz 1993). In response to an overloaded agenda at the central government level, governments seek to transfer state functions to lower administrative echelons, to quasi-autonomous agencies, to public–private partnerships and to private sector organisations. In England, the long Conservative period of rule (1979–97) witnessed a determined effort to shift service delivery functions away from traditional providers (central government departments and local authorities) to semi-autonomous agencies, public–private partnerships and private sector organ-isations. In France, political and administrative decentralisation was intended in part to redress the central state's incapacity to provide high-quality services and to increase its capacity to steer at a distance.

Local governance implies some degree of disengagement on the part of the central state. The willingness of central government to let solutions emerge and to learn from trial and error gives a measure of autonomy to local decision-makers. On the other hand, the willingness of central state actors to involve themselves in the detail of policy introduces new actors and decision-makers at the local level and makes local decision-making even more complex.

The greater involvement of private actors in public policy-making processes

Some writers declare that the nation-state has been 'hollowed out' (Rhodes 1996, 1997). In England the role of the state has been redefined by a long programme of privatisation of state enterprises, by reforms limiting the scope and form of public intervention and by the contracting out of services to the private sector. In France, not only has the private management of public goods long been a characteristic feature of French local governance, but public–private partnerships have extended their scope since the early 1980s (Lorrain and Stoker 1995; Cole 1999). In both countries, private sector actors can perform a public service mission.

The reshaping of local politics

In both countries, traditional forms of party political representation have declined and new types of political participation in local politics have grown. The diminished legitimacy and popularity of local representative democracy have taken different forms in England and in France. In England, this has been manifested by dangerously low rates of electoral participation in local elections and by a weakening of the two main parties; in France, participation in municipal elections is higher, but confidence in local and national politicians has been seriously shaken by a decade of political corruption scandals. In both countries, there has been an increase in local activity on behalf of new social movements, voluntary associations and new types of interests, such as consumers and business (Gyford 1991; Stoker and Wilson 1991; Archambault 1997). Although parties remain as the main vehicle for articulating interests during elections, the term local governance helps to identify complex and shifting forms of political participation. These novel forms of political participation have made the policy-making environment more complex and unpredictable. In England and in France, local political elites have had to adapt to new pressures and to accommodate new local actors.

Pressures to reform the quality of service delivery

At the same time as there has been pressure to decentralise, governments have become keen to improve the quality of public services and to obtain best value for money given the public resources available. This has led them to reform the structure of the state as it has decentralised power to elected or non-elected agencies. The pressure for reform is very familiar in England where new public management ideas and techniques, such as performance indicators, dominate debates and practice and where central government agencies have taken the place of locally elected ones. But France has seen some similar development in the post-decentralisation period: in policy sectors such as urban policy, central government has attempted to specify the relationships between public organisations in a series of contracts that demonstrate the concern of the central state to regulate the relationships between public bodies.

If the 'new public management' (NPM) was initially developed by New Right think-tanks close to the Conservative Party (Lowndes 1997), its central tenets have been more broadly diffused and have gradually filtered into mainstream organisational practice. The failure of traditional bureaucratic service-delivery mechanisms (such as the legendarily inefficient direct labour organisations in local government) is now widely accepted. In England NPM remedies have included introducing consumer 'choice' in public services (such as the creation of 'quasi-markets' in education and the provider/purchaser divide in the NHS); creating specific agencies deemed more adapted to flexible policy-making than traditional bureaucracies; installing competition between existing organisations (notably through competitive bidding regimes); inaugurating new regimes of policy evaluation; and enhancing decentralised budgetary management. The precise terms of the NPM are generally unacceptable in France. The framework of choice clashes with that of public service and republican equality. But many of the same underlying ideas have gradually emerged onto the policy agenda.

Thus far, we identify a mosaic of external and internal pressures that have reshaped patterns of public administration in England and – to a lesser extent – in France. We will now elaborate further our framework of analysis.

Governance: a framework of analysis

While often ambiguous, the concept of governance has a useful heuristic value. It highlights deeper processes of institutional fragmentation and the changing parameters of state action. It focuses analysis upon the blurring of boundaries between public and private and the creation of new policy mixes of markets, bureaucracies and networks. Governance implies change, but not from a *tabula rasa*. One obvious objection is that there is nothing new about governance. Organisational pluralism is not recent: public–private coalitions were at the forefront of city governance in Victorian and Edwardian England. Marcou (1999) traces the usage of governance (signifying simply public administration) back to the nineteenth century. In the case of France, Gaudin (1999) also insists upon the plurality of actors involved in city governance in the 1930s. The number of actors alone cannot be a criterion for measuring governance. The case for governance – tested in subsequent chapters – rests upon the argument that there has been a qualitative change in the course of the past two decades.

At the risk of oversimplification, we identify three main aspects to local governance: institutional fragmentation; blurred boundaries between public, private and societal actors; and the prominence of inter-organisational policy networks and new forms of co-ordination.

Governance takes place in a fragmented institutional context. Institutional change has modified previously more integrated patterns of local policy-making. This has taken different forms in England and France: in England, institutional fragmentation refers principally to the growth of non-elected agencies performing specific policy functions, often in competition with locally elected authorities; in France, fragmentation refers mainly (but not exclusively) to the creation of new layers of sub-national government. In both countries there has emerged a host of quasi-public agencies, an increased overlapping of responsibilities for service provision between distinct organisations, and new forms of public–private partnerships. We explain these developments in more detail in subsequent chapters.

There are increasingly *blurred boundaries between the public and private sectors.* Public sector actors act as entrepreneurs; and private firms can be tied into a public service mission. Other private actors, such as interest groups and voluntary associations, become more important: in England, the mixing of the public and private sectors has been driven by the policies of central government, such as the legal requirement to put out local authority services to tender; in the case of France, local fiscal pressures have forced municipalities to look to the private sector to provide services. In both countries, a key aspect of local governance is the manner in which private or voluntary sector actors have become more involved in the delivery of local services. In the English context especially, the belief in the market has affected local government, as demonstrated by deregulation, contracting out, public–private partnerships, the creation of new agencies and an emphasis on the individual as a consumer of services. In the French case, such ideas circulate less freely. The framework of public service (*service publique*) vests the public sector with far greater legitimacy than in England. This caveat aside, there have also been important French organisational reforms since the early 1980s, involving new contractual relationships between public sector organisations, administrative decentralisation, enhanced budgetary autonomy and the increased use of performance indicators. Chapters 3, 4 and 5 consider these reforms. These can be considered as functionally equivalent in certain respects to those undertaken in England. The greatest paradox, perhaps, is that the 'private' management of public goods is a long established feature of French local governance, a theme that we develop in chapter 4.

Governance involves *the greater prominence of inter-organisational networks.* Policy networks are a necessary feature of governance. As personal and organisational relationships are essential for managing a more fragmented institutional context, so regular contacts and relationships between key decision-makers have become important as a means of co-ordinating and producing public decisions. Actors engage in and invest in relationships with their counterparts in other organisations. Even if their co-operation is not required by statute, they often realise that benefits can be accrued by voluntary participation. English and French local networks contain many traditional actors, such as party leaders and local government officers or state officials, but they also have new participants, from the private sector and/or quasi-public agencies, whose co-operation is important if effective policy is to be made. These networks provide a way of promoting the co-ordination of public policies and they can help build trust and governing capacity. The linkages between policy-makers serve as means of communication and exchange of information, expertise and other resources. They allow public decision-makers to respond flexibly to the rapidly changing agenda.

Governing through regular relationships across organisations – policy networks – is a form of public decision-making that is a response to the complexity of modern institutional arrangements and the rapidity of policy change. While it should not be assumed that such networks were absent from older patterns of government, the essence of the politics of governance is that networked relationships take on a more important role. Whereas traditional local politics implied a pattern of negotiations with a limited set of agencies and party organisations, contemporary political leaders have to negotiate in a far more changeable and complex environment and they are involved in diverse sets of relationships which they cannot completely control. This raises various issues of leadership and democratic accountability.

Governance and democracy

While most writing and research about governance has examined such matters as the management of networks, new forms of community power, the politics of economic development partnerships and innovative management, less attention has been given to the normative implications of change. This is because governance is double-edged. It offers possible benefits to local political systems, but it has many costs as well. Underpinning our empirical investigation lie powerful normative issues of democratic legitimacy and effectiveness. Are some forms of leadership and patterns of institutions better placed to respond to the challenges of governance than others? Is secondary education or economic policy most affected by changing practices? Most of all, which country offers the most effective and legitimate form of local governance?

The incorporation of new decision-makers into public policy may renew highly institutionalised forms of politics. Traditional decision-makers have to build relationships with organisations and individuals who do not share their values or their ideas. Political exchange allows longer-term relationships to be built and new collective norms to emerge. Negotiations and relationships by themselves can produce legitimacy by increasing a sense of co-ownership on behalf of the various partners and by inciting policy learning. Learning produces common norms that go beyond positions and roles occupied in institutions. The ability to build trust between actors can be an important collective good in contemporary urban governance. Decision-makers have to exchange ideas as well as resources. Just as much as they need to refine the arts of political compromise, they must engage in debate if they are to find successful solutions to local public problems.

If networks offer a possibility for the renewal of local politics, they also pose a challenge to traditional notions of democratic accountability: in theory, a democracy requires transparency in political deliberation, participation by an active citizenry and political control over technocratic and professional decision-makers. The public sphere rests upon a consensus on basic norms, institutions and values; where disagreement exists, solutions should be sought by public argument. With reference to England, representative and responsible government (Birch 1964) depended on minimal political participation, but in theory there were clear accountability relationships, such as those between an elected council and the electorate or between ministers, civil servants and parliament. The doctrine of representative and responsible government reflected the nineteenth-century formulation of liberal democracy, such as that developed by J. S. Mill. The French republican tradition also insists upon the accountability of rulers to the elected National Assembly as the sole legitimate embodiment of popular sovereignty. During the Third (1870–1940) and Fourth (1946–58) Republics, the instability of French governments was attributed to the vigilance with which the National Assembly ensured the subordination of cabinets and individual ministers to its orders.

If complexity, indeterminacy and interdependence are the defining character-istics of modern governance, such doctrines of accountability would now appear to be even more inadequate than they were in more stable periods of govern-ment. Governance creates a crisis of accountability in the public sector because of the proliferation of non-departmental public agencies and other bodies. There is a lack of clarity about which decision is the responsibility of which public body as it is spread across many stakeholders. Most of all, the way in which decisions seem to be taken within networks of actors rather than in accordance with organisational practices and lines of control ensures that traditional mechanisms of accountability do not work in a straightforward manner. It is hard for a minister or an elected mayor to be called to answer for a decision which emerges from elaborate negotiations between public bodies and where the expenditure involved is shared between organisations, particularly when the contributors are both public and private sector organisations.

There is a sense in which the efficient functioning of networks or partnerships depends upon closure and secrecy. Pooling resources and building trust relies upon a mutual exchange of resources and too much transparency might force actors back to their institutional roles. Networks can shut out the public, create oligarchies and favour established interests. The accountability problem and the corresponding crisis of legitimacy emerge as the main challenge of contemporary governance. We suggest that the potential of political leadership can provide one part of the remedy though on its own it is not a panacea.

The possibilities of leadership

Local political leadership in England and France is embedded in distinctive and opposing institutional frameworks. As we will demonstrate in subsequent chapters, the strong personal leadership in the French townhalls contrasted with a more collective, less visible English style; in both cases, however, there are creative pathways leaders can take that can mobilise local communities for collective action. Able leaders can raise the capacity to govern.

Successful political leadership depends upon an ability to combine different roles. Urban political leaders have to perform many demanding and often contradictory tasks; the most important of these are as local chief executive, as public representative and as party manager. As local chief executives, leaders make executive decisions (either individually or collectively); as this involves deciding for or against local interests, they are often unpopular. As public representatives, leaders have a duty to express the unity of the urban space. Leaders must represent their cities by articulating in one coherent discourse the contradictory aspects of their locality. In their role as party chiefs, finally, leaders have to manage their followers in their political parties and to attempt to disarm internal party challenges.

The old institutional patterns and habits of governing created some certainty in what was already a complex task of combining executive, public representative and party manager roles. Local governance removes many of the old contours of governing by multiplying the numbers of actors in local politics, raising the level of complexity of local policy problems, imposing high costs on policy errors (especially in terms of the economic health of the city) and increasing the speed at which public problems need to be solved. While fragmentation means that some of these tasks can be offloaded onto other bodies, effective problem solving still rests disproportionately on the ability of the one person or team to mobilise resources and promote solutions to public problems. Local governance increases the demands made on the occupants of legitimate political authority. Citizens, associations and other local leaders target their attention on political leaders at the very time their hold on the reins of political authority have weakened and the burdens of office have increased.

Leadership is crucial to the new urban governance. The politics of decentralisation, networks, participation, partnerships, bureaucratic reform, rapid policy change and central intervention needs powerful but creative figures to give a direction to local policy-making; in a time of institutional fragmentation and complexity, local political leaders can provide direction and cohesion to the shifting framework of individuals and organisations involved in urban governance. While creating the need for better leadership, local governance also imposes strains on the people who exercise authoritative policy choices. They have to make sense of complexity and cope with rapid change and novel circumstances. Naturally, urban leaders are not necessarily up to the challenge, and there are different types of leaders appropriate for each context. We return to this theme in chapters 2, 3, 6 and 7.

Three dimensions to local governance

Local Governance in England and France engages in a thorough comparative investigation of changing patterns of sub-national governance in our two selected countries. Our book is based on extensive primary empirical research. The empirical data draw upon the results of interviews with political, economic and educational decision-makers in four cities, two in England (Leeds and Southampton), two in France (Lille and Rennes). Our approach is comparative. We aim to find out how politicians, officials, professionals, business people and representatives of interest groups in our four cities cope with policy change in the sectors of economic development and secondary education. The main task of our book is to investigate how decision-makers in England and France face up to the problems identified with local governance. In the right circumstances, we argue, decision-makers can overcome the challenges of policy co-ordination and political leadership. But over time the new framework of governing can itself cause a crisis of legitimacy. Policy-makers, operating in these new networks, often find their actions have little foundation in democratic practice. To restore confidence in their public service mission, local leaders have to search for new means of making public decisions and they must also invent new ways in which governance can conform to democratic norms. Such is the challenge of local governance.

Thus far we have explained the meaning of the term governance and we have examined the pressures for change and their implications for democracy. The labels we have used and the ideas we have discussed could be transferred to any context, as they address issues central to democratic politics at the end of the twentieth century. Thus an account of the politics of the European Union or national government could be couched in these terms. But in this book our focus is principally upon comparing local governance and here we stress three dimensions to the problem.

Country comparisons and contrasts

The first dimension of comparative local governance involves the continuing importance of national institutions and practices in defining the powers, functions and roles of local decision-makers. We have already referred to political institutions in our discussion of the traditional models of local government and how they have been challenged by international and national pressures and moved towards a pattern of politics called local governance. In terms of our comparison between local governance in England and France, each political system has a different pattern of central government control and has a unique political tradition underpinning it and, as we discussed, many writers contrast the two. In the English political system, local authorities have stocks of organisational resources and a high level of political legitimacy which no degree of central restructuring and incision of market forces can completely negate. Central governments, while they may wish to intervene in localities, still start from a position of little knowledge and history of controlling local politics. In France, locally elected government remains weak organisationally (notwithstanding the decentralisation reforms of the 1980s and the growth in city-wide metropolitan local government structures), but elected mayors can obtain political leverage as a result of their national connections. Local governance emerges in these tightly defined national contexts. Though the pressures for change are comparable in both countries, state traditions continue to structure the roles that new and old decision-makers adopt. We thus expect French and English policy-makers to adopt rather different solutions to policy changes and to building networks.

Sector comparisons and contrasts

The second dimension of our comparison relates to policy sectors. As at the national level, local policy-makers act differently according to the nature of the public policy problem; in the words of Lowi (1964), the 'policies make the politics'. The 'policy sector' is a useful metaphor to differentiate between different types of policy-making activities and the range of political and professional interests associated with them. Certain sectors appear closed and impenetrable. Activities such as civil engineering, sea defences or the water industry are highly technical; the role of professional communities is enhanced by the scarcity of their expertise. In these highly structured domains, cohesive 'policy communities' can emerge, based on shared values between professionals and their political interlocutors in ranking government ministries. Other sectors are less well defined, less professionally driven and more open to various sources of influence; in these looser, more pluralistic sectors – of which economic development is a good example – more actors are likely to interact.

Comparing policy sectors is a key preoccupation of the English policy networks literature (Marsh and Rhodes 1992; Rhodes 1997; Marsh 1998). The notion of the policy sector is also important in French public policy approaches, for example, Jobert and Muller in their classic work *L'Etat en action* (1987). Thus we expect to find that the sectors we study for this book, economic development and secondary education, have different relationships, distinct patterns of co-ordination, contrasting styles of political leadership and varying forms of accountability. Governance will take different paths depending on policy sector.

City similarities and contrasts

While cities and local areas are defined by their national contexts and by the type of activities their leaders try to regulate, they are also unique entities with political systems, administrative structures, historical memories, political traditions and cultures of their own which profoundly affect the practice of politics and decision-making. In spite of tendencies towards uniformity within nations, an influential school of thought prioritises the predominance of local factors in understanding urban politics, both in England (Harloe et al. 1990) and in France (Le Galès 1993, 2000). Cities differ according to their size, economic heritage and degree of distance from the centre, the solidarity of their political culture, the composition of their elites and their traditions of leadership, amongst many other factors. As with the influence of countries and sectors, these differences suggest various paths for local governance to take.

To map these paths of governance, we studied four cities. They comprised two large metropolitan centres (Leeds and Lille) and two medium-sized provincial cities (Southampton and Rennes). We compared pairs of cities. The pair of Leeds and Lille aimed to capture the politics of northern industrial cities of around a million inhabitants, with their socialist traditions and similar economic problems of industrial restructuring. The pair of Rennes and Southampton represented the politics of smaller but regionally important light industrial towns with large higher education sectors. While controlling for size allowed us to examine the effects of small versus big towns, there were contrasts between all the towns.

In the main body of the book we compare local governance across the three dimensions of countries, sectors and cities. To undertake this multi-dimensional comparison, we mapped out and observed in action eight specific local policy networks.[1] Our starting point is that there are different routes to comprehending local governance. For each of our networks is constrained by a combination of a national tradition, a policy sector and a local context. The particular pattern of national, sectoral and city influences shapes the parameters and governs the pattern of change, and provides a different starting point from which to build networks. These influences determine whether policy-makers can innovate, whether there is conflict or not, and whether there is capacity to solve public problems. While we identify common features of governance in all eight cases, the direction and course of change is particular in that each context promotes a certain form of change (Pierson 2000).

The influence of the context and the choices of the actors are the subject of our examination. Can political leaders overcome these constraints or are they slaves to their country and city traditions? Which set of conditions best co-ordinate public actions and are consistent with democratic norms? Are the politics of governance best suited to France, with its tradition of strong local political leadership, its pervasive central state and its practice of flexible negotiation? Or is England, with its professionalised local authorities, its market-based politics and its detached state, ahead of its European rivals in being adaptable to a more fluid and complex form of politics? Is governance the province of economic development, with its wide range of decision-makers and its important private sector dimension? Or are similar influences transposable to the sphere of secondary education, a sector that has traditionally required strong central government direction and bureaucratic control? Which city has the most propitious political culture and organisational structures to co-ordinate policy? Does effective governance occur only in places where strong municipal leaders are able bang the heads of local stakeholders together or is it more effective where power is already diffused?

We believe that answers to these questions are important because it is as local citizens, whether as consumers of local services or as employees in the public or private sectors, that people experience the major changes in the economy, politics and public organisations. It is local politicians and officials who have to face the tough problems of co-ordinating and implementing policy, and making sense of the succession of initiatives which come from central government. It is also at the local level that the crisis of democratic legitimacy first hits home, partly because local leaders cannot hide behind the power of national state institutions. Finally, because of the diversity of the local dimension, local variations offer many potential solutions and lessons that can be learnt at all levels of governance whether regional, national or supranational.

2 Local politics and policy-making in England

This chapter sets out the traditional model of English local self-government and considers the conceptual frameworks that have attempted to capture the essence of English central–local government relations. In the main part of the chapter we investigate the causes and controversies of English-style local governance, arguing that governance cannot be reduced to the radical reforming impetus of the Conservative period in office (1979–97), but forms part of a deeper evolution in English society. If England is the 'brand leader' (Andrew and Goldsmith 1998) of a certain model of local governance, comparable policy problems are posed in other European countries. The chapter concludes by highlighting the principal challenges of governance in English localities.

The English model of local self-government

From a comparative European perspective, the English model of local government is highly distinctive, the effect of a long process of historical evolution and incremental change. Three attributes set the English system apart from its European neighbours, whether those influenced by the Napoleonic or the federal states. These are the primacy of common law, the doctrine of parliamentary sovereignty and the principle of *ultra vires*. Common law refers to the accumulation of norms, conventions and precedents that comprise the English legal system. There is no English equivalent of the codified system of administrative law that exists in France, where the interests of public authorities are explicitly defined as being superior to those of private citizens. While administrative law exists in England, it has been modified by common law principles of natural justice and reasonableness. The Napoleonic model of regulation is different (Wunder 1995). The second principle is of parliamentary sovereignty, which affirms the legal supremacy of legislative decisions. The 'Glorious Revolution' of 1688 consolidated the victory of Parliament against absolutist monarchy. In spite of its limitations by international treaties, particularly after accession to the European Union in 1973, the doctrine conveys a powerful message to policy-makers and the courts that government can be both strong and democratic. English elites have always advanced the myth of a consensual, non-violent democratic evolution, yet the English state remains highly centralised and unrestrained, with power resting in the executive based in London. The legal and constitutional power and legitimacy of central government devalue local government and legitimates central intervention in the powers, functions and decisions of local government. In certain respects, the doctrine of parliamentary sovereignty performs a functionally equivalent role to that of republicanism in the French context; it legitimates an indivisible, democratic and ultimately centralised form of political power. The third principle, following logically from the second, is that of *ultra vires*: any public authority must act according to law as defined by parliament. This principle subordinates local authorities to the will of the legislator. Unlike their French counterparts, English local authorities do not enjoy specific, constitutionally embedded legal competencies and – in theory – they can only act where there is a clear legal basis for doing so. There is no principle of a general legislative competence for local authorities as there is in France (Delcamp 1997). Section 111 of the Local Government Act 1972, which empowers local authorities to do anything 'calculated to facilitate, or is conductive or incidental to' the carrying out of their functions, is not an equivalent. There is no legal limitation on a statute that removes the powers of local government. Central government can even legislate to abolish a democratically elected local authority, as occurred with the Greater London Council and the six metropolitan authorities in 1986.

The constitutional status of local government is double-edged, however. There is no real equivalent in England of the unitary and tentacular French state that is organised in an identical manner throughout the territory. English local authorities devote much energy to routine matters of administration that would fall to the field services and prefectures in France. English councils use their unrivalled knowledge of local circumstances to best effect and it is hard for any central agency to compete. Though local authorities in England are expressly subordinated to central government, they have evolved as multi-functional organisations, employing large bureaucracies and managing an array of services. In the end central government has found it convenient to allocate troublesome functions to local government, especially those that require local knowledge, and to let local politicians and officials get on with the job of providing public services.

Was there ever a golden age of local government? In the late nineteenth century local government pioneered many local services and it had a high status in its communities. It was at the centre of vibrant industrial cities, and some of its leading politicians, such as Joseph Chamberlain in Birmingham, were national figures. There was then what many people now describe as a pattern of local governance. Business and a wide range of community organisations were involved in politics. Private companies provided local services. There were small local bureaucracies and a complex pattern of jurisdictions and single-purpose public authorities. While localism was a powerful force in Victorian England and city governments became powerful and vibrant entities, local government owed its existence to statute. Parliamentary action gave it control over functions to regulate the social problems of an increasingly industrialised country. Rather than being an extension of communal life – as in France – English local government was always subject to central regulation, though not detailed day-to-day supervision. The leash has been long, but always strong. Central government, through parliament, continually changed the structure and functions of local government to suit whatever public priorities were dominant at any one time, whether it was the demand for public health or state education.

English local authorities are first and foremost agencies that deliver public services. While local political institutions have been a feature of English politics since 1835, having powers and the ability to raise finance to solve public problems, local government has ultimately depended on the will of the centre. Local authorities have implemented public tasks determined by the central authorities. Magnussun (1986) argues this tradition reflects the utilitarian bias to English and North American systems of local government. Reforms have usually been introduced not to enhance local democracy but to improve welfare: in the long-run the political legitimacy and power of local government has arguably been sacrificed in the name of greater efficiency of service provision.

The subordinate character of English local government became more apparent with the development of the welfare state from the 1930s onwards. Central government took away most of local authorities' powers to intervene in economic management and allocated them instead the newly expanded services of the welfare state. From managing local municipal transport companies and public utilities, local government came to administer state education, social services and largely centrally funded public housing. The most obvious consequence of this centrally driven change of focus was the expansion of local administrative services. Professional bureaucrats came to dominate local government, the agenda of which became increasingly subordinate to national policy initiatives. As the memory of local self-government receded, so did its self-confidence and its role as a local innovator. As the twentieth century proceeded, local government grew gradually more distant and it slowly weakened its links with local communities.

A dual polity?

The English version of the doctrine of political accountability requires clear responsibility for public decisions to reside with the central authority, which in theory is parliament but in practice means the incumbent government. At the same time, there is a non-executive tradition of the English central state. Parliament creates new powers and responsibilities, but local government or special purpose bodies provide and administer services. Central government departments would set the broad guidelines of policy and proposed legal changes from time to time, but they left the day to day administration of public affairs to local public authorities. With this relative freedom, local authorities allocated resources, set standards and made their own policies. This division of powers contrasts with the practice in some other European countries where responsibilities are shared between levels of government, both locally elected and the arms of the central state. While this division between 'high' and 'low' politics was always present during the nineteenth century, it was compounded by the expansion of the welfare state in the twentieth. With some exceptions (the bulk of health care and social assistance functions being the main ones), elected local government ran the welfare state.

This division of functions between local authorities and central government and the pattern of administrative devolution can be understood to be an aspect of what Bulpitt calls the 'dual polity' (1983: 147–52). This separation between the centre – the 'court' in London – and local and regional politics mainly comes about through the behaviour of political elites, the organisation of political parties and constitutional practice. Like France, local authorities were a recruiting ground for national political elites, but local government in England is a convenient staging post rather than a permanent power base. Most local councillors are happy to abandon their local roots once they enter national office. Political careers are built through party machines that do not depend upon local government for their survival and wish to conquer political power at the centre. Local political elites managed their spheres of delegated responsibility in relative isolation from central government. While local and central government came into contact with each other through professional networks of officers and civil servants, their political elites swam in separate streams.

Bulpitt's (1983) characterisation of the period from 1926 to 1960 as the 'dual polity' found backing in several empirical studies, such as the one undertaken by Gyford and James (1983) into the relationship between national and local parties. Local citizens tended not to bother central government departments with minor administrative details, and members of parliament who received such enquiries were very happy to pass them on to local councillors. There was little need for central government politicians to concern themselves with policy implementation locally. Likewise there was not much incentive for local politicians to access the central state to gain resources or to resolve local disputes. They could sort out most of the decisions themselves by making authoritative decisions in their councils. While life was easier for English local politicians than for their continental counterparts, the separation had its costs. It meant that central politicians had little wish to involve themselves in local matters and local political networks tended to be based on the local council rather than extending upwards and across into the organisations of the central state. Local government became weaker than in other countries because there were few political constraints on central reform as well as the absence of a constitutional *grundnorm*. As a result the lobbying power of national local government organisations tended to be weak (Rhodes 1986). Although there are many examples of local innovation, and of ideas and policies moving from local government to central government and back again, local policy-makers have tended to respond to the policy initiatives and financial incentives placed by the centre in a manner which reflected their role as agents of central government (Young and Rao 1997). Local interests were never really entrenched in central government machinery, notwithstanding the professional basis of intergovernmental relationships. There was a period of relative calm in central–local relations in the so-called 'golden age' from about

1950 to 1975, which disguised the political impotence of local government. The loss of political independence only became damaging when the period of relatively generous central government beneficence ended in the 1970s. Then local government had to fight its battles with central government and started to carve out a new identity of its own.

This account of the dual polity is, of course, a massive oversimplification. There have always been links between the services of local government, professional associations and central government departments. As many critics have commented (e.g. Stoker 1995: 103), the account of the separation between central and local politics does not take account of the varied interactions between central and local government and the great interest central government has always taken in the implementation of policies, such as housing and education. Nor does it reflect the interdependence of local and central government in both policy formulation and implementation. Nevertheless, the thesis captures an underlying principle governing political behaviour and was the basis for the exercise of power. The doctrine was expressed in a set of practices and understandings that have influenced the status of local politics in the political system as a whole. This was demonstrated just before the June 1997 general election when many elected Labour local politicians stood down from local office before standing for election to the House of Commons. Joint office holding between central and local government is still very rare. The culture of disdain by central politicians towards their localities is very much alive. Jones and Travers (1994) capture this in their colourful interview-based study of the views of central government civil servants and ministers. A large number of these people have highly deprecating views about local government. The two cultures and two realms of influence continue even in the era of local governance.

Local government in the community

The constitutional framework, the history of central control, the expansion of the welfare state and local government reorganisation constitute a sequence of developments which, by the 1970s, had fastened in place a particular form of local government. The pattern was broadly one where local councillors and officers were preoccupied with the delivery of services and which was imbued with the culture of professionalism. Public decision-makers operated largely within large and complex local authorities that exercised some discretion according to central government guidelines and professional standards. Local authorities generally had weak or hands-off links to other local organisations. Critics argued that the monopoly enjoyed by local government allowed it to retreat from the public it was supposed to serve.

The community power literature of the 1970s illustrated the restricted communal character of English local government. Researchers on English local politics were highly influenced both by the studies of the pluralists and by Hunter and the elite theorists. Though coming to different conclusions, pluralists and elitists shared common subjects of analysis. They investigated the complex relationships between mass publics, interest groups, and business interests over local public policy matters. While pluralists concluded that no overarching elite controlled local power, elitists pointed to a pattern of domination by private sector and established political interests. English researchers working in the pluralist tradition were unable to confirm the widespread involvement of local groups and interests in policy-making they expected to find; instead, they identified a narrow elite of bureaucratic officials and party politicians at the core of local power. Political parties tightly controlled local affairs (Green 1981). The leader of the council and a few powerful councillors usually controlled policy. Alongside local political leaders, key officials at the head of their departments were important actors in the decision-making process and they formed close relationships with the political leadership. Depending on the character of the locality and on its history of political control, power flowed from the significant autonomy these two small groups (politicians and officials) had over local policy formation. Councillors who did not hold senior committee positions and junior officers were hardly involved (Blowers 1980).

The pattern of party politics in England also helped consolidate a unified and insular form of politics. While party has been integral to urban politics in England from the beginning, the tradition of politically independent local councils in non-urban areas has only been gradually undermined during the twentieth century. Party control over most town halls is generally tight, with dominant local parties controlling the policy agenda of and providing the political support for the council and its committees (Gyford 1983, 1991). While parties are diverse coalitions, articulating many sets of interests and varying from place to place, they are highly centralised when compared to their counterparts overseas. Where single party administrations prevail, party caucuses usually control the allocation of committee chairs and decide policy in the party group away from the deliberations of council chambers. The legitimacy of these arrangements has been called into question, as parties have declining memberships and a much weaker connection to their local communities than hitherto (Game and Leach 1995).

The nature of party control has always differed markedly between urban and non-urban areas: in urban areas there has been a gradual strengthening of party control and a concomitant weakening of party competition (Boyne and Ashworth 1997). From the mid-1970s onwards, single parties often took control of city municipalities for sustained periods of time as urban England turned its back on the Conservatives. Indeed, in urban areas, the strong party system strengthened in spite of the political turbulence of the 1980s, when a new cohort, born of the radical political movement of the late 1960s and early 1970s, challenged the traditional local leadership. The Labour and Conservative local administrations of the 1980s used local government more effectively than their predecessors to introduce new policies (Gyford 1984), a local activism that provoked a concerted central government backlash thereafter. This phenomenon of single party control was less marked in non-metropolitan areas, especially in the counties; indeed, single party control has weakened since the early 1980s. Even in urban areas the tradition of single party control has weakened, the consequence of greatly increased electoral volatility and the growth of third parties since the 1970s (Rallings and Thrasher 1997).

The traditional pattern of party politics and the bureaucratic style of rule in the 'dual polity' tended to shut out the inclusion of a wide range of local groups. The involvement of pressure groups at the local level has been low, especially when compared with the United States of America (Gyford 1984: 91–8). Except for a small number of 'insiders' (Dearlove 1979), those groups with any influence had contacts only with local officials rather than with politicians (Newton 1976); local government elites regarded most groups as 'unhelpful' (Saunders 1980). That local government was freed from the checks and balances of local democratic influence, either through elections (see below) or through interest group pressures, compounded the portrait of a bureaucratised local administration.

In addition to party dominated councils and weak pressure group input, elections have had a low impact in English local politics. This is another instance where the English case stands apart from the classic pluralist model, for which elections are vital in sustaining a polyarchical type of politics. Dunleavy (1980) summarises the conventional wisdom that national opinion rather than local performance determined local election results. This phenomenon produced a feeling of local electoral helplessness in the face of national electoral tendencies, which may have proved a self-fulfilling prophecy. It certainly hastened the isolation of local government in the post-war years. For a variety of reasons, local councillors and officers paid scant attention to local representation and, partly as a result, local turnout in elections remains low (at about 30 per cent, much less than the European average of about 70 per cent), local interest in politics is weak and cynicism on the part of the citizens has been growing (Bloch and John 1991). If there are many reasons for the low level of local political participation in England (Rallings and Thrasher 1997), the arcane political organisation and structure of local government have played as great a role in discouraging local voting as the perverse electoral system, migration, economic change and the dominance of national politics.

The 'dual elite' model oversimplified the complexity of local political systems by exaggerating the extent to which local authorities were isolated from their environments. Several studies emphasised the links between English local authorities and other decision-makers (Friend et al. 1974). Dunleavy (1980) challenged the conventional wisdom that community power structures had dissolved under the weight of national influences. Many 'networks of community influence' continued to exist, taking the form of links of local party organisations, cross or joint membership of local councillors on other elite organisations and committees, interest groups and networks of corruption. Dunleavy's account of mass housing in the 1960s and 1970s revealed the connections between local political leaders and business interests (Dunleavy 1981), though this was rather a closed kind of relationship, away from the community and public scrutiny, and which had some disastrous consequences for public housing policy at that time. Saunders' (1980) research in Croydon also indicated strong links between the council and business groups; these links occurred on an informal basis, and were monopolised by the officer cadre. Newton's (1976) study of Birmingham confirmed the importance of interest groups, elections and public opinion, although he concluded that the 'dual elite' still exercised considerable autonomy over policy. Bassett and Harloe's (1990) study of the growth coalition in Swindon is a reminder of the close relationships which emerged between local political leaders and business as both sought to attract inward investment and promote economic development. In spite of these qualifications, the 'dual elite' model of power has much validity in describing the centralisation of local political parties and bureaucracies in local politics. As Dunleavy (1980: 156) argues, the community networks 'underpinned and legitimated the insulation of local political institutions from electoral control or developed mechanisms of control by ordinary citizens'. It is against this background of an entrenched dual elite at the heart of English localities that we can appreciate the extent of the transition to local governance.

From local government to local governance: causes and controversies

The debate about the move from local government to local governance derives from a dramatic decade in English politics. Few thought in May 1979 that the election of Margaret Thatcher as Prime Minister would lead to the restructuring of the key institutions of public life. But, after a shaky start, the 11 years of Conservative governments under her leadership reformed established public bodies and changed them beyond recognition. Locally elected councils were one of the government's prime targets as they appeared to embody the bureaucratic state and the inefficient provision of welfare services. The resurgent radical right despised local government; in the place of large, overbearing bureaucracies run by unaccountable professionals, it wished to empower smaller agencies that, aided by the market mechanism, would favour consumers. With this background set of ideas, many policies and much legislation in the 1980s undermined the foundations of democratically elected government. The Conservatives attacked the basic principle of the elected local authority. They did not approve of an organisation with the freedom and discretion to provide a complex range of services and the ability to levy local taxes to pay for its decisions. The current pattern of institutional fragmentation, the importance of quasi-markets in the local public sector, the role of the private sector and the co-existence of myriad competing local agencies appear to originate from this radical ideological experiment in English politics.

If the paragraph above alone summed up the path from local government to local governance, there would not be much point in writing a comparative book on the subject. The exercise would show only the unusual character of English politics. Its party system throws up radical leaders and its constitutional framework allows such a far-reaching set of radical legislation to be put in place. When the reforms are portrayed in such an ideological manner, the English experience – one of emaciated local government and growing private sector provision – has nothing in common with the path of the decentralisation of central power to elected local government followed in other countries. England, as ever, stands out as the odd case. It is a warning about what not to do.

However, the radical changes in local politics, while owing much to the policies of the governments in power in the 1980s, were not just the result of the ideology and statecraft of one political party. The reforms derived from the broader economic and political changes affecting western democracies. The Thatcher governments operated within and were propelled by wider changes in the economy and by the political logic of reforming public service provision. Writers on English politics have now questioned the notion that Conservative governments had a clear plan to restructure the welfare state along market lines (Marsh 1995). Ministers adapted policies as they went along. The Conservative reforms of local government were a series of incremental changes that took on a life of their own and ended up by being far from incremental. Conservative governments followed policies that seemed to work in particular contexts; and the politicians and civil servants experimented and sought to learn from the successes and the failures. In fact, the time when ideological Conservatism was at its height between 1987 and 1990 was when the strategy went drastically wrong. As the policies did not seem to work, Prime Minister John Major and his colleagues continued a slower but more manageable pace of reform after 1990, a policy continued and elaborated by the Labour Party when it came into office in 1997.

Many of the changes governments introduced in the 1980s were already well in train in the 1970s, and continued in the late 1990s long after Margaret Thatcher's cabinet colleagues ejected her in December 1990. The reforms emerged from the broad cross-national trends we discuss in chapter 1, but they have taken a particular form in England because of its constitutional arrangements and traditions, the history of local government as a service provider, the parlous local tax base and an ill-sorted set of technocratic reforms introduced in the 1970s. In the context of our comparison, it is vital to observe the form the evolution towards local governance took in England. This evolution combined an original policy mix of structural reforms, financial retrenchment, central restructuring and organisational change.

Structural reform

Before 1972 English local government had a complex and fragmented patchwork structure of local authorities which it inherited from the waves of reforms that occurred from the mid-nineteenth century onwards. Particularly characteristic of the fragmentation were the 79 county boroughs and the 1,086 boroughs, urban districts and rural districts. The lack of an apparent relationship between size, function and the type of population frustrated a generation of reformers who wanted large local authorities to administer services effectively. What the technocratic debates from the 1940s to the 1970s neglected was the importance these apparently ill-thought-out jurisdictions had to their local communities and to the range of public and civic organisations that occupied them (Sharpe 1978). But the reformers largely got their way in the proposals of the Redcliffe-Maud

Commission in 1969, and the technocratic solution remained even in the watered down reforms of 1972. England created some of the largest local authorities in Europe. Almost immediately, their lack of relationship to settled community patterns caused the government to try to reform the system again in 1977, 1985 and 1992. The 1972 reform reflected the political weakness of English local government that was held in sway by central government and expert opinion. Only the counties were able to exercise power to retain – by and large – their original identities. The reform compounded the weakness of local government by creating organisations that were even more bureaucratic and out of touch with local communities than before. These large authorities, which seemed so appropriate to the needs of a technocratic era, are one of the sources of the problems of English local government as it relates to local communities. It is also the reaction to these forms of government that characterises the English road to governance with its stress on new forms of inter-organisational relationships and the quest to decentralise and to reinvent democratic mechanisms.

The bugbear of local finance

If there is one factor that caused the reform and change in English local government since the 1970s, it is finance. This chapter is not the place for a detailed history of local government finance (see Travers 1985). However, the tensions caused by the English system of funding local government overshadowed central–local relations. While other countries have experienced tensions over financial matters, and this has caused central governments to become more interested in the delivery of public policies (see Newton and Karran 1985), nowhere has this assumed similar proportions as in England. This was in part caused by the 1974–9 Labour government's spending cuts, particularly on capital expenditure, when Tony Crosland famously declared 'the party's over'. As a result local authorities reduced their expenditure and put up taxes. During the 1980s the Conservatives struggled with the issues of central control and local independence in financial matters. They introduced a series of ill-fated reforms to control local expenditure. Central grant controls, central grant penalties, the capping of local taxes and expenditure and then the experiment with the single person local tax, the poll tax, were, to varying degrees, failures. In part, the normal conflicts in central–local financial relations which occur in every country were heightened by the division of power within the English state between the finance and economic policy ministry, the Treasury, with its desire to reduce government expenditure as part of a macro-economic strategy, and the rather weaker demands of spending ministries, such as the Department of the Environment (now Department of the Environment, Transport and Regions) which is responsible for much central spending on local government. The conflict was intensified by the reaction of Labour-run local councils to resist the cuts and the attempts by the Conservatives to counter their strategies.

Tensions in the financial relationship between central and local government were responsible for much of the central intervention in local politics and the particular form it took in England, with controls over rates, reforms of housing finance and experiments with new taxes, many of which were counterproductive. More than anything else, local government reforms in the 1980s were a by-product of the central obsession with finance. That the issue was always on the agenda partly explains the depth and vituperative nature of the conflicts between central and local government. The introduction of rate capping from 1985, the transfer of the business rate to central government in 1990 and the introduction of tough new spending formulae (Total Standard Spending) represented a new level of central control over local government finance. But the enhanced legal regulation of local government finance also represented a settlement of sorts. Once the highly unpopular poll tax had been shelved, political radicalism began to ebb and central–local relations settled down to a less frenetic existence.

The central restructuring of the 1980s and 1990s

While the reform of local government finance generated much of the conflict in central–local government relations in the 1970s and 1980s, many more profound changes occurred gradually. These reforms did not stem just from party politics or even only from central government, but they culminated to affect the structure, functions and ways of working of English local government as it had evolved since 1945. The reforms had many origins, which derive from the general factors discussed in chapter 1. The internationalised character of the English economy made central intervention in local economies almost inevitable. Central ministries have been under pressure to improve economic performance since the mid-1960s, and these imperatives became more prominent in the 1970s with economic recession and incipient inflation. The concern with economic performance also started to ripple into other public services that affect economic efficiency, such as education with its impact on human capital. The economy also helped create a crisis of public finances and encouraged the government to place limits on public expenditure. The Conservatives adopted a particular response to these forces that involved making the public sector more efficient and less of an apparent burden on the private sector, and they tried to involve the private sector in public decisions. But it is likely that even had the Conservatives not been in power, any government would have reformed local government, encouraged more efficiency and sought better performance in public services. To show that the reforms did not just emerge from one party, the Labour government elected in 1997, while accommodating local government participation in its new programmes, has continued much of the obsession with performance and tendency towards central regulation of its Conservative predecessor.

The first set of reforms the Conservatives started was to require local authorities to contract out services to the private sector. At first this was directed against the highly inefficient direct labour organisations, responsible for the building and maintenance of highways. Once successful, the practice was extended to nearly every aspect of local government services in the 1988 Local Government Act, in particular to refuse collection, leisure management, street cleaning, catering and park maintenance. It was expanded to white collar activities in 1992. Contracted-out services also figure implicitly, such as in the relationships between the purchasers and providers of community care. Here the providers carry out services on behalf of the local authority. The result is that many new organisations have emerged at the local level, both public and private, and they have a very close relationship with local authorities. Local authorities need to cultivate a wider range of horizontal sets of relationships in order to prosper in this organisational environment.

Competitive tendering has brought about profound changes in accounting and management practices which in turn have had an influence on the internal culture of local authorities by reinforcing the trend towards leaner bureaucracies and the use of measures of performance evaluation (Walsh 1995), all of which have been enhanced by the Best Value regime of the Labour government since 1997. Best Value allows local authorities to provide services themselves, but they must observe a highly restrictive set of guidelines should they do so.

Conservative governments in the 1980s created many special purpose organisations, some of which took powers away from local authorities. The first of these were the much-discussed Urban Development Corporations (UDCs), introduced on a small scale in 1980 and expanded in subsequent years. These took over local planning and housing functions from local authorities in designated areas, and had large sums of expenditure to invest in capital projects for economic regeneration. They were headed by a board and chief executive accountable to the Department of the Environment. While they were few in number, as there were never more than 11 at any one time, they represented a new implantation of direct central control and challenged the monopoly of elected local authorities. They were also part of a more general centralised direction in economic policy (Harding 1989). There were other examples of centrally organised and funded bodies, such as the Housing Action Trusts, introduced by the Housing Act 1988, which supervised the regeneration of run-down public housing estates, and the City Technology Colleges introduced by the Education Reform Act 1988 as new forms of state school. These initiatives were short term. They reflected ministerial initiatives and did not cover the whole country. Rather different was the creation of Training and Enterprise Councils (TECs) in 1989. The TECs were uniform across England and Wales, and had responsibility for co-ordinating and financing local training policies and programmes. Though each TEC was headed by a chief executive and a privately led board, there was a direct line of accountability to the Department of Employment, now Department for Education and Employment. The TECs have performed a less central role under the Labour government elected in 1997, but the practice of special purpose and centrally directed public bodies has continued. This was demonstrated by the creation of partnership organisations to run the bodies designed to improve educational performance: the education action zones, for example. The direct result of this framework is to create a maze of new organisations that often have functions very similar to those of elected local government. The multiplication of organisations with similar tasks is one of the sources of the co-ordination problem of local governance.

Structural reform has never ceased being a theme of debate and policy. The technocratic edifice of 1972 was gradually dismantled, but the costs and obstacles to reform prevented a thoroughgoing restructuring of the system. In 1977 the Labour government tried to promote a further reform by its proposals for organic change, but it failed to generate enough energy and enthusiasm to get its proposals off the ground. More drastically, the Conservatives' disenchantment with the reformed local government system and with the structure and politics of metropolitan government, together with Margaret Thatcher's antipathy to the Greater London Council, led to the notoriously politicised decision to abolish the GLC and the metropolitan counties in the White Paper. *Streamlining the Cities*, implemented in 1986. The removal of these strategic councils created many new authorities, often called joint boards; these are co-operative arrangements, often required by law, between the lower-level authorities that remain in these areas to administer metropolitan-wide services. Examples are in the public transport, fire, planning and civil defence fields. While local authorities and other bodies have adapted to these reforms, there is a highly confusing level of governance in England's main cities which the Labour government's mayor and a strategic authority for London are partially designed to address. Yet the new Greater London Authority is a slim-line body that leaves much of the multitude of London quangos and special purpose agencies intact.

Reorganisations did not stop with the metropolitan areas, but continued in England in 1992 when the Conservative central government set up the Local Government Commission. The Commission was an advisory body that roamed non-metropolitan England making recommendations in the light of central government guidance to simplify the structure of local government. As the Commission moved around the country, central government policy changed away from recommending one tier of local government. As a result the commission produced an inconsistent structure for local government – single tier in some parts of the country, two tier in other counties, and a hybrid structure, with some big towns gaining 'unitary status' while the rest of the county remained two tier. Rather than simplifying English local government, the 1992–5 re-organisation made it much more complex, in many ways returning England to the pre-1972 local government system. To remedy the confusion caused by structural change and the absence of planning in the 1980s, local authorities have increasingly participated in partnerships over such matters as land use and waste disposal, creating a non-statutory set of networks (Travers 1995).

The privatisation of public utilities has created new organisations at the local level, which no longer fit into a centralised framework. Water, electricity and gas companies make a number of decisions that affect public policy, and these organisations are present at the local or regional level. At levels above the local authority there has developed an increasingly complex tier of governance which incorporates the government offices for the regions, created in 1994, regional organisations of business and trades unions, regional organisations of local authorities, and a wide range of non-elected bodies, such as the 'Next Steps' and similar agencies. All of these bodies have a set of interactions at the city level, the main focus of this book. The proposal by New Labour to create regional chambers of representatives of local authorities will not replace the network, but will add another body that will only be able to co-ordinate regional matters to a limited degree. Regional Development Agencies are yet another co-ordinating body that has to liaise with the other regional and local bodies.

These diverse trends all imply that the field of local politics is far more disparate, changeable and multifarious than it was in the 1970s. The number of organisations has multiplied many-fold. There are different types of organisations. Some are very small while others are large; some have the micro areas as their remit, yet others relate to the county or the region; some have a mandate from elected local government, while others have lines of control to central government or are privately run. All these bodies occupy the urban space, particularly in the cities we study for this book. The further implication, which we test, is that they need to co-operate in order to foster effective local policies.

It might appear that the 1980s and 1990s was a period of unfettered central control that witnessed the domination, if not destruction, of local government. Indeed central government reduced local government discretion, took away its powers, replaced it with its own agencies and removed its financial discretion, but central government still needed the co-operation, expertise and legitimacy of elected local government when implementing its reforms. There were periods of conflict between central and local government, when central government agencies tried to implement policies without the co-operation of local institutions, such as in the 1980s when the government first introduced urban development corporations. But there were other periods when locally elected authorities pragmatically forgot their resentment at their loss of powers and worked with the new agencies. Likewise, the boards, chief executives and employees of these organisations soon realised that they had to talk to and build trusting relationships with the existing local organisations if they were going to stand much chance of implementing their policies. The classic example was the urban development corporations that gradually wrestled a place as part of a public sector led coalition in English cities (Imrie and Thomas 1993). It was through the need to work together to solve common problems that the pattern of English local governance started to emerge.

Democracy, leadership and the governance of localities

Local governance in England cannot be reduced to a set of reforms launched by central government. There have also been profound changes at the level of localities, in line with the various influences on governance overall; there are many influences upon the local dimension of governance. Some of these are largely external, such as greater economic and political competition between localities and the influence of new ideas from the European Union and other bodies. Other changes come from within localities that have adapted to new funding regimes, adjusted to Europeanisation, engaged in local experimentation, witnessed the increased activism of local interest groups and introduced important management changes within local authorities.

Adapting to new funding regimes has introduced a new element of competition between cities which takes several forms. The first is the growth of competition for inward investment that is a feature of the internationalised economy with its footloose capital. This process illuminates how private companies have much more freedom about where to relocate their plant and their administrative offices. This is the subject of chapter 4, so we do not discuss it here, save to note the importance it has in creating coalitions of local public and private interests which can mobilise resources to tempt these national and international businesses to a particular location. Less discussed is the competition for public resources, which takes two forms. The first involves mainly national sources of public finance in the form of programmes in areas such as road schemes, and the favourable allocation of central government formulae grants; the other is funds from the European Union.

Lobbying for national resources by local politicians and their political contacts at the centre has not been a public activity of English politics and is officially frowned on by national politicians and civil servants. There is no equivalent to the pork barrel in US politics where national legislators try to ensure the best allocation of resources to their locality, or the close relationship between local politicians and central bureaucrats as in France. But there is evidence that local politicians increasingly seek to represent their interests at the centre because of the more competitive environment within which they operate. Local decision-makers see themselves as local emissaries to obtain public investment and favourable decisions from Whitehall and Brussels (Stoker and Young 1993: 151–78). The change in central government funding regimes, away from general grants allocated according to a formula to discretionary ones, creates an incentive for local politicians and officers to use their contacts at the centre to maximise the chance of obtaining a favourable allocation. In the 1990s, central government introduced funding regimes that were much more explicitly competitive, where local authorities had to bid for resources from a limited pot (John et al. 2001). The first 'challenge funding' initiative was City Challenge established in 1991; in 1994 competition was introduced for the annual sum of £2 billion of urban funding in the Single Regeneration Budget scheme administered by the newly created Government Offices for the Regions. 'Challenge Funding' regimes were subsequently extended to a wide range of programmes, such as capital spending for local government. In 1997, while the Labour government sought to reduce what it saw as the wasteful competition of these schemes, it continued and enhanced the Single Regeneration Budget and extended competition to new government policies, such as Best Value pilot authorities, the 'beacon' authorities (that have special freedoms to act) and Education Action Zones.

The competition for resources has created new incentives for co-operation among local partners. This is essential as many of these schemes need to demonstrate that effective partnerships exist. Local councils have everywhere set up partnerships to reach out to local interests such as business. Likewise local businesses sought to become more involved in local affairs to ensure that their cities benefit from government and EU largesse; inter-city competition has also affected roles of local political leaders and administrative officials. Rather than act as just party politicians, they have had to look outward from their authorities – upwards as lobbyists of central government and across their cities as leaders of partnerships and as representatives of the whole of the city. Local leaders are becoming rather like continental mayors in this respect, though without a national power base. The 1997 Labour government's legislation on new executive structures, which includes provision for directly elected mayors, formalises the changing informal roles rather than introducing a new practice of leadership.

The second factor that has affected local decision-making has been international policy transfers. In the main this has been through the European Union that allocates funds for local areas and makes policy affecting local government (Goldsmith 1993; John 1996, 2001). The influence of the European Union has encouraged local authorities to lobby for funds, to enter networks of national and European policy-makers, to employ European liaison officers and to set up European committees, and to open offices in Brussels. It is rather hard to judge the effect of these activities. It is tempting to regard them as essentially financially orientated and a trend in local government which will come to the end of its lifecycle. The alternative scenario is that Europeanisation encourages local government to create more effective partnerships, to work more closely with the private and voluntary sectors, to engage in networks and to take a more European approach to policy problems (John 1994). In short, the Europeanisation of local government is one of the factors that have influenced the shift towards governance; in particular it has encouraged more positive attitudes towards partnership and policy-making.

Europeanisation is linked to a third set of changes in local government. These are the developments of new fields of activity or sub-sectors in advance of central government regulation. As our very brief treatment of nineteenth-century local government showed, local government was first and foremost an innovator. The nationally regulated services and even private sector activities were often started by municipal governments. We argue that this sort of activity ebbed during the twentieth century. It continued in some policy sectors, such as experiments in secondary education in the 1950s and with personal social services, but it was not until the 1980s that local experimentation became the norm. The rise of the urban left in the 1980s brought a host of new concerns, such as women, policing, race and sexual orientation, which were fostered by links to new interest groups. Particularly after the election of radical administrations in London and the metropolitan areas, these concerns turned into new policies, run by committees. Thus police committees, women's committees, race committees and their like became common in English local government and were frowned upon by the right-wing press and by Conservative politicians (Gyford 1985; Lansley et al. 1989). Most of these experiments were short-lived, reflecting the lifespan of radical experiments at the local level, and were attenuated by abolition of the

Greater London Council and the metropolitan counties in 1986. They also suffered as easy targets for spending cuts during the financial constraints that faced local government in the late 1980s. But many new policies continued. The main example was the new economic development function (see chapter 4) which was eventually recognised by central government in 1989. The European Union function discussed above links closely to economic development, given the regeneration focus of many of their programmes. Another example is crime prevention that has increasingly a local dimension, with local authorities working closely with the police. Local authorities have expanded their role in environment policy, particularly in response to local agenda 21 (Young 1996). While these sectors can be isolated areas of innovation within local government, the argument is that they are 'change drivers' (Mills 1994), typically working across local government and staffed by activist officials who argue for priority to be given to the new sector and convert others to the new cause. Many officers and councillors have close contacts with new interest groups and a range of community and voluntary organisations.

The fourth factor that has affected local politics has been the changed orientation of local interest groups. We noted earlier that the impact of pressure groups in local government has been weak. There is some evidence to suggest that community groups, business representatives, single issue groups and the voluntary sector have become more active and assertive since the 1970s. Stoker (1991) suggests that the community-based activism of the 1970s did not ebb away but carried over and developed during the 1990s. He also argues that local authorities have opened up to more interest groups through management reforms, decentralisation and extensive forms of consultation. It also seems that the stock of local associations has increased (Maloney et al. 1998). The multicultural character of local communities is now increasingly expressed in interest group representation, as ethnic minority groups organise themselves and gain experience in local politics (Ball and Solomos 1990). Many issues raised by interest groups – such as local crime or environmental policies – have now become part of the agenda of local authorities. The pattern of local networks and associations has expanded. The policy-making arena is more complex and changeable. Local authorities face further challenges to their dominance as they have to negotiate and respond to these diverse demands.

The business community re-awakened as a local political interest at the end of the 1980s. After a period of alienation from the radical local authorities that ran English cities, business started to make more effort to improve contacts with local politicians and officials. This was partly spurred by central government that wished to encourage local partnerships, but businesses have also become increasingly conscious of the local dimension to their survival and of the links between public sector activity and local competitiveness.

The fifth aspect of change which has indirectly affected inter-organisational politics is the internal management of local authorities. We have already mentioned the influence of contracting-out. Much of the impetus to reform the structure of local government came from central government organisations, such as the Audit Commission, set up in 1983 to run local government auditing. The Audit Commission has carried out research, has created indicators of local authority performance and has disseminated local information. But many of the changes originated from within local government and its allied organisations, such as academics, consultants, accountants and the private sector. Management changes have broken up or weakened the hierarchical organisation of local government (Leach et al. 1994; Stoker and Rhodes 1999). Examples include the split between purchaser and provider, the decentralisation of customer access to smaller neighbourhood units, the delegation of financial management and the growth of cost centres. Other reforms (such as the use of performance indicators and local charters) are based on a desire to listen to the consumer of local government services. Labour's Best Value regime for local authorities maintains the managerialist and competitive focus. Local authorities must develop a vast array of performance indicators to ensure they are offering best value for money. A related development has been the involvement of users in public services (Pollitt et al. 1998).

These changes have reduced the presence of local authorities as departmentalised and hierarchical organisations; the local authority has become as institutionally fragmented as its external world. The complexity of relationships requires a more networked pattern of decision-making if local government is to be effective. Management reform has introduced permanent change as part of the life of local authorities; this has made them more responsive to outside influence, brought them closer to the practices of the private sector and other public organisations, and encouraged them to accept complex and shifting networks as a permanent feature of policy-making.

Conclusion

Taken together these changes amount to a fundamental reshaping in the organisation, practices and culture of English local government and the context in which it operates. The revival in interest group activity, new sectors of policy intervention and the fragmentation of local authorities are part of the environment of local governance. They demonstrate that the English version of governance did not just emerge from radical reforms of central government in the 1980s; it has its origins in the reconstitution of local bureaucracies and changes in political behaviour. It was influenced by transnational pressures, policy change and finance from the European Union and by the growing competition for resources and investment.

Of particular interest for local government is the potential for renewal of local government itself. Policy and management change may have disheartened many participants – the third of councillors who stand down after one term of office is testament to the burdens of office in the new management culture (Bloch 1992). The central controls and scarcity of resources appear to limit local democratic choice, to reduce the role of local government and to hand over responsibilities for co-ordinating policy to local quangos or to the government offices for the regions. But as the new policy experiments show, there is also much scope for local government innovation. Local government remains the largest local public organisation with the biggest slice of public finance and vast stores of expertise in matters of organisation and service delivery. Most of all, it retains its democratic legitimacy by virtue of local elections, in spite of low turnout and low public interest in local affairs. If it is able to renew itself as a democratic organisation in the 2000s as much as it renewed itself as a service delivering organisation in the 1980s it will have a future as the key body that can co-ordinate the vast array of local groups and organisations. It has the ability to give identity to local communities and to articulate their needs. All the conflict of the 1980s, the mounting central government controls and the emergence of competing organisations may have had the paradoxical effect of renewing the institutions of local government itself.

3 Local politics and policy-making in France

Following on from the discussion of English sub-national politics and policies in chapter 2, we now examine French-style local governance. The chapter starts with a historical survey of the evolution of central–local government relations in France and describes the changing environment within which local and regional authorities operate. While the changing external environment has called into question important features of the traditional French model of politics and policy, we contend that internal changes have led more directly to French local governance. We identify three main internal causes for French-style local governance (section two): the diminishing capacity of the central state as a policy actor; the far-ranging institutional reforms of the early 1980s; and changing patterns of local political participation and local innovation in public policy. The principal features of local governance in France (section three) are greater institutional fragmentation, the development of networks and partnerships in an effort to enhance local governing capacity and efforts at new types of policy co-ordination, notably in the form of contractual relationships. After addressing the issues of the leadership of the new French urban governance and its political accountability, the chapter concludes that the republican model of territorial administration has gradually given way to a more complex pattern of sub-national governance.

Centre, periphery and locality in the indivisible Republic

One of the central paradoxes of post-Revolutionary France is the coexistence of rigid centralised judicial norms and rules with the rich diversity of local and regional cultures and practices. French sub-national authorities have operated within the confines of a highly centralising state tradition that emphasises the indivisible nature of political legitimacy and the organisational pre-eminence and legitimacy of the state. As a consequence of the Revolution and the ensuing Napoleonic period, the French state gradually crushed regional identities and centralised political power in Paris. The Napoleonic regime established the model of territorial integration that governed centre–periphery relations throughout most of the nineteenth century. The prefect was the pivot of this system. The prefect was the representative of the central state in French localities, charged with controlling local communes, implementing central government policies and maintaining public order. Underneath the prefect, the sub-prefects exercised an even closer control over local authorities. Government departments were organised in an analogous manner, with decentralised units usually operating at the departmental and sub-departmental levels. For example, taxation offices were arranged around a departmental division, with sub-divisions at the level of the *arrondissement* (electoral constituency) and officers at the level of the commune (Mabileau 1991). This tentacular organisation brought forth metaphors of the 'honeycomb state' (Dupuy and Thoenig 1983).

As the Republic was 'one and indivisible', local government units were long considered to be the antennae of central government. The 38,000[1] municipal councils in the communes and the 96 general councils in the departments were instruments of central regulation before becoming locally elected authorities. The 96 departments were the product of Napoleonic centralisation. They were sufficiently large to allow for the efficient territorial administration and implementation of central state policies; they were small enough not to pose a challenge to central state direction.

In practice, the pattern of sub-national politics contained a rather more subtle mix of centralising ambition and local influence than implied by the Cartesian model. The 38,000 French communes – based on the parishes of the pre-Revolutionary *ancien régime* – were the foci of local identities and community interests that persisted in spite of the centralising ambition of the Republic. The pre-eminent figure in French small town society was the mayor, the personification of local identity. Local influences became more important with the gradual move to democratisation and economic liberalism in the 1870s and 1880s (Tudesq 1983). The Departmental (1871) and Municipal (1884) Government acts recognised 'local liberties' for the first time, permitted democratic elections and consolidated local influence.

Prefects, notables and cross-regulation

The emblematic figure of this state-centred model of public administration was the prefect. There is no English local government equivalent. The roles performed by the French prefect included those of 'lord lieutenant, emergency security commissioner, director general of the field services, of the ministries, political agent for the government, and executive officer for the Departmental council' (Machin 1976: 237). Before 1982 the prefect was able to exercise a considerable degree of supervisory control – *la tutelle* – over local authorities. As representative of the central state, the prefect retained formal hierarchical control over local authority budgets as well as being an important source of inspiration and assistance when implementing public policies. The prefect was also in formal charge of the ministerial field services that administered most government policies at the territorial level. As the executive authority within the 96 departmental councils, the prefect drew up the budget, and prepared, approved and implemented the decisions of the council chamber (meeting formally for only six weeks a year). Favoured by the central state as the principal level of sub-national administration, the departmental councils were vested with important formal responsibilities from an early date. From 1852 onwards, they had the right to raise their own budgets; in the 1871 Departmental Act, the departmental council was recognised as the sovereign authority on 'all matters of interest to the departments' (Mabileau 1991: 34). Since prefects were the executive officers, they were generally favourable to expanding the responsibilities of the departmental council.

The 1884 Municipal Government Act recognised the responsibility of municipal government for 'the affairs of the commune'. The Act sanctioned municipal councils as entities with their own legal character and the right to raise budgets. The prefect was less directly involved in the management of the communes than the departmental councils. Day-to-day relationships with the mayors of small communes were usually carried out by sub-prefects, whose number varied according to the size of a department. Prefects confined their relationships to genuine *notables*; these were either the mayors of important communes, departmental councillors representing cantons (the administrative sub-divisions of departments), the local representatives of parliament (deputies and senators) or – more usually – individuals combining these offices. The most important unwritten duty of the prefect was to act as an arbiter between conflicting local interests, especially between competing localities. An ability to maintain good relations with the most prominent local actors was an important source of the prefect's influence.

While prefects formed an integral part of the French pattern of territorial administration, French mayors have been subjected to the most sustained attention as the focal actors of local political communities (Dion 1986; Rondin 1986; Garraud 1989; Fontaine and Le Bart 1994). As embodied in the 1884 Municipal Government Act, the French mayor is a local political leader and the representative of the central state in the commune. In the ensuing section, we will consider these two separate but related aspects of mayoral leadership: the mayor as a local *notable* and the mayor as an intermediary of central–local government relations.

The mayor as a local notable

There were certain stable features of French mayoral leadership that helped define the office. These were social notability, the stability of political personnel and the practice of political clientelism. The first prerequisite of mayoral leadership was social notability. Directly nominated by central government during the Second Empire (1852–70), only individuals from higher socio-economic categories were eligible to be mayors. The phenomenon continued throughout the nineteenth century; mayors were prominent representatives of local society, such as lawyers, doctors and businessmen (Tudesq 1983). This pattern gradually weakened with the rise of political parties in local government, but it never disappeared completely, especially in smaller communes. *Notables* were valued insofar as they could negotiate effectively with the exterior, especially with central government. Social prestige was a valuable resource to be exchanged with prefects. The second characteristic of the mayoral office was longevity. Once elected, mayors (and presidents of departmental councils) were notoriously difficult to dislodge. This characteristic has remained valid, as demonstrated by the high rates of re-election for incumbent mayors, and the longevity of some political cohorts. Powerful individuals have traditionally occupied the post of mayor for decades; in the post-war period, many mayors first elected to office in 1947 continued to hold municipal office 30 years later. The 1977 cohort promises to be equally durable. The third feature of traditional mayoral political leadership was that of clientelism. Writers such as Mabileau (1991), Faure (1991) and Dion (1986) describe clientelistic practices as being primordial to the functioning of municipal power during the nineteenth and early twentieth centuries and beyond. Clientelism was based on personal relations, personalised political machines (allowing for the distribution of favours) and social prestige.

Case studies of cities have demonstrated the importance not only of the local environment in shaping the character of local political leadership, but also of the ability of local leaders to shape their environments. In his study of Bordeaux, Lagroye (1973) explored the interactive relationship between the mayor Jacques Chaban-Delmas and the local business community. Chaban-Delmas captured the townhall in 1947 with the financial and ideological support of local business. Though Chaban-Delmas pursued policies in favour of business interests once elected mayor, this was a two-way relationship. As a leading Gaullist politician during the Fourth and Fifth Republics (successively deputy, minister, President of the National Assembly and Prime Minister), Chaban-Delmas was able to use his positions of national influence to channel resources to Bordeaux. Local economic and political interests came to depend upon his ability to deliver goods for the locality. While the alliance with local business was important, Chaban-Delmas' power was based on a close partnership with the local Gaullist prefect, who occupied the post from 1958 to 1972. Other powerful local actors gravitated around this central dyad, which insulated itself from the pressures of local elites.

The mayor as an intermediary of central–local relations

As demonstrated in the example of Bordeaux, the importance of personalised mechanisms of central–local linkage has been a key feature of French political traditions. The French literature argues that the political prestige of the local *notable* with national connections facilitates access to other policy-makers: the prefect, the ministerial field services, the departmental and regional executives, and the local and national civil servants. The high point of the *grands notables* was during the Third Republic (1870–1940). These individuals usually combined a national parliamentary office (deputy or senator) with an important local mandate: that of departmental councillor or the mayor of an important commune. The *cumul des mandats* (multiple office holding) provided a safety valve for the expression of local influences in a centrally driven central–local order; indeed, it became the principal way in which local interests were taken into account. Politicians were judged on their ability to defend local interests in a nationally orientated system; hence the importance of a local mandate for a successful national political career. Through the power of the *grands notables*, the 'periphery' became incorporated into national policy-making. As a result local political representation became highly personalised.

The dependency of local democracy on the central state attracted academic attention in the 1960s and 1970s. Specifically related to local administration, Crozier and Thoenig (1975) developed the 'cross-regulation' approach to describe relations between local political and administrative actors in this state-centric and bureaucratic system. Three pillars supported the system. First, the rules governing centre–periphery relations were defined by national politicians and officials; in the state-centric view, the control of society required uniform administrative rules and a hierarchical method of making and implementing public policy. While local politicians and officials could negotiate concessions and exceptions, the rules had to remain intact. Second, there was a long-term dialogue between state officials (notably the prefect) and several *notables* to allow for adjustments to nationally defined rules to reflect local circumstances (Worms 1966). Third, local relationships were limited to a 'dual elite' of political and administrative actors; there was no place for 'third parties, whether they were economic interests or voluntary associations' (Duran and Thoenig 1996: 588). The principal local relationships were thus between political *notables* (parliamentarians, mayors, departmental councillors) and state officials (either prefects, or officials from the ministerial field services). At any given level, such relations were unequal because one partner dominated the other. However, power was exercised with caution since the subordinate partner could often mobilise resources by appealing for support from higher-placed representatives of political or administrative authority. Powerful deputy-mayors, for instance, could call on their national political contacts to override the objections of departmental prefects. There was an incentive for ambitious politicians to accumulate elective offices (*cumul des mandats*) as office gave access to higher levels of authority and consolidated local power bases. Multiple office-holding was especially important during the Third Republic where the presence of the deputy in Paris gave opportunities for accessing favours and resources.

French localities from technocratic modernisation to decentralisation

The pattern of central–local relations known as the French 'system of territorial administration' was a key feature of the traditional French model of policy and politics (Sadran 1992; Cole 1998). It rested upon the principle of administrative uniformity across the nation. It recognised the superiority of central state interests over those of parties, regions, interest groups and localities. It formed part of a hierarchical mode of top-down organisation, whereby public policies originated within government departments or administrative corps, were implemented in localities by state field agencies and local authorities, and were co-ordinated by the prefect, the representative of the French state in the departments.

Dynamic post-war modernisation occurred in spite of local government. The administrative organisation of French local government lagged far behind the challenges of democratisation, industrialisation and urban change. The period 1945–74, known as *les trente glorieuses*, was a period of strong demographic growth, and technocratic modernisation. The orthodox account of French public policy, as developed by Jobert and Muller (1987), described determined central state action, uncovered the existence of tight policy communities and diagnosed a specific form of French state corporatism. It had important ramifications for territorial public policy-making. Armed with a modernising ideology, French state technocratic planners piloted most significant public policies in the 1950s and 1960s (Lorrain 1991). The French state combined various forms of direct and indirect control over urban policy; in a direct sense, central actors determined territorial planning priorities and ensured a steady flow of financial resources to fund centrally defined projects. Urban planning activities were the policy province of the bridges and highways (*ponts et chaussées*) corps that controlled the engineers working in the Equipment ministry (Thoenig 1973). The Equipment ministry (especially the DAFU division) also tightly controlled town planning procedures and regulated activities such as the development of new towns. Indirect methods of control of central government were even more effective. Adopting a standard-setting role, central actors dictated technical norms in housing, road-building and equipment. The state could rely on a network of field services and para-statal agencies to implement its will in French localities. The most significant of these were the *Caisse des dépôts et de consignations*, the state lending bank that controlled most finance, and the *Directions départementales d'équipement* (DDE), the departmentally based field services of the Equipment ministry (Jeannot and Peraldi 1991).

The dominant players in the modernisation of French localities were found in the national ministries and within innovative state structures, such as the DATAR (Burnham 1998). The rules and pecking orders within the state affected the determination of policy, notably between the rival *grands corps*. Decision-makers would be much more likely to deal with public problems if they were associated with a particular technical corps. Thus, the importance of the bridges and highways corps (*ponts et chaussées*), which dominated the Equipment ministry, ensured that urban modernisation remained a salient policy domain; in contrast, environmental policy suffered from its inter-ministerial nature and the unwillingness of any of the technical *grands corps* to be associated with it (Muller 1992; Thoenig 1996). Each ministry jealously guarded its expertise and areas of policy competence, as well as a range of client interest groups.

Local strategies

Local influences could be brought to bear in numerous manners. The effects of *cumul des mandats* and of the need for local adaptations to national rules ensured a space for negotiation, for compromise, even for the building of local coalitions between mayors and prefects in 'local politico-administrative systems'. City case studies (such as those of Lagroye (1973) on Bordeaux, Biarez (1989) on Lyons and Lille, and Phlipponneau on Rennes (1977)) emphasise the importance of local actors in mitigating the effects of national policies. More detailed examination demonstrates that there was no single type of local influence: local actors engaged in pork-barrel politics, lobbying strategies and confrontation.

At their most successful, the activity of nationally prominent politicians in delivering goods and services for their cities recalled models of pork-barrel politics. The role model for such influence was provided by Edmond Herriot, the Radical mayor of Lyons for 40 years and a pivotal figure of the Third Republic: as premier, Herriot stoutly defended the interests of Lyons (Mabileau 1991). Such a pattern was repeated later by Chaban-Delmas, combining the offices of mayor of Bordeaux and Prime Minister. Aside from the example of Chaban-Delmas in Bordeaux, other city case studies have highlighted the role of Gaston Defferre in Marseilles (Bleitrach 1980), Pierre Mauroy in Lille (Bruyelle 1991) and Edmond Hervé in Rennes (Le Galès 1993). Even nationally prominent mayors were usually at their most effective when deploying a strategy of close co-operation with state actors. Thus, the Popular Republican (MRP) mayor of Rennes, Henri Fréville, co-operated effectively with central planners in the modernisation of the city from 1953 to 1977 (Phlipponneau 1977). Co-operation was a more fruitful strategy than conflict. The alternative model to that of co-operation was that of confrontation. The oppositional strategy was most likely to prevail in the Communist municipalities that governed many of France's largest cities during the post-war period. If the traditional model of territorial administration allowed for the expression of local differences, it did so at the margins. The advent of French-style local governance implies qualitative change, the analysis of which follows.

Local governance French style: causes and controversies

If we are to understand the causes of French-style local governance, we must first identify specific external and internal pressures for policy change. In chapter 1, we identify external pressures as including the development of internationalisation (Scott 1998), increased transnational policy-making in bodies such as the EU (Cole and Drake 2000) and trends towards institutional and policy convergence (Bennett 1991). While external pressures have an obvious impact on decision-making, we are more concerned here with the internal changes in the structure and operation of local government. As in England, these internal changes in France have involved pressures for more decentralised forms of public policy-making, new forms of private sector involvement in policy delivery, changing patterns of political participation in local politics and reforms in public service delivery based on proximity and improving quality.

Most specialists agree that the traditional 'republican' model of public administration has been undermined by an increasingly complex and polycentric policy process. Thus Gaudin (1996, 1999), Duran (1999) and Duran and Thoenig (1996) all stress the emergence of new forms of institutionalised negotiation, contracts and policy learning. On the other hand, there is much disagreement over which perspective best makes sense of the new sub-national realities. Expert French opinion is divided on the pertinence of the governance perspective. There is an instinctive fear of importing Anglo-Saxon concepts irrespective of context (Jouve and Lefèvre 1999; Thomas 1999). An orthodox political scientist such as Mabileau (1991, 1997) is highly sceptical of imported commentary on 'governance', which glosses over the specificity of French political traditions. For Mabileau the end of the 'territorial model of administration' has quite simply produced genuine French local government. This he defines according to three criteria: the existence of precise sectors of policy intervention; a genuine decision-making capacity for local authorities; and access by local politicians to national decision-makers (thanks to *cumul des mandats*). Marcou (1999) argues that 'governance' is not new, a point reiterated by Gaudin (1998, 1999). The term first appeared in the nineteenth century, when it signified quite simply public administration. In a sustained critique, Borraz (1998) criticises modish governance theorists for applying inappropriate models irrespective of context. Borraz considers that governance can be a useful descriptor of changes occurring in French localities, but it is by no means the only model of local power.

Those broadly favourable to a governance approach place much emphasis on informal processes, new actors and horizontal networking, while stressing the importance of French state traditions and institutional structures (Le Galès 1995b; Biarez 1996). The case is defended well by Lorrain (1993), for whom the new type of governance is urban, local and contractual. It is urban, in that large cities have emerged as powerful, indeed central actors. Almost all public policy questions have an urban dimension. Contracts determine relations between two or more actors involved in public policy. Relationships are negotiated and horizontal rather than hierarchical. This has been a considerable change in a country with a top-down policy style and a strong administrative law tradition. It is decentralised. The state no longer has a monopoly on making policy and local actors have actively promoted their agendas.

While much ambiguity rightly surrounds the concept of governance – especially as applied to the case of France – it has a useful heuristic value as a description of an ongoing process incorporating internal and external pressures for policy change, the appearance of new policy actors, the growth in institutional fragmentation and the development of new types of inter-organisational relationships. The principal causes we identify for French-style local governance are: (i) the diminishing capacity of the central state as a policy actor, leading to (ii) the far-ranging institutional reforms of the early 1980s and (iii) changing patterns of local political participation and local innovation in public policy.

Bureaucracy, proximity and the capacity of the state

During the post-war period the French state was committed to a top-down model of modernisation. Though local authorities were weak, the problems of post-war construction and urbanisation were real. The period from 1960 to 1975 was one of heightened activism on behalf of the urban policy technocratic planners. The central state had many powers. It could rely on powerful agencies (especially the Equipment ministry and DATAR). It had a coherent discourse on urban planning. It implemented ambitious urban development policies with minimal local consultation. The mainstays of central policy included the creation of urban communities in 1968, the ambitious structure plans of the late 1960s, the creation of new towns (such as Villeneuve d'Ascq in Lille) and the establishment of the first generation of urban development agencies. The principal tools by which local actors were involved in urban renovation and economic development projects were in the mixed economy societies (SEM), considered below.

This phase of ambitious top-down urban expansion was interrupted by the economic crisis of the 1970s. From the 1970s onwards, the state no longer had the means to realise its ambitions; in this sense Crozier's (1992) description of decentralisation as a 'reform of the state' was accurate. The growing complexity of decision-making called into question the central state's capacity to deliver services alone. The belief was widespread that excessive centralisation in service delivery produced inefficient services, interminable delays and a lack of flexibility to deal with local circumstances. This was manifest in a domain such as secondary education, where exclusive central state control left school buildings in desperate need of repair (Marcou 1992). Proximity itself was a means of improving the quality of public services; this belief came to be shared not just by local policy actors but by powerful interests within the state.

Though active in defence of their localities, the financial subordination of local authorities greatly limited their autonomy. With sparse local resources, local councils depended on state grants for specific investment projects (often implemented by the technical field services); on loans from the state-lending bank the *Caisse des dépôts*; or on collaboration with the private sector. Growing local experimentation in municipal governments did occur from the 1960s onwards, an evolution that was greatly strengthened by the decentralisation laws themselves.

The politicisation of local politics

The model of cross-regulation between prefects and *notables* affected small-town and rural France. The account depended in part on the weakness of political parties and upon the *notable*'s domination of his local political community. While this was an accurate description of politico-administrative relations throughout most of the country, certain types of municipal government never corresponded to this model. Those cities (especially in the Paris region, and in northern and southern France) controlled by the Communists, for instance, became citadels of opposition to government policy, with the municipality subject to tight control by a disciplined party organisation (Lacorne 1980; Dion 1986). Party politics was always far more important in large cities, where the left-wing parties had a weighty presence. Rapid post-war urbanisation and industrialisation created more complex cities, and produced more specific politics in the large cities.

For much of the post-war period there was a manifest dissociation between national and municipal politics. From 1947 until 1977, many large cities, such as Lille, were led by centre–left coalitions (SFIO, MRP and Radicals) aimed against the Gaullists and the Communists. These municipal coalitions were a legacy of the Fourth Republic 'third force' alliances against PCF and RPF. Most other cities were controlled by the Communists or by independent (conservative) *notables*. The failure of de Gaulle's UNR to capture many important municipalities in 1959, 1965 and 1971 contrasted with the successes of Gaullism on a national level. Only after 1977, with the capture of the Paris townhall, did Chirac's neo-Gaullist RPR establish solid bastions in municipal government.

During the 1970s, the municipalities finally caught up with national politics. Local elections developed an increasing tendency to become referendums on the performance of national parties in office. There was a noticeable politicisation of local government in the 1970s as the consequences of partisan bipolarisation at the national level filtered down to the localities. The watershed in the govern-ance of French cities occurred in 1977. In the 1977 municipal elections, the united left (PS, PCF and MRG) ran joint lists in 202 out of 221 towns of over 30,000 inhabitants. Socialist mayors who refused to end centre–left alliances were expelled from the party. Long-standing 'third force' townhall alliances were replaced by united left municipalities, with precise, nationally regulated political programmes. After the 1977 municipal elections, the left ran almost three-quarters (153) of large French towns (221). Though the united left alliance collapsed at a national level shortly afterwards, Socialists, Communists and their allies (such as the Greens) governed many of France's large cities during the 1977–2001 period. The left's capture of Paris and Lyons in the 2001 municipal election was offset by the loss of a string of medium-sized towns and by a serious decline in the number of Communist-run localities.

Left municipalities were not content to engage in traditional lobbying practices. Many of the new municipal teams were strongly influenced by the ideas of the May '68 movement, notably those of self-management and social experimenta-tion (Viveret and Rosanvallon 1976; Viveret 1977). By local social experimentation, we signify municipalities that engage in innovative, experimental policies not approved or initiated by central government. This practice was not in itself new. During the inter-war period, ambitious municipalities launched road-building and electrification programmes; certain Socialist-controlled cities adopted local anti-unemployment policies against central government opposition. In the 1960s, Socialist-led municipalities were again in the forefront of innovation; the case of Hubert Dubedout and the municipal action groups (GAM) in Grenoble was exemplary in this respect. The 'Grenoble model' became synonymous with a model of close co-operation between townhalls and voluntary associations, and a belief in the virtues of grassroots political participation. During the 1970s, the

French Socialist Party revived within the municipalities (in 1971 and 1977) before achieving national victory in 1981. Old-style municipal socialists were gradually replaced by innovators determined to use local government as a policy laboratory. With the left in charge of most French cities and departmental councils by 1977, prefectoral authority was increasingly resented and effectively bypassed. Municipal activism was particularly focused in the sphere of local economic development and in developing new forms of political participation – at a rhetorical level, at least. One product of the belief in the need to *gouverner autrement* was to create a dialogue with voluntary associations. Networks of associations close to the new municipal teams were encouraged; indeed, not only were representatives of associations co-opted onto policy committees, local councils also provided the mainstay of financial support for the survival of many local pressure and citizen's action groups. The themes of proximity, democratic empowerment, citizenship and local self-reliance were thus important facets of a changing ideological and policy climate that was highly conducive to institutional reform.

Institutional reforms

The French Socialist government's ambitious decentralisation reforms of 1982–3 were a catalyst for French-style local governance. Interpretations differ about how to place the reforms along the spectrum of continuity and change. While the Socialist interior minister Defferre claimed that decentralisation 'would put an end to a century of centralisation', others stressed elements of continuity. The 1982 law certainly ratified an evolution that had been gathering pace since the late 1960s. Prefectoral *tutelle* had been softened in 1970. Though the *tutelle* system allowed them to reject the decisions of the departmental and municipal councils, in practice the prefects could do little to prevent decisions they considered to be unwise. During the 1970s, the localist case began to be won at the level of ideas. The Guichard (1976), Peyrefitte (1976) and Bonnet (1978) reports gave support for more decentralisation, as did the Barre government's Green Paper of 1978. There was a measure of elite-level consensus in favour of change, though powerful opponents persisted within the Interior ministry and the Senate and amongst the *grands corps*.

The decentralisation reforms of 1982–83 were highly complex. Amongst the numerous laws and decrees, the most prominent decisions involved the creation of directly elected regional authorities as a separate tier of sub-national government; the transfer of executive authority from the prefect to the elected heads of the 96 departmental councils and 36,500 communes; the right of communes and departmental councils to set their budgets without prior prefectoral oversight; and the transfer of some staff from the prefectures and the ministerial field services to the departmental councils. The decentralisation reforms did not alter the basic structure of French local government. This remains a highly fragmented system. Policy-making responsibilities were henceforth divided among three tiers of sub-national authority as well as a varied array of ad hoc and intercommunal bodies; in contrast to the pattern of ongoing change in England, there has been no root and branch structural reform of local government in France. Rather, a process of incremental accretion has taken place. New structures have been added to existing ones, without a fundamental overhaul of the territorial system as a whole. The 1982 decentralisation legislation added further layers to the institutional cake.

The reforms created 22 elected regional assemblies and greatly enhanced the decision-making powers of the 96 departmental councils and of the larger communes. The reforms increased the responsibilities of local decision-makers. They extended local influence in policy fields such as urban planning, social affairs, economic development and secondary education. Each of the three tiers of French sub-national government – the region, the department and the commune – emerged with enhanced responsibilities. Decentralisation empowered local authorities in various other ways. Subject to certain legal and administrative safeguards, they were given full executive authority in their spheres of policy responsibility. The reforms gave councils greater budgetary autonomy by abolishing the prefect's tutelage (*tutelle*) and by making important fiscal transfers to allow councils to accomplish their new duties. Decentralisation also created a specific statute for local administrative staff (*fonction publique territoriale*), allowing councils to recruit more qualified personnel. A central plank of the first Mitterrand presidency, the decentralisation reforms have won the lasting approval of the French electorate (Dupoirier 1998a).

The decentralisation reforms highlighted the apparent contradiction between the dual aims of embedding micro-territorial identity and of providing for more effective service delivery. The communes remain the foci of local identities. As Nemery (2000) argues, all reform projects that have been based purely on technical/economical imperatives have failed. Thus the 1971 law (on the fusion of communes) had a very weak impact, so much so that the 1982 Defferre law did not even address the issue of fusion. However deeply embedded in French political culture, the commune is rather ineffective in delivering services. The extreme fragmentation of French communes – there are over 36,500 – requires co-operation between them to provide basic services in sectors like transport, road maintenance and waste disposal. At its most elementary level, such co-operation is ensured by single function (SIVU) or multiple function (SIVOM) inter-communal syndicates whose role is to provide essential services. The large number of French communes remains a source of weakness. Despite the transfer of land use and town and country planning duties to the communes, for example, they often lack the technical competence to decide upon the merits of planning applications. Even large communes have not fully developed their technical, informational and bureaucratic resources. They are often forced to turn to private sector operators to provide services such as sewerage, heating and incineration. In practice parochial, political and fiscal rivalries have often prevented inter-communal collaboration.

There has been a growing impetus behind the development of city-wide local government structures as a tool for tackling problems of urban governance. Various laws and regulations since the 1960s have attempted to adapt local government structures to take account of sociological and demographic change. While large cities typically contain 30–80 communes, public policy problems do not respect such small communal boundaries. The most complex of these city-wide inter-communal structures are the urban communities which have taken over many of the traditional communal functions in France's largest cities, such as Lyons, Marseilles and Lille. Created by central government in 1968, the urban communities have gradually become key players in the governance of the larger French cities, though their development has been hampered by their indirect method of election and their narrow fiscal base.

The 1990s witnessed a major legislative effort to strengthen further inter-communal structures, particularly through developing the inter-communal public corporations (*Etablissements publics de co-opération intercommunal* – EPCI). In French public law, the EPCI has the status of a public corporation. It is not a fully constituted local authority – such as a commune, department or region – but it has an independent executive and certain tax-raising powers. The principal EPCI are the urban communities, the urban districts and the new city-wide communities (*communautés d'agglomération*). Moves to strengthen the EPCI – during the 1990s in particular – were driven by the desire to discourage local tax competition, to ensure a more equitable distribution of resources and to promote appropriate structures for tackling organisational weakness.

One of the principal problems of French sub-national governance lies in the combination of an imperfect democratic legitimacy and the divisive impact of local government finance. In France – the country of top-down administration – almost 50 per cent of local finances is raised by local taxation, a far higher percentage than in the UK, the self-declared country of local self-government. Though councils are recipients of four separate taxes, most local taxation is raised by the *taxe professionelle* (TP), a tax levied on local businesses. The business tax produces obvious territorial inequalities. Richer communes with fewer social problems are attractive to business and hence draw more taxation resources, while poorer communes, less attractive to business investment, have the greatest social needs. In the absence of an overarching system of fiscal transfers, communes compete with each other for business location decisions. Many of the most obvious inequalities occur within cities, where richer communes are often resolutely hostile to sharing the fiscal resource with their less endowed neighbours.

In the morass of laws and regulations addressing issues of sub-national governance in the 1990s (including the Pasqua law of 1995 and Voynet law of 1999 which dealt with rural areas), two important laws explicitly addressed the combined problems of inter-communal co-operation and local government finance. The Joxe law of 1992 gave the urban districts, the urban communities and the new 'communities of towns' and 'communities of communes' the possibility of implementing fiscal transfers from richer to poorer communes by levying the business tax on a city-wide basis. The Chevènement law of 7 July 1999 went much further, by creating new city-wide communities (*communautés d'agglomération*) wherein the business tax would be levied and distributed at a supra-communal level. For the first time, recalcitrant communes could be forced to join these communities; in a move interpreted by many as a return of the state, the prefect could insist that individual communes form part of a city-wide community. The Chevènement law was considered by close observers as a major success: in the first six months of its existence, 51 *communautés d'agglomération* had come into existence, encompassing 763 communes with a total population of over 6 million (Marcou 2000). The EPCI are gradually replacing the older functional syndicates (SIVU and SIVOM) as the principal agencies of inter-communal collaboration, not only within the main cities (urban communities) but across medium-sized towns as well (city-wide communities) and to a lesser extent within rural areas (communities of communes, *pays*).

Decentralisation conferred new functions on the 96 departmental councils in mainland France, but these authorities were not new institutions. As the principal sub-national entity, the departments symbolised the tradition of rational, hierarchical administrative uniformity throughout France. Before decentralisation, the budgets and agendas of the departmental council were controlled by the departmental prefect. The departments emerged as clear victors of the decentralisation reforms. They were given larger budgets, more staff and more service delivery responsibilities than the regions. While powerful entrenched interests already operated through the departments, the regions were untried and untested; indeed, central government preferred to deal with the relatively subservient departments, rather than strong regions that might contest its authority. After the decentralisation reforms, the departments took charge of most of the civil servants previously attached to the prefectures, as well as benefiting from generous financial transfers from central government. The departments were able to rely upon experienced bureaucratic personnel while the regions had to experiment and innovate.

Dreamt up by Parisian technocrats, the French regions were initially conceived with the aim of modernising the 'periphery'. Regional levels of state action – the regional programmes – were first created in 1956 to facilitate the implementation of central state planning policies. Administrative 'deconcentration' thus came well before political decentralisation. The important 1964 reforms created the regional prefects, whose role was to co-ordinate the economic development of the departments and the economic planning of the regions. For Parisian modernisers, the regional sphere would provide a rational sub-national structure – closely controlled by the state – to facilitate national territorial planning. Administrative regions were favoured by Parisian innovators over departments and localities, where entrenched local interests provided obstacles to change. Regional prefects would spearhead industrial innovation and economic co-ordination. In the event, efforts at regional administrative decentralisation ran up against powerful Parisian and departmental interests. Vertically organised ministries were determined to prevent the regional prefects – general administrators – from having too much influence. The regional prefectures had very little influence in affecting public investment decisions; these continued to be determined nationally, by national ministries. Nonetheless, the regional idea made headway throughout the 1960s, as demonstrated by General de Gaulle's rallying to the cause of directly elected regional assemblies in the unsuccessful referendum of 1969.

Initially created as co-opted bodies in 1972, France's 22 metropolitan regions became fully fledged, directly elected sub-national authorities in 1986. The regions could also claim to be victors of the decentralisation process. They benefited indirectly from the removal of the prefects' control, and from the creation of an elected assembly with its executive. They became legally constituted local authorities for the first time, exercising statutory responsibilities in spheres such as transport, education and economic development. Notwithstanding these claims, however, French regions have remained weak institutions (Loughlin and Mazey 1995). The 22 regions are authorities without a strong link to a territory; in most instances, regional boundaries are artificial, not corresponding to pre-existing territorial identities (Le Galès and John 1997). Moreover, up to and including 1998, regional councils were elected on a department-based proportional representation system. This had two effects. First, ever since the first direct elections in 1986 many regions have been deprived of working majorities. The 1998 regional elections proved devastating in this respect, with the far-right National Front holding the balance of power in many regions. Moreover, regional councillors are elected on departmental lists; they are representatives first and foremost of their departments, rather than their regions (Nay 1997). The regions have neither the organisational heritage nor the bureaucratic resources available to the departmental councils. Unlike the departments, they are unable to rely on the transfer of state personnel, although many state civil servants opted for the challenge of serving the new regions. In contrast to the sizeable bureaucracies serving the large cities, and the departments, there are fewer than 100 salaried staff in most regions. As they have become established, the regional councils have added new responsibilities, notably that of adult training policy. But rather than being a major service delivery institution, the region consults, co-ordinates and plans; in most respects, regional councils remain outsiders in the French system of local governance. But partly because of their functional weakness they seek coalitions with other local and regional actors.

Rather as in the English example, the immediate impression from this overview of French sub-national public administration is one of institutional fragmentation and organisational complexity. This has implications for democratic practice in French localities. It has also encouraged policy-makers to develop new methods of policy co-ordination.

Characteristics of French local governance

The principal characteristics of local governance in France are those of greater institutional fragmentation, as a result of overcrowded policy-making and an increase in the number and change in the nature of policy actors; the development of networks and partnerships in an effort to enhance local governing capacity; efforts at new types of policy co-ordination, notably in the form of contractual relationships, and a changed policy-making environment influenced by Europeanisation and global economic change.

Institutional fragmentation and competition

Decentralisation added more layers to an already multi-layered institutional cake. The Socialist decentralisation laws of 1982–3 greatly increased institutional fragmentation and the complexity of the system. There are a larger number of local actors than ever before. The proliferation of policy actors has blurred responsibilities and diminished political accountability. There remains much confusion about the division of policy-making and administrative tasks between central and sub-national units and amongst the local authorities themselves. While decentralising major areas of responsibility, the laws did not specify clearly which body was responsible for what activity. The 1983 law on the division of responsibilities was very general. It attributed specific spheres of competence (*blocs de compétence*) to each type of local authority. These spheres were services that were best executed at a particular level of government. The 22 regions were given important powers of economic planning, infrastructure development, transport and secondary education. The 96 departments took over from the state the responsibility for social affairs and post-primary education (excluding matters relating to staff and curriculum). The communes acquired the functions of urban development, decisions over planning permission, land use and primary education.

In practice, this orderly division has proved impossible to implement. The various sub-national authorities have overlapping territorial jurisdictions and loosely defined spheres of competence. There is no formal hierarchy between them; in theory, no single authority can impose its will on any other, or prevent a rival authority from adopting policies in competition with its own. Even when responsibilities are clear, they are not respected (Thoenig 2000). Communes, departments and regions compete openly with each other and adopt policies designed to appeal to their electorates. Ambitious mayors have been determined to demonstrate their capacity to govern across the whole range of policy areas likely to affect their cities (Muller 1992; Lorrain 1993; Mabileau 1997). The same political imperative applied to the presidents of the departmental and regional councils. The idea of an ordered division of responsibilities made little sense in this respect (Téqueneau 1991).

As local authorities have developed their decision-making authority, so new policy actors have emerged within localities, particularly those from the voluntary and private sectors; this is especially relevant in the local economic development and related spheres. The narrow 'politico-administrative' alliances of prefects and *notables* have been replaced by much broader coalitions involving economic interests and representatives of voluntary associations and local pressure groups.

Partnerships, networks and contracts

French local and regional authorities are involved in a complex array of partnerships, which come in all shapes and sizes. While public–private partnerships are more common in the UK, there are also many new forms of private sector involvement with the public authorities in France. These arrangements are especially apparent in the sphere of economic and urban development (in the form of the mixed economy societies that we consider in chapter 4) and in environmental policy. Closer co-operation between political actors and those from voluntary associations forms a second important feature of French local governance. Attempts to involve local associations in the formulation of policy or even to co-opt them into the local decision-making machinery have been apparent in experiences throughout French cities. The ability of local councils to fund local associations directly gives them a powerful means of developing supportive local clienteles; likewise withholding municipal grants from local associations can be an overt means of pressure.

Public sector partnerships are a defining feature of French-style local governance. Public sector partnerships are a means of restoring policy coherence in an inherently unstable environment. Faced with the reality of diminished control over local authorities, the central state has imposed public sector partnerships in an attempt to improve policy cohesion and co-ordination. The quinquennial State–Region Contracts, for instance, determine the rights, responsibilities and financial contributions of public sector partners in relation to a broad range of policy areas. The State–Region Contracts outline in great detail hundreds of precise initiatives, many of which go beyond the regions to include the departmental councils and city-wide structures such as urban districts or urban communities.

There are differing interpretations of these public sector partnerships. Gaudin (1996, 1999) concludes that State–Region Contracts rely upon genuine bargaining between different public sector actors, an inference close to that drawn by Duran and Thoenig (1996) for whom contracts embody a new form of 'institutionalised negotiation'. The opposing view is that the State–Region Contracts are a new form of central state domination. They tie local government finance to state-directed policy initiatives. They represent a recentralisation of policy after the confusion of the early post-decentralisation years. Whichever interpretation is favoured, no one denies that a qualitative shift has occurred. Before the 1980s, there was no need to set out detailed contractual relationships, since power relations between the centre and the localities were 'entirely one way' (Gaudin 1996). This changed with decentralisation. Local authorities are now vested with powerful resources and with precise statutory policy-making responsibilities. Because they can refuse partnerships and contracts (the example of the departmental council in Nord is a good one), genuine bargaining between the state and the sub-national authorities has occurred. Apart from the global State–Region Contracts and the City Contracts (see below), other contractual processes have included University 2000 (co-ordinated by the Education ministry), Environmental Charters (Environment ministry) and Cultural Development

Conventions (Culture ministry). Planning contracts are a good indicator of French-style governance. The French tradition is one of bureaucratised, centralised and uniform public services. Procedures such as City Contract and the State–Region plans challenge this principle, recognising a diversity of local circumstances and priorities (Le Galès and Mawson 1995).

At the sub-national level, negotiations and bargaining occur in a more networked governing style. This change has been fundamental. In the 1950s, the state dominated the policy agenda. It imposed uniform solutions on areas such as housing, roads, schools and monopolised resources. In the 1990s, a negotiated policy style prevailed; the state produced guidelines, inviting other partners – business, associations, local authorities – to co-operate in achieving commonly defined goals. These objectives were defined in State–Region plans and in other types of urban policy programmes such as City Contracts (Le Galès and Mawson 1995).

Through the City Contract and other programmes, the French state invented a new role for itself as a catalyst for urban networks in the 1990s. These programmes were principally the work of the Socialists from 1988 to 1993. State urban policies such as the City Contracts were co-ordinated by state actors within the localities, generally the sub-prefects nominated for this purpose (Main 1991; Morgensztern 1991; Le Galès and Mawson 1995). City-based actors were not particularly active in state-driven urban policies, though there were some exceptions. Those state actors with a role in urban policy networks were not the traditional ones, such as the engineers of the bridges and highways corps. They comprised the regional field services of the Environment ministry (DIREN), specialist services within the prefectures, and inter-ministerial bodies such as the Inter-ministerial City Delegation (DIV). The Environment ministry in particular developed close relations with associations, local councils and firms. Contractualisation has to some extent focused upon new actors – both within and beyond the state.

The challenges of policy co-ordination

Policy co-ordination is conceived of as a problem primarily at the level of central state. State–Region plans and City Contracts demonstrate the new belief that the effectiveness of the state depends upon its ability to co-ordinate diverse actors and policy initiatives. Traditional hierarchical methods of policy co-ordination are inappropriate in a more differentiated polity. State actors cannot co-ordinate policy alone; they have neither the organisational nor the financial resources, nor the coercive potential. The prefectures have been definitively weakened, in the sense that the ties binding local political actors to local representatives of administrative authority have been broken. The French prefects are in no real position to co-ordinate governmental activity, though their prerogatives were strengthened by the 1999 Chevènement law. They continue to preside over a plethora of field services in each department and region, and their contacts with their local political communities have been weakened by decentralisation. On the other hand, processes such as the State–Region plans and urban policy programmes (City Contracts) demonstrate that state actors (regional prefects, sub-prefects, officials with specific 'missions', such as the Economic Commissars interviewed in the Nord department) can often bring together the myriad range of local actors behind common projects better than divided local elites themselves.

As we established above, one of the principal dynamics of French-style local governance is the affirmation of newly established institutional identities and the pursuit of local public policies. While top-down co-ordination is imposed by the central state (as in State–Region Contracts and related programmes), bottom-up co-ordination can be observed in the growth of partnership bodies, such as the Greater Lille Committee (see chapter 7) and similar entities in most French cities. These bodies bring together the principal social, cultural, economic and educational actors. Co-ordination can usually be assured only by an active and vigorous local political leadership, which is critical for mobilising the range of local interests that affect the vitality of a city (John and Cole 1999; Baraize and Négrier 2000).

Europeanisation and global economic change

Governance can also be understood as signifying a changed generic context within which local public policies are formulated, shaped by an increasing cognisance of the importance of Europeanisation and global economic change. These themes are developed in chapters 4 and 7. As in the English case, French localities have also adapted to new European funding regimes and adjusted to Europeanisation. The development of the European Union as a multi-level polity has encouraged local authorities to lobby for funds, to enter networks of national and European policy-makers, to employ European liaison officers and to set up European committees, and to open offices in Brussels (Jeffery 2000). We should be cautious, however, before assuming that moves to a more differentiated European polity have necessarily empowered regions and localities. Consistent with French models of tight policy co-ordination on all European matters, structural fund negotiations are officially co-ordinated by the DATAR at the national level and the regional prefectures in the regions. As the state holds the key to unlocking matching funding, the negotiation and allocation of structural funds appear to empower state actors both at the regional and at the national levels. A less state-centric reading is possible. Fieldwork uncovered evidence both of direct contacts between the regional prefectures and Brussels (thereby pre-empting the national level, except in a formal sense), and of negotiations between regional prefectures, elected regions and sub-regional local authorities. In so far as we understand Europeanisation to signify a changed context within which policy goals are formulated and new arenas of negotiation are developed, it is consistent with the main features of French-style governance.

Political leadership, democratic accountability and transparency in French localities

Having established the causes and characteristics of local governance, we conclude this chapter by considering the governance of French municipalities themselves. Decentralisation enhanced the power of urban mayors by loosening tight state controls on their financial capacity and by increasing their legal and political scope for policy innovation. French mayors often appear to give a political direction to urban networks, building horizontal relationships with other public and private sector actors. At the same time, the more complex policy environment produced by decentralisation has made the mayoral function far more complex.

While observers agree that French mayors have always been a natural focal point for local political communities, two rather different interpretations of municipal government, and the mayoral role in particular, have emerged after decentralisation. The first concentrates upon the internal operation of French municipal government, stressing the ascendancy of mayors within their organisations. The second approach considers mayors as policy entrepreneurs, building horizontal relationships with other public and private sector actors. These views are not mutually exclusive, but there are subtle differences between them. In the former, attention is centred on the institution of municipal government; in the latter, mayoral political leadership is orientated beyond the institution; it depends upon building networks and cultivating relationships.

The chief exponent of the first approach is Mabileau (1995), whose central thesis is that the 'republican monarchy' of the Fifth Republic's presidential system has been exported to the localities. A system of virtual direct mayoral election and modern communication strategies has reinforced the power of mayors. The checks and balances on the powers of mayors are few; democracy is lacking in French localities. The mayor is elected for a long period of office, with practically no possibility of being deselected between elections, except in (rather frequent) cases of criminal misdemeanour. As a result of the electoral system (which guarantees the leading list a majority of seats whatever its score) and a restrictive municipal code, no genuine opposition exists within the communes, as opposed to the regions. The mayor is head of the local executive and selects a list of associates (*adjoints*) before a municipal election (*adjoints* are the equivalent of the committee chairs in the UK). The selection of *adjoints* can result from a fierce bargaining process; a mayoral candidate must respect coalition partners, party factions and increasingly issues of gender when determining the electoral list. Once elected, however, *adjoints* are usually subordinate to the mayor's executive leadership role, and mayors can dismiss *adjoints* from their responsibilities.

The election of the mayor by the council chamber is usually a formality, since the electoral system automatically produces a majority for the leading list. The council chamber has little decision-making power, though formally speaking it votes the budget and approves those texts presented to it by the local executive (the mayor and the *adjoints*). There is no real equivalent to the English committee system; the *adjoints* substitute themselves for the decisions of council committees. The mayor controls the appointment of the main officers and tends to have both a political and an administrative role, straddling politics and administration within the council (Lorrain 1989; Fontaine and Le Bart 1994). Mayors face the outside with solid control over their councils; the French case is far more predictable than the English one in this sense. Unlike in the English case, where the more collegial style of English local government sometimes encouraged a party to overturn its leader, there is no mechanism between elections whereby a fractious local party can rid itself of a municipal leader. This can lead to the creation of mayoral dynasties, whereby the local political party becomes an appendage of the townhall, which is central for the distribution of local patronage. Power within townhalls is held by a narrow elite: the mayor, the members of his office, key *adjoints* and leading officials. There is no real equivalent in France to the institution of local government in the Anglo-Saxon countries. Officials – the US City Manager or the English Chief Executive – play a less important role in the French context and political parties are less influential.

The presidentialisation of local government is at first sight a persuasive argument. As local authorities have become increasingly complex, however, it has become less realistic to believe that mayors exercise a tight personal control over all aspects of local policy-making. Specialisation has diversified the structures of local power. With decentralisation, the *adjoints* have become central actors (Borraz 1998). As local authorities have developed their policy capacities, the *adjoints* have become real specialists in their chosen areas, enabling them to engage in a dialogue of equals with technical experts and representatives of local pressure groups. Size matters. It is far less easy for a mayor to control a city-wide structure such as an urban community than a small municipal council.

In the context of local governance, problems of co-ordination and leadership are the inevitable effect of an increasingly complex charge. French mayors are judged on how effectively they are able to build networks and to harness local governing capacity (Garraud 1989; Le Bart 1992). Successful mayors have become more entrepreneurial (Faure 1991), determined to implement local public policies. Across France, mayors have placed themselves at the head of new-style development coalitions, mobilising large-scale public and private resources for ambitious development projects. The leadership role of mayors depends upon the extent to which they can mobilise political and financial resources, develop new partnerships and invent new forms of governance.

Successful co-ordination and leadership continue to depend on visible structures of local political leadership. French municipal government remains the focus of local identities. The high rate of voter participation in municipal elections, and the popularity of the institution of the French mayor in particular, suggest a strong legitimacy for this elective structure, which remains at the centre of the French pattern of sub-national governance. Nonetheless, serious problems of local political accountability have arisen in the period since decentralisation. The granting of control over new resources to local politicians (mayors and *adjoints* especially) gave rise to a series of highly publicised local corruption scandals; in several cities (for instance Grenoble), the role of the mayor in determining public works contracts, or in granting land use permission for development was exposed as a powerful incentive for corruption. In important respects, decentralisation has strengthened the role of mayors, while weakening the checks on their abuse of power. Powerful local politicians have bypassed or completely ignored prefects; they are aware that prefects usually prefer not to use their regulatory powers for fear of retaliation. The 1980s demonstrated that powerful mayors often did not respect environmental norms or those relating to building permits. Political corruption scandals in cities such as Lyons and St Etienne revealed the legal authorities (investigating magistrates) and the financial regulatory bodies (regional courts of accounts) to be more effective counterweights to the abuse of municipal power than the administrative system from which prefects draw their legitimacy.

By attempting to restrict *cumul des mandats*, the Jospin government recognised the need for more transparency and accountability in local government. This move did not go unchallenged. Many critics from within his own party accused Jospin of undermining French mayors by attacking a system (*cumul des mandats*) which has allowed French local leaders a degree of political support and national political visibility that is generally not available to their English counterparts. Jospin's inability to proceed with a rapid reform of *cumul des mandats* revealed the persistence of deeply ingrained national traditions.

Conclusion

In France, as in England, local governance implies that change has occurred, even though its precise direction and dimensions are not identical. In the French case, the historical context shapes current political powers and arrangements. Writers such as Mabileau (1997) argue quite convincingly that contractual processes and partnerships are fully consistent with French top-down administrative traditions, whereby the state gives a lead, but relies on local authorities and other partners to finance and implement policy programmes. There is stiff resistance to administrative decentralisation from many Parisian civil servants; hence the weakness of the prefectures and ministerial field services. Powerful local and regional authorities do not have in face of them effective regional or departmental state structures. The central state intervenes directly in the form of steering the State–Region and other public policy contracts. When interpreting changing patterns of sub-national governance, we must not lose sight of established French politico-administrative traditions.

The French state retains enormous regulatory and fiscal powers, and remains deeply involved in local affairs. Through its control over resources and planning processes, the state acts as an arbiter between the conflicting claims of different localities and sub-national authorities. The state defines the conditions under which decentralised units function. It retains control over much local government finance and continues to determine apportionment criteria for grants to sub-national units. The taxation instruments available to local councils are crude;

and councils are not at liberty to avail themselves of new instruments. France remains very much a unitary system of government, at liberty to increase or reduce the prerogatives of local government according to the perceived interest of the centre.

To conclude that change is artificial would be unsatisfactory, however. Whether interpreted as the logical outcome of developments of the previous two decades or as fundamentally innovative in themselves, the institutional decentralisation reforms of the early 1980s were an important landmark in French local governance. In conjunction with parallel evolution of the orthodox practice of French public policy-making, decentralisation has allowed a more pluralistic form of sub-national politics to emerge. The central state can no longer claim a monopoly of expertise and legitimacy. There has been greater access to knowledge and resources, allowing local authorities to develop local public policies. All local authorities emerged with strengthened powers, budgets and staffs from the decentralisation reforms. We would highlight the enhanced role of cities in urban development as being particularly indicative of the new patterns of French urban governance. This has occurred at the expense of central planners and engineers, whose influence has undoubtedly diminished (Morvan and Marchand 1994).

The republican model of territorial administration has gradually given way to a more complex sub-national environment. We have discussed the emergence of separate layers of sub-national authorities with overlapping responsibilities, and the growth of joint financing of urban projects partly as a consequence of this. We have also observed the rise of contractualisation as a new form of central state 'steering at a distance'. These themes each pose distinct questions of political accountability. How can decision-making be identified? How can partnerships and networks be held to account when policy-making processes are secretive and ownership of policies is inter-organisational? Is the private management of public goods legitimate? What forms of accountability best safeguard against the abuse of local political power? We respond to these normative questions in our concluding chapter.

4 The governance of local economic development in England and France

In the first three chapters of this book we set out the broad contexts and elements of the change from local government to governance. We focused on the sources of change in each country and we charted the varied paths of institutional reform. We described the manner in which public decision-making in the two countries has become, in different ways, more complex and fragmented, less institutionalised and more dependent on horizontal networks. The task of the next two chapters is to explore how this transition affects two very different policy sectors in order to compare the different forms of governance which are emerging, both within the countries and between them.

We begin with local economic development. Although, in explicit terms, it is a relatively new field of public regulation, it cuts to the core of urban governance as it seeks to affect what is most subject to change – the economic livelihood of cities. Partly because it is driven by wide economic forces and is subject to influence from different levels of government and from the European Union, the sector is probably more closely linked to the emergence of local governance than any other. Partly because of the multiform organisations involved, the large number of sectors of activity affected by economic development issues and the likely involvement of the private sector, it is most likely to resemble local governance. It is thus a strong test case for the transformation of governing systems, something which the more statist and bureaucratic sector of secondary education is designed to correct in the next chapter.

The logic of internationalisation

The less local government directly intervenes in the local economy, the more attractive its city becomes as a location for inward investment. This is the logic of Peterson's argument, made in his book, *City Limits* (1981). Cities are forced to compete with each other to attract footloose capital. This compels cities to adopt similar supply-side policies as capital will migrate to the most attractive environment. It excludes radical social policies, and encourages local welfare state retrenchment. International business circles will turn against cities that adopt interventionist policies designed to protect the jobs of local workers, to ensure equality of opportunity or to protect traditional industries. This deterministic thesis highlights converging, economically driven pressures on city administrations. If true it would demonstrate that economic change poses new governing challenges for all cities. There is now intense competition between cities and regions within Europe. Cities attempt to attract investment by deliberate strategic decisions (Harding 1994a). Effective urban governance requires strategies to co-ordinate the activities of a wide range of interests and agencies operating at a local level. One of the most visible effects of the internationalisation of the economy has been to create a hierarchy of large and medium-sized cities, within and across nation-states (Sassen 1994: 39–47). Just as there is competition and specialisation between mega-cities like New York, Tokyo, London and Paris, so internationalisation can affect the economic chances of the smaller urban centres.

The Peterson thesis, adapted in this manner, should not be pushed too far; internationalisation has a differential impact on cities. Not all cities compete in the same league; medium-sized cities are far less affected by these exogenous constraints and opportunities than larger metropolitan centres. Internationalisation has also produced varying political responses. Local politicians must deal with the concrete problems of poverty, social exclusion and unemployment arising from the abstract pressures of the international economy. An ability to address such issues can be essential for their chances of re-election. Rather than mechanically responding to international economic pressures, urban governments attempt to balance the requirements of economic competition with those of social cohesion. Indeed, there is a strong linkage between social and economic problems as the salaried middle classes will desert areas with grave social problems.

The importance of the external environment on the governance of cities cannot be disputed. In the context of greater internationalisation, many more key decisions that have an impact upon local economic development fall outside of the control of locally elected bodies. Cities have to react to the economic consequences of macro-economic decisions over which they have little say. Whether an industrial plant opens or closes may depend upon a decision made in London, Paris, Tokyo, Seoul or New York, rather than in the city, region or nation-state. If nation-states are not able to affect these decisions, certainly smaller units of cities are less able to do so. To an extent, it was always the case that cities were dependent upon economic decisions made elsewhere.

Economic development policy in times of change

The changing nature of the world economy has altered the manner in which local politicians perceive of economic development. In the UK, local politicians pursued interventionist local economic development policies in the 1970s and 1980s, partly for ideological reasons. City administrations in Sheffield, London and Liverpool hoped to create local economic growth based on local capital and workforce participation. By the late 1980s, such efforts had proved illusory, broken by the controls exercised by central government, the weakness of municipal finances, the antipathy of the Conservative-controlled central state and the hostility of the business community.

Policy fashions and political beliefs have changed, including those of traditional left-controlled councils. The increased pace of economic change, the failure of interventionist policy experiments and the greater circulation of policy ideas in a more transnational system of political exchanges have affected all localities. The beliefs of local politicians have shifted away from municipal socialism towards public–private partnerships, the politics of compromise and coalition building. After a difficult learning process, left-wing local leaders have proved more willing to accept markets and competition, and, within limits, to modify their traditional commitment to welfare and to the demands of its declining working-class constituency.

Closer partnership with central agencies and business interests can also empower lower-level decision-makers, as they form strategies to revive their local economies. Local economic development strategies have become more diverse. They have relied not only on traditional economic development schemes (such as urban regeneration projects, land reclamation and business support), but also on the recognition by public and private actors of the various ways in which public decisions link with private economic decisions, in sectors such as transport, strategic planning, education, housing, waterways and tourism. These activities are to a degree controlled by public sector actors which are either locally elected authorities – as in the UK – or a mixture of central and local state actors as in France. Public sector decisions are critical in affecting the vitality of a city and how it is perceived by inward investors. Research by Parkinson and his colleagues (1992) showed that some cities in the EU were able to respond to new economic challenges, while others were not. The key variables for maximising local economic opportunities forwarded by Parkinson were, first, local political leadership, which can mobilise local political and bureaucratic actors, and second, organisational capacity, which is facilitated by links and partnerships between public and private sector bodies.

The very rapidity, change and dynamism associated with internationalisation presents opportunities as well as constraints. As Lash and Urry write: 'The specificity of place, of its workforce, the character of its entrepreneurialism, its administration, its buildings, its history and especially its physical environment, become more important as temporal and spatial barriers collapse' (1994: 303). Even though economic change is ultimately structured by wider forces, policy-makers must understand the unique factors shaping economic activity in each locality (Wilson 1995). There is a strong argument that global trends strengthen the importance of urban-regional economies. As they are no longer able to use traditional dirigiste or Keynesian policy instruments in an age of budgetary retrenchment, national governments welcome endogenous economic initiatives as a source of public policy innovation. Combined with the opportunities provided by Europeanisation (notably through structural funds and other financial transfers), this makes the sub-national arena an important one for economic development.

There is no single model for ensuring local development. Certain cities are highly sensitive to the impact of internationalised political and economic processes; others are more self-sufficient, dependent either on past public sector investment decisions, or – as in the case of the Italian industrial districts – on a dense network of endogenous businesses and close links between businesses and the local community (Benko and Lipietz 1992). Thus the processes of internationalisation have a differential impact upon local economies and on the patterns of local economic development networks.

Such a belief in the importance of local development is widely held in the French literature (Pecqueur 1989; Benko and Lipietz 1992; Le Galès 1993) where concepts of territorial identity and specialisation demonstrate the importance of the politics of place. Sociological and psychological causes are 'invisible factors in local economic development' (Benoit-Guilbot 1991), explaining why certain cities achieve economic prosperity, while others decline. Economic performance cannot be explained by neo-classical economic explanations alone; it depends upon the existence of specific sociological and psychological conditions favourable for economic development. For Benoit-Guilbot, these include the particular social composition of a city, notably its ability to sustain a strong professional and middle-class population; whether or not it enjoys a dominant geographical position with respect to its immediate environment; its access to higher networks, notably those for channelling state and European aid; and whether it has a history of opposition to central power. In his comparative study of Rennes and Coventry, Le Galès (1993) also pointed to local factors to explain differential economic performance. Le Galès explained the weakness of local economic dynamism in Coventry by the working-class nature of its local electorate and the trade union mentality of local council officials. This contrasted with Rennes where the progressive municipal council fully incorporated the social and cultural demands of the new middle-class electorate into its policies. In these French studies, sociological explanations usefully complement those based on economics and politics.

In spite of its unclear effects, local economic policy has a high party political salience in both countries. Central and local politicians wish to be involved with decision-making and to receive any credit associated with economic growth. Local economic policy is a networked policy sector almost by definition. Public and private sector actors both have a role in economic development; as this chapter demonstrates, the particular mix of public and private actions varies between countries and between cities within countries. No one public sector decision-maker can claim a monopoly of provision in this complex field. In any city, the number of organisations directly or indirectly involved with local economic development is very large, covering a range of quasi-public, public and private actors. These include agencies whose specific function is local economic development – such as the economic development officers and units in local authorities. They also include other local public sector bodies (such as universities, hospitals and theatres) whose economic development function is ancillary as well as the range of non-governmental and private actors. At the same time, central government ministries attempt to promote local economic development, and modify disparities across the national territory. Because of the cross-sectoral nature of economic development, several government departments have an interest in economic development policy – especially in the planning, transport, housing, education/training and industry ministries. These central departments have decentralised offices in the regions (and/or departments in France) and may have special purpose agencies that compete with other local ones. When trade and industry organisations are added to the plethora of public bodies, colourful metaphors spring to mind to describe the pattern.

Local economic policy in England

The economic development of English cities illustrates well the salient characteristics of English-style local governance. Many new organisations have become involved with local economic policy, along with older institutions having to redefine the roles they perform. There is some evidence that institutional fragmentation has gradually encouraged closer co-operation, as autonomous but interdependent decision-makers attempt to co-ordinate policy. Four main types of actor might be identified in English local economic development policy: locally elected bodies, the field services of central government departments, central government special purpose agencies, and economic interests.

Locally elected bodies

At the beginning of the 1980s, local authorities were the main actors in economic development policy. With their land use, planning and transport activities they had control over the major decisions affecting the economic health of the cities. The creation in 1972 of large strategic authorities – the metropolitan counties and the county councils – as well as the existence of city-wide local authorities, made local government the natural arena for developing local economic development strategies. Indeed, their statutory obligations in strategic planning gave local authorities considerable technical expertise in related areas. Before the 1980s, planners sought to balance the economic development objectives of planning with other social values, such as free living space, the environment, and the pace and type of development. When some leading metropolitan authorities first became interested in economic development, policy was designed to remedy the blight of the inner cities, to replace the loss of manufacturing jobs, and sometimes to meet more radical objectives, such as countering poverty and increasing the economic opportunities of minority groups. Some leading local authorities, such as the Greater London Council, set up boards or companies to oversee municipal investment; most appointed economic development officers; and many, especially all the large strategic authorities, created special economic development units – either as separate departments or as parts of planning or chief executives' departments.

As there is such a profusion of initiatives which an authority can carry out under the auspices of economic development, so there is a wide variety of activities undertaken, varying from place to place. Policies range from land development, urban renewal, business support, attraction of inward investment and city centre initiatives, to the attraction of central government funding. In important respects, economic development occurs across sectors. Because many aspects of economic development relate to what appear to be traditional policy sectors, such as education, housing, transport, tourism and European liaison, so economic initiatives link with many other local government policies.

Under political pressure in the 1980s, the interventionist and radical focus of local economic policy initiatives diminished and was gradually replaced by a greater search for inward investment and a series of interrelated policy initiatives designed to improve the local economy. Rather than direct intervention, the stress was now focused more on co-ordinating policy, responses to initiatives from central government and the European Union, links with transnational organisations and the improvement of the image of local areas. Such activities meant that economic development activity needed to be carried out more in partnership with other bodies, particularly with the private sector, in bidding for public funds and in assisting with inward development.

The transformation of local government in the 1980s reduced the providing role of local government and decreased the budgets it could deploy directly on local economic development. Moreover, central government limited the freedom of local authorities to act directly, notably their power to set up local authority companies. In spite of these constraints, local authorities have continued to find ways to involve themselves in the local economy. The Local Government and Housing Act 1989 created a statutory provision to act in the field of local economic development. The requirement to publish a local economic plan actually stimulated local authorities to think more about the co-ordination of economic activity, both in relation to internal local government structures, and with respect to other organisations seeking to stimulate local economic development. In spite of the reduction in the powers and finance of locally elected government since the mid-1970s, the emergence, consolidation and adaptation of local economic development activity by elected local government from the 1980s onwards is witness to its resilience and dynamism. Local government will always play an essential role in this policy sector.

Central government departments

At the same time as in the municipal world, in the 1980s local economic development emerged at the forefront of central government's attempts to restructure local politics. The departments of state involved in economic development issues are mainly the Department of the Environment, Transport and Regions, with its planning, transport and local government remit; the Department of Trade and Industry with its concern with inward investment and market dynamism; and the Department for Education and Employment with its training function. As we noted in chapter 1, up until 1994 there were separate regional organisations of these departments and to an extent they still operate separately after the creation of the new government offices for the regions. The Labour government, elected in May 1997, inherited, but did not seek radically to change this framework. The use of local authorities as one of the main organisations to implement the New Deal reflects a gradual shift back in favour of local government since the early 1990s.

Economic development issues dominate the regionalisation of the English state since 1997. Labour set up Regional Development Agencies in 1999 as the first step towards the regionalisation of the English state alongside regional consultative chambers. They will over time, and in conjunction with the appropriate regional Government Office, assume an important role in supporting, coordinating and stimulating economic development in the English regions. In some more peripheral regions there was disappointment that the RDAs were given relatively circumscribed powers, that their board membership was both dominated by business people and appointed by the Secretary of State (rather than regionally elected). On the other hand, the creation of the RDAs means that powerful organisations now exist at a regional level, with precise responsibilities for making some of the most important decisions affecting economic development, such as deciding appeals over planning decisions, approving new transport schemes, deciding urban redevelopment grants and administering training initiatives.

More politically, the regional offices remain as the main official connection between local bodies and ministers who have a special interest in a city, particularly if they are from that city or nearby or have a housing or urban remit as part of their portfolios. As there is a plethora of bodies that have non-elected appointees at their heads, there are varied contacts between local political actors and the government office civil servants who act as the conduit for communication between elected and non-elected actors. This brokerage between ministers, local politicians and officials has increased the role of the regional directors, who oversee the four departments of state in the government offices for the regions. Regional directors advise ministers about appointments, such as the chairs of Training and Enterprise Councils. The regional offices also perform essential supervision functions over the central government agencies that have a local presence. The regional offices control the administration of the Single Regeneration Budgets and the funding of European programmes, such as the European Regional Development Fund and the European Social Fund. However, it is important not to over-emphasise the extent of the integration of activities in the regional offices. Most functions remain in the regional organisations of central departments that have lines of command to Whitehall, and of course, all budgets are controlled departmentally and are ultimately sanctioned by the Treasury (Mawson 1995). Thus, to an extent, local actors have to liaise with regional civil servants in each department of state, depending on whether the problem is a housing, urban funding or transport matter. This is partly because of the nature of economic development policy, which cross-cuts a range of government functions. It also reflects central government activism mentioned earlier, in that the regional organisations of government have to get involved locally to implement government initiatives.

Central government special purpose agencies

During the 1980s the government set in motion a series of departmentally based initiatives which bypassed locally elected agencies. While early programmes, such as the Department of the Environment's Urban Programme, were designed to distribute grants to local authorities, initiatives in the 1980s often were contrived to exclude them, the most famous example being the Urban Development Corporations which took planning and housing powers away from local government and set up organisations with generous central funding to redevelop areas like the Docklands and Merseyside. In addition, task forces, enterprise zones, city technology colleges, housing action trusts and city action teams were attached to different central government departments. On top of these are the partnerships of organisations seeking to access European Union funding co-ordinated by central government regional offices (previously the Department for Trade and Industry). Thus there has emerged a complex set of agencies with overlapping functions at a sub-national level, a local replication of the competition between government departments at the centre. These agencies are to some extent in competition with those from the locally elected sector.

The most important of these agencies are the TECs, created by central government in 1989 to co-ordinate centrally funded training programmes. TECs were supposed to perform a dynamic role in relation to local economies. They were to be managed by a business-dominated board and a chief executive drawn from the private sector, though most of the staff were drawn from the former public sector training bodies and TECs retained their public agency cultures and working practices (Bennett et al. 1994). As each TEC has a budget of about £20–30 million they are significant players in the cash-starved local development scene. The Conservative government sought to make TECs the main or lead partner in local economic development initiatives, such as the single regeneration budget bids. Thus the TECs became the essential partners for most local economic development projects and initiatives. They endeavoured to act as co-ordinators of the complex matrix of agencies, but they have found it hard to win the trust of local bodies as they report to the Department for Education and Employment and are subject to the vacillations and rapid changes in central government policy. Also in order to fulfil their mission the TECs had created their own organisations, such as single regeneration budget working groups and business link agencies, which again added to the 'patchwork' of local agencies already in existence, and threatened other local organisations. Since 1997 the TECs have had a rather narrower remit; to deliver central government training policies and to assist in funding projects from the New Deal and the Single Regeneration Budget. They have had to develop new relationships with the Regional Development agencies and their future is rather uncertain.

Economic interests

Business organisations have traditionally been weak at the local level. In the nineteenth century business people took a leading role in local politics, but as local government became more professional their role declined, though perhaps not as much as is often believed. The Chambers of Commerce which represent all local business sometimes have a parochial outlook and usually have a weak financial base (Grant 1993). Some are financially dependent on administering Department of Trade and Industry funded business support schemes. In recent years, however, business actors have returned to public prominence and have invested their energies in reviving the Chambers as representative business institutions. Business actors have become part of the policy-making community, both within and outside the more formal relationships co-ordinated by Chambers of Commerce. Some large businesses now seek to become strategic actors in the belief that participation in local governance processes is essential for the survival and prosperity of their firms (Useem 1984). The Chambers of Commerce themselves have become better organised and expanded their staff numbers. New roles have encouraged some to merge, while others have combined with TECs, to create more continental-style para-statal types of business organisation. Since 1988, after the government's White Paper, *Action for Cities*, most centrally funded programmes have required business to be a necessary financial partner for state funding projects, a policy endorsed by the Labour government in 1997. European funding policy regimes are now similar. These incentives explain why certain business leaders sought to enhance their power in local economic policy communities. Because of the fragmentation of business interests, the number of public sector organisations, the wide range of projects requiring partnerships and the multiple territorial policy-making arenas, there is no limit in the number of public–private partnerships that can emerge. Thus many cities have partnerships involving different sectors and functions, with different organisations jostling for position. The important question is whether the recent growth in participation is symbolic or whether it represents a real input into the policy-making process.

Developments in English local economic policy have produced an extreme case of 'local governance', in the sense that central reforms, municipal initiatives and business activism have multiplied the number of institutions at work. There are incentives for the key individuals within these agencies to form networks in order to make co-ordination possible. But such co-operation is not preordained. To local authorities, with constrained budgets, with less direct responsibility for services and facing central controls over the exercise of their discretionary powers, it makes sense to build good relationships with central government agencies. The realisation that local economic development policy requires the participation and co-ordination of actors across various policy sectors – most of them controlled by central government – necessitates cultivating good relationships with central state actors. From the central government's point of view, the setting up of new local institutions was initially intended to bypass or replace locally elected bodies and to exclude elected local government from the main decision-making local policy networks. But in fact, after some initial hostility, most central government organisations developed close, if not necessarily good relationships with locally elected bodies (UDCs: Imrie and Thomas 1993; TECs: Bennett et al.

1994; Thomas 1994). While the UDCs had powers over planning and housing, they could not operate as islands apart from the local authorities, which had so much power to determine matters outside their boundaries. TECs are small organisations with low legitimacy which depend on the goodwill of local authorities and Chambers of Commerce to ensure central government policy is implemented.

In some senses the strategies adopted by local government and business interests evolved in response to shifts in central government policy-making. But central government policies themselves have evolved. Whatever its initial intentions, Whitehall discovered it was impossible to exclude local authorities from central government initiatives. The tensions in central–local political relationships gradually eased in the 1990s as local authorities became more pragmatic and central government realised the limits of its 'top-down' strategies. Imposing urban policy from central government without local participation simply did not work. Central government also came to realise that it had created a far too fragmented institutional framework. Reports, such as those from the Audit Commission (1989), highlighted the lack of co-ordination in urban policy. There was a consensus that urban policy had become too complex. The result of this was an attempt at co-ordination at the regional level, through the creation of the single regeneration budget in 1994 which is administered by the government offices for the regions. But the apparent centralisation has its paradoxes – there is no unravelling of local governance. Hence the regional director has become a new actor, to some extent part of local economic development networks. New initiatives in urban policy, such as the single regeneration budget, have produced new agencies, in the form of single regeneration budget working boards. This demonstrates the complexity of urban policy-making: while the government endeavoured to unify urban funding in one procedure, it had to create yet another new organ to attempt to achieve this. Another new policy has created another new organisation, English Partnerships, to administer another part of urban funding. Thus the management of local economic development policy in localities continues to be based on co-ordinating a vast array of agencies and individuals. On the other hand, the new local economic development function gives an added legitimacy to local authorities that often end up as the only organisation with a vested interest in seeking a city-wide focus to the many initiatives.

Though institutional reforms have multiplied the number and nature of policy actors, it is possible to identify the key players in UK local economic development networks. As in France, there are four principal clusters of policy actors. These are locally elected councils, central government-run organisations, central government and business interests. In spite of all the reforms of the 1980s and 1990s that have reduced the functional role of local government, it remains as the main service provider and the source of much of central government and local funds. This particularly applies in metropolitan areas where large unitary authorities control or are involved with all local government services. Thus it would be surprising if locally elected people and the officers did not form an essential part of local economic policy networks. The essential question involves the extent to which the roles these actors perform have changed, as they have lost many of their traditional decision-making functions and have been forced to operate in a new inter-organisational context. Are UK local leaders becoming rather more like French mayors who broker between the central and local state?

Local economic policy in France

Consistent with its dirigiste traditions in economic and industrial management, and a post-war ideology of technocratic modernisation, French economic and urban development policies were largely centrally driven during the first three decades of the post-war period (Muller 1990b; Téqueneau 1991; de Courson 1994). The weakness of local economic activism reflected the dependency of local authorities upon central state actors, as well as the fragmented structure of French local government. Local actors were not entirely absent; they were to be found in the mixed economy societies and amongst professional groups (architects and property promoters notably) as well as within local authorities. Economic intervention of various sorts preceded the 1982 reform. Communes invested resources in land reclamation as well as in creating industrial zones and small business centres, for which tax exemptions were granted. The departments created economic expansion committees (*comités d'expansion économiques*) as a means of attracting state grants. The regions were formally established as public agencies with strategic planning and investment powers in 1972. By the end of the 1970s, local authorities and regions had invested considerable sums in local economic development, in spite of regular circulars from the Interior ministry to the prefectures that such direct and indirect aids were forbidden (Gerbaux and Muller 1992).

While certain cities (those controlled by municipal socialists) engaged in economic policy experiments during the inter-war period, post-war modernisation either precluded local activism or depended on close collusion between powerful mayors and state administrators (Phlipponeau 1977; Mabileau 1991). During the 1970s the large French cities became more self-assertive, not least Paris, which obtained its first directly elected mayor in 1977 (Knapp 1994). A new generation of local politicians came to office in 1971 and 1977. They were concentrated above all in the new Socialist Party (PS). Many mayors elected to office for the first time in 1971 and 1977 demanded greater local participation in policy-making. They regarded municipal office as a laboratory for implementing the left's agenda in preparation for the rise to power at a national level. A new ideological climate thus preceded the formal decentralisation programme of the early 1980s.

The 1982 decentralisation law gave greater freedom to the communes and departments to engage in economic development activities, but promoted the regions as actors with specific responsibilities for economic policy-making. The 1982 law distinguished between direct and indirect forms of economic assistance.

'Direct aids' consisted in employment and business creation grants, which were to be allocated by the regions. Departments and communes could top up regional grants but not initiate them. 'Indirect aids' were a broad set of measures whose content was left to the discretion of local authorities. Typical 'indirect aids' include loan guarantees, the provision of industrial sites and buildings, tax exemptions for periods of up to five years, and business advice centres. In addition, the 1982 law allowed communes to 'help firms in difficulty'. The regions and departments have used direct grants to account for most of their aids; this type of direct grant only ever had a marginal role in communal finances (Douence 1988; Gerbaux and Muller 1992).

Local economic development policies have evolved during the period since 1982. To some extent, the experiments and reversals of the Mitterrand presidency (1981–95) affected the sub-national level, as there was a sequence of ideas about the appropriate form of municipal interventionism. While government policy initially exhorted local authorities to help firms in difficulty, and to boost local employment by direct municipal intervention, such demands became less audible as national policy shifted away from Keynesian expansion to economic austerity. The early belief that direct municipal intervention could have an effect on employment policy gave way to attempts to improve the business environment as local authorities embraced policies aiming to encourage inward investment and to attract new firms. Local authorities (especially communes) came to consider all aspects of public activity as contributing to their broader economic development aims. To this extent, the economic development function of local authorities has become an accessory to their principal responsibilities (in urban development, land use, training, research, education, roads, transport) rather than a separate activity.

In France as in England, several different types of organisation have an impact upon local economic development policy. These comprise locally elected bodies, the field services of government departments, economic interests, and various types of public–private partnership.

Local and regional government actors

There are powerful structural incentives for competition between territories in France. There have traditionally been good reasons for communes *not* to co-operate over economic development. Competition to attract firms – and thereby to obtain the product of the business tax (*taxe professionelle*) – has traditionally set communes against each other: individual communes compete with each other to offer tax and buildings incentives to entice business investment. The key resource that all communes share is that, within limits and subject to certain safeguards, they control the development of the land over which their jurisdiction is based (Priet 1992; Ferré-Lemaire 1996). As befits a country with over 36,500 communes and a honeycomb state, there are limits to communal autonomy in the economic development sphere. In theory – and to some extent in practice – planning permission for public or private sector developments is an increasingly important resource as the demand for development land intensifies. However, communal control over planning permission is limited by various forms of inter-communal, regional and central state oversight.[1]

The enhanced role of cities in economic development can be seen as a weathervane of new patterns of French urban governance. The emergence of city-wide inter-communal structures, with their own planning and taxation instruments, was greatly strengthened during the 1990s, notably by the provisions of the Chevènement law of 1999 (see chapter 3). Urban governance also rests upon the adoption of broader city visions of the type that we investigate later in Lille and Rennes. The technical expertise of the larger communes has greatly improved owing to the rise of urban development agencies, bodies staffed by planning experts, economists and urban geographers to provide technical information and to help municipal authorities to develop structure plans (*schémas directeurs*). Such agencies have reduced the reliance on state field services such as the field services of the Equipment ministry (DDE). Large communes have also developed sophisticated place marketing agencies, often in association with business interests, and on occasion in competition with the state's own agencies.

Unlike the communes or the regions, the departmental councils have no statutorily defined economic development function. But they have actively sought to be involved in economic development activities. In our case studies, both departmental councils engaged in their own place marketing activities, either in co-operation with state or city-wide structures, or independently. Both had small economic development bureaux, with modest budgets. Most departmental councils consider themselves 'associate-rivals' with the regions and the communes in the economic development sphere. They will associate themselves with prestigious initiatives, such as inward investment. In Ille-et-Vilaine, for example, a strict protocol ensured that all local actors were given equal credit for the decision of the Japanese Sandon firm in 1995 to invest in the department. But this association is underpinned by rivalry. The departmental councils have retained a specific identity. They have often become the defenders of rural and small town interests, adopting policies aimed at preserving non-metropolitan economic activities; *de facto*, the departmental councils and the leading city are more often rivals than associates. Diverging territorial interests are reinforced by political rivalries; while many cities are run by the left, the departmental councils are overwhelmingly the province of the UDF or RPR.

The 1982 law conferred specific responsibilities on the 22 regional councils: those of regional economic planning, training, and the allocation of business creation (PRE) and employment (PRCE) grants. The law also allowed the regions to participate in financial institutions (*Sociétés du développement régional* – SDR) to raise capital and to invest in regional businesses. However, expenditure on economic development by the regions trails well behind that of the communes (INSEE 1999). In an era of fiscal retrenchment, the regions have preferred to replace direct grants to businesses with loans and usually have a symbolic presence in regional investment banks.

It was unlikely that the regions would ever become strategic planning agencies once they had lost out to the departments in the 1982–3 legislation. The central state was genuinely fearful of *land*-style regions emerging as powerful policy-makers. The regions have not been able to control or federate the economic development activities of the other layers of local government. They have suffered from weak political legitimacy and modest financial resources (Le Galès and Lequesne 1998; Nay 1997). The state has prevented the regions from emerging as stronger entities. Though EU regional policy in theory favours the regional level of sub-national administration, in practice EU structural funds are allocated to sub-regional areas (Smith 1997). In the case of the Nord/Pas-de-Calais region, for instance, only Valenciennes and the mining areas of the Pas-de-Calais had objective 2 status. Regional actors performed a marginal role in this process; negotiations were concentrated between state officials in the SGAR (advised by city-based actors) and representatives of the Commission.

The principal tool of regional economic policy is that of the State–Region Contracts. Originally conceived as instruments of joint democratic planning, in practice the quinquennial State–Region planning contracts usually favour central state funding priorities (Loughlin and Mazey 1995; Pontier 1998; Fontaine and Warin 2000). In the round of negotiations prior to the 2000–2005 plans, it was made clear that the release of central government funds would be conditional upon the elected regions agreeing to co-finance programmes in areas such as road-building and universities where they have no formal policy responsibilities. Refusal to follow central government priorities would endanger regional funding, a prospect made all the more daunting since the Jospin government decided (in 1999) to suppress the region's share of the local property tax (*taxe d'habitation*) and replace it with a direct grant. The five-year contracts effectively force the regional councils to commit a proportion of their budgets to priorities determined by the central state, thereby lessening their ability to engage in autonomous public policies. Moreover, the State–Region Contracts are a misnomer; the state deals with departmental councils and city-wide structures as well as regions.

State actors

Through contractual processes such as State–Region plans and more direct forms of intervention, the French state remains very much an actor in local economic development. The cognitive norms of state activity lie somewhere between those of classic administrative regulation and new styles of partnership politics. The range of state agencies with some input into economic development policy is bewildering, the main ones being the SGAR (the economic service of the regional prefecture), the DATAR (the delegation for regional and territorial planning, an inter-ministerial agency with offices in the regions) and the DRIRE (the regional service of the Industry ministry). Other agencies, such as ANVAR (the research and innovation agency) or individuals (such as the Industrial

Commissars) also have an impact. These agencies exercise subtly different roles and functions, ranging from classic bureaucratic control to partnership-style joint ventures.

The SGAR is the service of the regional prefecture charged with strategic economic planning. The 1992 Joxe law conferred upon the regional prefect the co-ordination of the activities of the field services in the economic sphere. This task is carried out by the General Secretariat for Regional Affairs (SGAR). The SGAR is a light structure headed by a General Secretary. It is charged with co-ordinating the state's economic objectives at the regional level; to achieve this, SGAR officials oversee the work of several government departments at a time. The SGAR is also responsible for distributing economic development credits and monitoring the State–Region plans (Bernard 1992; Antony and Bourgeois 1995). The SGAR performs an important role in preparing and negotiating European Union structural fund grants. In the case of the Nord/Pas-de-Calais region, for instance, the SGAR prepared the necessary documents to assist Douai, Avesnes and Valenciennes in their bid to obtain EU regional fund objective 2 status. The SGAR is also responsible for managing European funds and evaluating EU-funded projects. In its other major role, the SGAR represents the French state in the quinquennial State–Region plans.

The DRIRE is the decentralised field service of the Industry and Research ministries. It has significant powers of factory inspection and control of technical standards; this ensures a continuing influence in local economic development. It also performs an important role in advising businesses over grant applications, and in administering EU, national and regional grants. It is a fairly classic bureaucratic structure, heavily dependent upon the transmission of orders from the national ministry, and subject to the influence of the Mining and Highways and Bridges technical corps. The DATAR is a governmental agency created in 1963 to assist the state in its territorial planning role. An obvious loser of decentralisation, the DATAR is a Parisian administration that has learned to adapt to changing circumstances (Burnham 1998; Guigou 2000). It has survived by developing new roles: as the overall co-ordinator of EU structural fund policy; as a residual source of central government expertise on urban planning (the 1995 Pasqua law was drawn up by the technical services of the DATAR) and as an active player in partnership-style joint ventures with local actors. Thus, in our two case study areas, the DATAR was the driving force behind ambitious place marketing agencies, where it participated alongside other public and private sector actors.

Whatever formal powers of co-ordination the 1992 law conferred on the regional prefectures, powerfully organised ministries, such as Industry, continue to resist inter-ministerial regional co-ordination. They have the means to do this as their budgets and resources are considerable and the regional prefectures do not have the financial or administrative authority to challenge national Industry ministry policy. In the sphere of economic development policy, there is extensive bureaucratic competition between state agencies – just as in England.

Chambers of Commerce and business interests

Though they are powerful local actors, the French Chambers of Commerce must not be confused with their English counterparts. They bridge the public and private sectors; in the words of one Director-General, they are 'public sector organisations run by private firms'. They are semi-statist, corporatist organisations. They represent local business and commerce in their dealings with other public authorities. Because each locally registered firm must pay taxes to its local chamber, this relationship is one which often causes resentment. Local business ambivalence towards the chambers is expressed through a participation rate in consular elections that rarely exceeds 15–20 per cent of local businesses.

As hybrid actors, the French chambers perform three separate roles. They are important economic actors in their own right, notably through their role in managing ports and airports. The chambers are also powerful as local commercial and business lobbies. In their most statist version, the chambers represent the Industry and Commerce ministry in cities across France. As agencies performing a public service mission, they are subject to administrative, rather than civil law. The central state retains powerful means of control over the chambers. It can modify the missions of the chambers by decrees or laws. It must approve all property developments undertaken and loans contracted by a chamber. The annual budget of each chamber must be approved by the Commerce ministry (Waters 1998). Although they can charge for services provided, there are strict limits up to which the chambers can raise their own finance, in the form of additional taxation on their constituents (Schulz 1994).

Though constrained by regulations, the chambers represent place-bounded business interests better than any other organisation. They are the natural economic partners of local authorities. In their capacity as economic developers, the chambers reserve certain rights to expropriate land for development purposes which can make them valued partners for local government. They are in permanent contact with industrial, commercial and service interests. Voluntary co-operation between chambers and large cities has developed as rivalry has given way to partnership and as chambers have been forced to recognise the economic importance of French local authorities in the post-decentralisation period.

The more powerful and less place-bounded business interests often reject co-operation with the chambers on account of their corporatist and parochial outlook. Unlike in the US, French business interests are strongly centralised, focused on lobbying activities in Paris or in relation to EU institutions. The weakness of strong indigenous firms in most French cities encourages this perspective. Business prefers to lobby upwards to the region, the central state and the EU. The principal employer's association, the MEDEF (formerly CNPF), has a highly centralised structure within which local or regional interprofessional employers' federations have little influence. The horizons adopted by powerful business interests are usually wider than those of local political communities. Surprising as it may seem, however, there is a long history of private sector involvement in French public service delivery that we will now consider.

Private interests and public goods

From the beginning of the twentieth century, the French Council of State recognised the distinction between direct public management and the private management of public services (Gugliemi 1994). Pragmatism has underpinned this mixed economy policy style. Two forms of private sector involvement in French localities are especially relevant to the comparative debate on local governance. French joint venture companies have become important actors of local economic development; private firms have managed French local public services for far longer than their counterparts in the UK.

The closest French equivalent to a formal English public–private partnership is the mixed economy society (SEM); this is a joint venture company between public and private partners, within which local authorities hold a majority of the capital (Ascher 1994; Mitchell 1996; Cole 1999). Such joint ventures are not new. SEMs have existed since the Poincaré decree of 1926. They have always involved partnerships. Prior to the decentralisation reforms, however, they were closely supervised by the prefectures. A new generation of SEMs was created by the 7 July 1983 law. They are now easier to set up (the prefect no longer has to approve of their creation). They can have varied objectives, rather than being created for a single purpose. Their operating modes were made far easier as they are allowed to set their own fees and draft their own constitutions. As mixed economy societies are subject to civil, rather than to administrative law, they are much more flexible than local authorities themselves. Mixed economy societies facilitate the introduction of private sector management techniques (such as the freedom to recruit part-time and temporary workers and more flexible accounting practices) while retaining overall public sector control of joint ventures.

The range of activities undertaken by SEMs has increased dramatically, as has their number – a 100 per cent increase from 1983–93 (Bizet 1993; Pivet 1993). Apart from classic urban and industrial construction projects and public service delivery functions, the new generation of joint ventures has allowed local authorities to become economic entrepreneurs in their own right. Joint ventures have been used for purposes of transport, museums, theatres, sporting facilities, tourism, conference centres, even hotel chains. The flexible structure of a joint venture is more suitable for economic development activities in particular than the more rigid local authority bureaucracy. As in the case of the SEM Euralille (see chapter 7), the SEM format can cover very high-risk economic development strategies.

A more direct involvement of the private sector in the governance of French localities concerns the practice of communes 'contracting out' the provision of local services to private sector operators in spheres such as water, drainage, waste disposal, industrial heating, school canteens and transport (Coing et al.

1989; Lorrain 1991; Ascher 1994; Caillose and Le Galès 1995; Burnham 2000). The most common form of delegated public service is that of the 'concession'. The local authority confers – through contract – the operation of a public service to an external party (the 'concessionnaire'). After a stated period (usually from 25 to 75 years) during which the concessionnaire recuperates the initial investment, the good resorts to the public sphere. As is the case for the PFI in England, the 'concession' minimises the initial costs for the local authority, while the concessionnaires recuperate their investment by levying charges for services.

Thus far, the similarities with the PFI are striking. Unlike in England, however, in the French case there is a much weaker practice of competitive tendering, an ingrained tendency to identify a 'favoured bidder' and a less rigorous regulatory regime to police service delivery (Burnham 2000). In its most complete form, this private sector penetration of French localities has led to the development of the *ensemblier* practice; this involves highly specialised and concentrated public utility firms (Vivendi, Générale des Eaux-Suez, Bouygues) offering a complete range of urban services to municipal authorities, allowing councils to overcome their own organisational and financial weaknesses. These public utility firms comprise an oligopoly, with the power to define an urban product and to sell it to local authorities. Such strong and nationally present public utility firms benefit from economies of scale that local councils cannot match.

Private sector influence in local management has become pervasive. French-style partnerships have been stimulated by the weakness of local authorities and the complexity of normal administrative procedures; by the impact of decentralisation, which conferred new powers on mayors; and by the increasing complexity of economic development operations themselves, necessitating the mobilisation of public and private resources. Joint venture companies and other forms of private sector involvement are a staple feature of urban governance in the main French cities.

Conclusion

While France and England have differed greatly in their approaches to the economic development of localities during the post-war period, in neither country do specifically local economic development policies have a long history. In the French case, the economic development of localities was supervised by the modernisers in the administrative corps and Parisian ministries and implemented principally by their field services. In England local authorities began establishing economic development units, partly in reaction to the reforms of the Thatcher governments. The logic of central state-driven modernisation traditionally discouraged French cities from undertaking bottom-up economic policy experiments. Even before the 1982 decentralisation reforms, however, the mayors of certain large French cities were engaged in proactive economic development strategies; this was particularly the case for Dubedout in Grenoble, and Defferre in Marseilles (Bleitrach 1980). Local economic interventionism gathered pace during the 1970s under the impact of the economic crisis, the development of a 'localist' ideology, and the renewal of municipal government in 1971 and 1977. The advent of a new generation of (mainly PS) mayors committed to practices of social experimentation, political participation and local economic development gave a major push preceding decentralisation. In the early stages, local economic development took the form of municipal subsidies to fight unemployment and to assist sectors in difficulty. In the English case, early local economic development policy – in the form of municipal socialism – had similar origins and objectives. The energy of activist Labour councils in the 1980s was dedicated to pursuing local economic strategies to counteract – or combat – the effects of Thatcherism at a national level.

Franco-English differences appear to confirm not only the contrasting state traditions in each country, but also the divergent inspirations of the particular policies followed by the Thatcher and Mitterrand governments. In England after 1979, the Conservative governments pursued a neo-liberal policy agenda, producing a market-led set of policies aiming to place business in the centre of local policy-making. In France, the Socialist governments of the 1980s initially adopted a more interventionist approach to economic development: localities were valued partners in the fight against unemployment.

A shift in ideas and practices occurred in the mid-1980s and by the end of the 1980s many of the sharper differences between England and France had faded. The anti-local government stance of English centrally directed local economic policy became less apparent once John Major replaced Margaret Thatcher and even more so once Blair succeeded Major. In the French case, there has long been an acceptance of market or mixed economy solutions, in the form of joint venture companies, the contracting out of local services, and – in certain cases – the development of closer relationships between local political and business communities. Local political leaders in both countries see themselves as policy entrepreneurs, building alliances with other local decision-makers. The prospect of European Union funding has encouraged local actors to co-operate as local authorities, state agencies and business interests all stand to benefit from EU grants.

The two countries face many common policy problems of economic competition, de-industrialisation and a lack of match of skills to employment. In France and England, both locally inspired and centrally directed economic policies have rapidly evolved. The speed of change reflects the high level of salience of economic policy for politicians at all territorial levels of the state. The politicisation of the local economy has led to very rapid changes both in the content of central and locally inspired policy and in the institutional framework within which policy is implemented. Local economic policy has had an impact upon change in other sectors; it has also been influenced by changes in other spheres of public action such as education, health and housing. The new local environment requires the ability to manage shifting inter-organisational relationships, as well as developing sustainable long-term strategies.

The direction of local economic policy in England bears certain similarities to the French experience. The creation of the single regeneration budget and the government offices for the regions introduced a centrally approved partnership approach, in certain respects similar to the French State–Region planning contracts. In both countries central government tried to introduce a form of inter-governmental management which would counteract the problems of fragmentation and lack of co-ordination. While institutional structures have remained distinct, substantive policy differences have thus narrowed. Urban policy-makers in both countries face similar problems of unemployment, industrial decline, inward investment, urban deprivation and the need to build the image of their cities. In both countries, local economic development is perceived as part of a more general effort to strengthen the identities and improve the social cohesion of local communities in the face of rapid international economic change.

5 The governance of sub-national education in England and France

One of the central themes to the study of policy networks is that policy-making differs according to the field of public activity. Each 'sub-government' has a unique power structure and set of relationships. In contrast to other sectors, relationships between policy-makers in secondary education have tended to be less open to influences from actors outside of the educational policy community itself. In so far as it addresses processes of governance within education, this chapter investigates a policy field with specific qualities. Education is unlike other public services. Not only does it reflect and shape social and occupational mobility, but it also embodies ideas of citizenship, social equity and national identity. We begin the chapter with a brief presentation of the distinctive historical pathways that have shaped the educational debate in the two countries. We then discuss in some detail the changing parameters of educational management in England and France. We conclude the chapter by considering whether governance fits the case of secondary education.

Education and state traditions in England and France

Each education system has a specific national context. Franco-English educational studies posit England and France as examples of the most different comparison. Thus Archer (1979) contrasts the two countries as exemplars of decentralised and centralised decision-making systems. Broadfoot et al. (1985) assess three analytically distinct but mutually reinforcing aspects to the national context: prevailing educational policies and priorities, institutional infrastructure and dominant ideological traditions. The logic of the national distinctiveness argument is that changes in both systems are dependent upon nationally specific institutional structures, unique political configurations and the ideology of public service against the ideology of 'choice'.

Secondary education clearly illustrates the different state traditions in England and France. Duclaud-Williams (1995: 3–4) contrasts 'an active, interventionist French state with the capacity to employ and control education with a view to producing modernisation and a reluctant non-interventionist limited English state, certainly unwilling and probably unable to intervene in similar fashion'. For reasons of nation-state building, ideological control and economic performance, educational issues had a far greater salience in nineteenth- and twentieth-century France than in England. By the early twentieth century, one French ministry concentrated educational provision, while there was a plethora of central bodies in the English state: the Charity Commission, the Treasury, the Board of Education and the Science and Art department. As early as the 1830s, French education minister Guizot was able to interest himself in primary and university-level teaching. English elites adopted different attitudes to education. Partly because the traditional social and political order was never destroyed, education was not used as blatantly for social engineering. The state feared expanding its educational role for fear of alienating the religious orders that ran the denominational schools and had extensive political clout, particularly at the national level. The state was reluctant to intervene too closely in the autonomy of the micro agencies. This benefited English local authorities and teachers who were free from central state supervision. Both systems were predicated upon a particular path of historical development and a contrasting pattern of church–state relations.

Arguments based on immutable national contexts assume that strong national traditions will persist and change will be limited. It is difficult to comprehend the variable structure of the educational policy communities in the two countries without understanding the distinctive institutional contexts, political relationships and ideas that underpin educational policy-making. These differences are addressed in the main body of the chapter. National traditions have an obvious bearing upon the structure of the policy communities involved in both countries. In England, educational professionals and administrators operated mainly at the local government level in accordance with the 'dual polity' tradition observed in chapter 2. While teaching unions engaged in national pay bargaining, much educational policy and all of its administration was conventionally carried out by the local education authorities, the traditional focus of professional educational expertise in the English system. In France, the existence of a nationally regulated and hierarchically regimented state education system forms a powerful symbol of French republican culture. The national educational policy-making community traditionally consisted of a strong administration – the Ministry of National Education – and several corps of teachers organised into powerful trade unions. These partners were determined to preserve the centralised character of policy-making and its independence from local and societal pressures. While in France long traditions of educational centralisation and the independence of the professions have been mutually reinforcing (Archer 1979), the decentralised English system has been much more open to external influences (notably from elected politicians).

While the institutional starting points are highly distinctive, some experts observe common problems confronting education systems in both countries that are sometimes more important than the structural properties of educational systems themselves (Moon 1990; Legrand and Solaux 1992). Both countries have experienced the shift from an elite to a mass education system; moves to comprehensive forms of secondary education; the expansion of higher education; and the implementation of curriculum change (Barber 1996). Notwithstanding their nationally distinctive educational traditions, we also find evidence of some cross-fertilisation and the transfer of ideas between the two countries. Thus reforms to French classroom teaching methods in the 1980s and 1990s borrowed from the English experience of child-centred learning (Legrand and Solaux 1992). On the other hand, explicit contrasts have been drawn between the move to more central regulation in England from the late 1980s onwards and the weakening of a traditionally more directive French model of school governance (Judge 1990). This chapter takes as its starting point the dynamic tension between the distinctive national contexts of education policy-making in England and France and the similarity of common policy problems. Moving to the main body of the chapter, we now examine in more detail the local governance of secondary education in contemporary England and France.

The governance of education in England

The history of the government of English public education is one of central government legislative action and local democratic administration. Central government set out the broad outlines of the system, but locally elected government administered educational provision. The localism of the system was explicit between 1870 and 1944, when local education committees, set up by the Forster Act of 1870, had substantial autonomy. In the run-up to the landmark 1944 Education Act, local autonomy appeared to be threatened by the proposal to nationalise public education and bring it under the control of central government. The 1944 Act set up the duty of the Minister for Education as 'to promote the education of the people of England and Wales and the progressive development of institutions for that purpose and to secure the effective execution by local authorities under his control and direction'. As many have commented, the 1944 Act set up a partnership between central and local government. The former was the senior partner, but the latter had much discretion and autonomy (Regan 1977). Once the reforming impetus died down at the end of the 1940s, local education authorities had extensive autonomy in such matters as secondary school organisation, curriculum administration, school funding, training and management (Saran 1973). The role of central government was as a promoter rather than a director of policy (Griffith 1966). By virtue of their independence, local authorities exercised a strong influence over policy-making, either individually or in national communities of professionals in partnership with central government.

The direction local policy-making took owed much to the political orientation of the particular local council. Urban Labour councils and rural Conservative ones followed different policies. The senior officers of the local education authority, who had a high level of prestige, expertise and legitimacy in the post-war education system, were key actors in determining local education policies. Chief education officers were powerful people, both locally and as a national force. In some places chief officers held sway over the councillors. In general, however, there was a close alliance between local politicians and the chief education officers that resulted in locally adapted solutions to education problems during much of the 1950s and 1960s. Local education authorities were embedded in various close relationships with teachers, parents and other community organisations (Saran 1973) as well as in local political relationships. Most education areas retained selected education under the influence of elite and parent pressure for grammar schools.

The 1960s witnessed the height of local education authority dominance of educational policy-making. In many ways the decade saw the culmination of local education authority influence through the adoption of comprehensive education, which the government encouraged through its famous circular 10/65 in 1965. The advocacy by education professionals of comprehensive solutions to problems of educational underachievement and social equity became the new professional consensus. In spite of a vigorous campaign of parental opposition, comprehensive education gradually spread throughout the country through central encouragement, financial incentives and, finally, legal power. The manner in which school reorganisations took place showed a large degree of local discretion (James 1980). Even when central persuasion turned into a mandatory policy, local education authorities were able to negotiate their own reorganisation schemes (Ranson 1980).

The pattern of local education authority dominance gradually declined from the late 1960s onwards. The policies of the 1960s and 1970s led to the reforms of the 1980s. The voice of the 'consumer' started to be articulated against the decisions of the local education authority in the form of resistance to comprehensive reorganisation schemes. At the national level the concern for the voice of parents was expressed in such forums as the Taylor Committee, which argued for an enhanced role for parents on the governing bodies of schools. At the same time, central government started to become more concerned about educational performance. Here the influence of economic pressures drove central government policy. Fiscal pressures caused central government to look closely at the levels of expenditure and the value taxpayers were getting from it. These fiscal pressures were, in part, caused by the international crisis of the 1970s that had affected the UK economy more than its competitors. Controlling public expenditure was essential to the government's economic policy strategy. The other economic impetus for reform was a concern for standards in education. Poor generic standards were perceived to have a detrimental effect on economic performance. As early as 1975 the central government started to review standards and advocate a more focused curriculum. In a famous speech in October 1976 Prime Minister James Callaghan lamented the 'state of state education'. The proposals for reform and the public rhetoric that ensued became government policy in the 1977 Green Paper, *Education in Schools*, which stressed the national basis of education, its relationship to the world of work, the role of central government in ensuring standards and the importance of the curriculum. At the same time the Department of Education enhanced the Assessment of Performance Unit (set up in 1974).

It is important to mention these initiatives of the 1970s in order to add further criticism to the view that the Conservatives made a massive break with the past when they entered office in 1979. They extended developments and worked with parts of the education policy community to introduce a series of reforms, many of which were gradually gaining acceptance. The Department of Education and Science led many of these changes, and gradually changed its strategy from persuasion, to pressure and finally to control (Ranson 1985). Just as Mrs Thatcher presided over the move to comprehensive education when she was Secretary of State for Education in 1973 in spite of her personal opposition, so she pushed along the reforms of education in the 1980s. It is important not to overplay the cohesion of Conservative education policy, which was shaped by a struggle for influence between traditionalists, modernisers and market-liberals (Barber 1996; Kenyon 1995). The resulting mix of reforms was an uneven one, as organisational decentralisation co-existed with rule-enforced central regulation, justified in the name of either choice (its ideological rationale) or efficiency (in deference to the canons of the new public management).

The Conservatives came to office with a belief in the role of parents and criticism of bureaucratic organisation that gave an additional bite to policies affecting the power and legitimacy of local education authorities. Right-wing pressure groups and think-tanks were influential on education policy, for example the Hillgate Group, the Institute for Economic Affairs and the Adam Smith Institute. This affected the provisions of the Education Act 1980 that gave representation and power to parent governors, who were strengthened in 1986. The government also enacted measures designed to make the curriculum more responsive to employers by setting up the Training and Vocational Educational Initiative (TVEI), and also the Youth Training Scheme (YTS) under the control of the Manpower Services Commission.

The 1988 Education Reform Act was a particularly important staging post of Conservative education policy (Lawton 1992; Ranson 1992; Ball 1994). The 1988 Act engaged in the parallel process of decentralising to 'below' the education authority and centralising 'above' it. The main sections of the 1988 Act included open enrolment, the creation of grant-maintained schools, the national curriculum and local management of schools. School autonomy was enhanced by local management schemes with pupil-weighted formula funding and the gradual delegation of budget and staffing decisions to school governors. Schools henceforth had control over most of their budgets. This broke the umbilical cord with the local education authorities, though LEAs continue to set the overall formula for funding schools and the total amount of the education budget. The Act extended parents' ability to choose their school and allowed some schools to 'opt out' of local authority control by obtaining direct funding from central government. The Act also set up city technology colleges, established the National Curriculum Council and introduced testing at 7, 11, 14 and 16 years. While local management embedded local schools, the national curriculum has provided the stimulus for further moves to central regulation and for the exercising of a much tighter central supervision over local school management. The creation of a national agency for school inspections (OFSTED) and a national teacher training agency (TTA) further removed functions previously exercised by the local authorities.

The obvious losers of the 1988 Act were the local education authorities (LEAs). The LEAs were weakened through the provisions for formula funding (which reduced their financial discretion), 'opting out' (which removed some schools from their tutelage altogether) and open enrolment (which made future planning more difficult). The link between the formula for the budget for schools and the freedom of parents to choose where to send their children created a 'quasi-market' whereby schools receive more resources if they attract more children and fewer resources if they become unpopular. These changes encouraged the expansion of popular schools and provoked the closure of several unpopular ones. Critics argue that the needs of longer-term educational planning have been sacrificed to those of short-term choice. They also point to the unintended consequences of open enrolment, in terms of environmental policy (the 'school run'), local property markets and selection criteria.

The effects of these changes on local authorities have been profound. They no longer run the government of education. Education officers and politicians share responsibilities with headteachers, chairs of governing bodies, professionals, parent groups and other pressure groups such as private sector businesses. The empowerment of governing boards and school headteachers has created new, unpredictable centres of decision-making within schools. Local education authorities have shed their direct training function, and many of their other personnel and support functions are bought in by the schools themselves. Their powers have been reduced to those of special education, setting the budget and formula, closing and opening schools, transport and capital programmes. Some commentators initially thought that the LEAs would go into permanent decline or even be abolished, but their powers and democratic legitimacy remain considerable. Local education authorities continue to be a powerful force in local education policy-making and spend by far the largest proportion of local authority budgets.

The strengthening of schools as autonomous actors has had an unpredictable impact on the functioning of the educational system. Decision-makers have had to address new issues of regulating school management and reconciling greater school autonomy with the broader objectives of the public education system, and the implementation of a prescriptive national curriculum. The requirement since 1992 for schools to produce (and for the government to publish) a range of performance indicators to inform parental choice and to encourage efficiency has demonstrated the central government drive for increased regulation as the corollary for micro-decentralisation.

National regulatory styles have strongly influenced organisational responses to regulating school governance. Strong models of administrative control have prevailed in France while market-based forms of evaluation have progressed in the UK. The agency model has been most prevalent in the governance of education in England. The national curriculum acted as a catalyst in this respect. Various non-governmental agencies (such as the Funding Agency for Schools, and the

Qualifications and Curriculum Authority) were created to implement the 1988 Act and manage its consequences. The most controversial of these agencies is the Office for Standards in Education (OFSTED), the agency in charge of the school inspection service. OFSTED was created in 1992 as a 'non-ministerial department independent from the DfEE' (OFSTED 1998). OFSTED could have been invented to provide a case study in the new public management, a central plank of English-style governance. OFSTED operates as an independent regulatory agency. It awards school inspection contracts on the basis of competitive tender from qualified inspectors. In line with the market-principles characteristic of the new public management style, inspectors having undertaken OFSTED training and agreeing to its Framework for Inspection are eligible to bid. Its powers to intervene in failing schools (such as the Ridings School in Calderdale in 1996) have demonstrated the force of OFSTED as an agency. Its acceptance by the incoming Blair government ensured its organisational survival. But OFSTED is highly contentious and dissatisfaction with the agency is high. School-teachers see its members as not properly trained and complain that OFSTED inspections undermine the confidence of the teaching profession. Local authorities highlight OFSTED as an example of their diminished status. Not only have local authorities lost control of the function of co-ordinating academic inspections in the schools they control, they are subject to regular OFSTED visits themselves.

Although these reforms were formulated and implemented during the Conservative period of rule, there have been strong elements of continuity under the Blair administration. The Labour government has accepted the national curriculum, local management of schools (rebaptised 'fair funding'), open enrolment, OFSTED and the slimming down of local education authority functions. There have also been several significant changes: most notably the repealing of the assisted places scheme (financial assistance to the private school sector) and the restoration of grant-maintained schools to local authority control. The Blair administration has its own educational style, emphasising the role of training and the importance of transferable skills with the same ardour as its Conservative predecessors stressed choice. If anything, the New Labour government has increased central direction in its focus on standards and has moved further towards a partnership model in tackling educational problems through Education Action Zones in which local education authorities may play a role but do not necessarily lead. These Education Action Zones are a cornerstone of New Labour's secondary education policy. There are clear similarities with the French experience of *réseaux d'éducation prioritaires* (REP), introduced by the French Socialist government in 1981. In both cases, less favoured status areas can qualify for specific regimes, wherein central government targets increased resources to schools with special educational needs. In the English case, Action Zones are run as partnership bodies, with the main partners including participating schools, the LEA, local and national businesses, the TECs, religious bodies, voluntary and community organisations and other local government agencies. The Secretary of State retains the right to appoint a representative. The emphasis on partnership within the community responds to the political imperative for New Labour of being seen to promote joined-up government.

The acceptance by the Blair government of the main reforms of its predecessor confirmed the lasting impact of the Conservative period in office in the sphere of educational governance. An imperfect and uneven consensus has built up around the highly controversial reforms of the late 1980s and early 1990s – local management, the national curriculum, testing and evaluation – as comprising essential reforms addressing the long-term trends of the English economy and the need to broaden the skills base in a more flexible labour market. Stripped of their ideological overtones, developments in England were comparable with those in countries as diverse as Canada, New Zealand, the Netherlands and Belgium (Hill et al. 1990). Whatever their economic or educational merits, patterns of school governance and of local decision-making have been transformed by these countervailing pressures.

Decision-makers in local English education policy networks

The structure of the educational policy community in England was consistent with the 'dual polity' tradition observed in chapter 2. While teaching unions engaged in national pay bargaining, much educational policy and all of its administration was carried out by the local education authorities, the traditional focus of professional educational expertise in the English system. The reforms of the 1980s and 1990s disrupted this policy community. In certain accounts local management of schools was aimed primarily against educational professionals and local authorities, the core of the post-war educational policy community (Hill et al. 1990). Though traditional actors remain important (local education authorities), the centre of gravity has shifted downwards towards micro-organisations (school heads and school governors) and upwards towards a plethora of semi-autonomous agencies.

Local education authorities

Local education authorities are the functionally specific branches of elected local government dealing with the management of school education. Consistent with the collegial organisation of English local government, decisions are taken by locally elected politicians in committee, aided and assisted by an expert officer cadre. The most important elected politician is the chair of the education committee, though the leader of the council and other leading members of the ruling party group will also play a role. Other councillors seek to influence education policy by representing the interests of schools in their areas. Given the size of the council bureaucracy, a large number of council officers are involved in policy-making, the most important of whom are the director of education and her or his deputy; the heads of the financial and schools sections within the local education authority; and the LEA schools liaison officers.

Local authorities have learnt that, to be effective in the new environment, they have to reinvent their roles and shed the hierarchical and paternalist orientation that came from years of unchallenged dominance. The new organisational culture encourages local authorities to think in terms of enabling schools to provide education rather than directly controlling them; in terms of giving advice rather than direction; and in terms of ensuring a high level of quality. Governing secondary education requires new skills of liaison and networking. The speed of change and the existing diversity within local education authorities means they have reacted to the changes very differently. Some proceeded very quickly to adopt a partnership style; others have retained a more traditional role (Rao 1990). In general, however, most authorities have moved a long way in the direction of a partnership mode of operation. Nonetheless, in spite of these reforms, local education authorities have few political friends at the centre. The Labour and Conservative parties both threaten to abolish them.

Headteachers and governors

As administrators or managers of their schools, school headteachers have formidable power in the new system. They shape decisions over budgets, hiring and firing, and planning. Headteachers represent the school in the local market place, adapting the school profile to the imperatives of local supply and demand. Along with the chair of the governors, headteachers shape the agenda of the governing body, the legislative instance of decentralised school management. Decisions supported by the head and the chair of the board of governors usually prevail. Headteachers are also the repositories of professional expertise, with unsurpassed knowledge of how the decentralised system works in practice. In their capacity as the new educational professionals, heads sit on various expert committees, and, when allied with other headteachers, they can form an effective lobby group.

School governors have also been invested with powers in the new system. A headteacher must have a co-operative relationship with the chair of the board of governors, if the school is to be governed effectively. Governors (formally) make many decisions within the school, particularly the hiring of staff, budgets and development plans. Governors also exert power within the broader local education authority area and, like headteachers, sit on committees charged with formulating policy, either of their own or set up by the local education authority.

Semi-autonomous agencies and the central state

Conservative educational policy produced a more powerful pattern of central regulation and constraint. Consistent with the new public management reforms, the agency model has become a central feature of the governance of education in England. The national curriculum has acted as a catalyst in this respect. Various non-governmental agencies were created to implement the 1988 Act and manage its consequences. The Funding Agency for Schools (FAS) directly funded grant-maintained schools until their abolition in 1999. The School Curriculum Assessment Agency (SCAA) manages the national curriculum. The Office for Standards in Education (OFSTED) has taken charge of the school inspection service. We observed above how this semi-autonomous agency has assumed direct responsibility for functions previously partially exercised by the LEAs. The introduction of a more directive style of school inspectorate (OFSTED) into a traditionally decentralised UK model of school governance has produced new tensions between central agencies, educational professionals, local authorities and other interested actors. Though officially separate from the Next Steps agencies, OFSTED shares many features with them, such as open competition for recruiting managers, management by objectives and target-related missions (Hood and Jackson 1991). These agencies have had difficult, competitive relationships with existing actors, notably in the DfEE and amongst the local education authorities.

In spite of the centralisation of the 1980s, the English state still plays a marginal role in the day-to-day life of education policy. The Department of Education did not even have a regional organisation until 1995. Where liaison was necessary between local education authorities and central government – such as over approval for school closures – this occurred directly between LEAs and civil servants in Whitehall. Since 1995, the renamed Department for Education and Employment has inherited the Department of Employment's stake in the Government Offices for the Regions, but the linkage between the regional structure and the LEAs remains weak. The education divisions within the department have remained distant from regional educational policy communities, though there have been greater links between the training and education functions through the government offices. There have also been more links between other training organisations, such as the Training and Education Councils (TECs) and the main education policy-makers.

Other interest groups

Most pressure group activity within the sphere of secondary education has traditionally come from those closest to the education system: from teaching unions, parents groups and religious organisations. With the partial exception of the teaching unions, these have operated principally at a local level. In the past two decades, business interests have become somewhat more involved in educational issues – encouraged in part by central government and partly from their own initiative. Business involvement has taken two principal forms: participation in the training programmes administered by the TECs and the co-optation of business representatives onto the boards of school governors. Business has generally taken an enhanced interest in educational performance, as levels of human capital and the local skills base are seen to be essential for successful economic development. But there remains some distance between the rhetoric of government policy and the extent of business involvement.

More than in any other domain, political reforms in English education have challenged the traditional model of local self-government and have laid bare the myth of the 'dual polity'. The management of secondary education has been a laboratory of English local governance. Over the course of the past two decades, power has ebbed away from the locally elected authorities to central government, to agencies and to schools, and has created a far more complex and unpredictable form of policy-making. Education is arguably the sector in England where the transition from local government to governance has been the most marked, given that economic development is almost by definition one which cannot operate within bureaucratic hierarchies. We shall now consider the extent to which educational change is nationally unique or part of a broader European movement.

The governance of education in France

The French and English systems of secondary education represented two contrasting examples of educational governance. While in England and Wales, the central state defined general principles without intervening closely in the day-to-day running of schools, France had a far more directive system of school management. According to one of the most prominent authorities (Durand Prinborgne 1990), four principles traditionally underpinned the French educational system. First, the state has a pre-eminent role, recognised in the constitution, and it directly administers a public education service. Second, there is freedom of choice in education; private, mainly confessional schools exist to provide an alternative to the state sector. The bulk (95 per cent) of such schools choose to contract themselves with the state in exchange for financial assistance. Third, the Education ministry regulates all teaching, including in 'contracted in' private schools. Fourth, local authorities must contribute to the functioning of the state education system; in specific circumstances, they may also give forms of assistance to 'contracted in' private schools.

Centralisation and uniformity have traditionally been presented as the key principles underpinning the French secondary education system. As it had developed by the end of the nineteenth century, the French model of secondary school management was extremely centralised. Central government was responsible for the general organisation of the education system, the building and maintenance of secondary schools (*lycées*), the setting and regulation of national examinations, the content of the curriculum from the primary to the university sectors, the training of teachers, the organisation of school timetables and the close control of teaching methods.[1]

The tradition of educational centralisation is usually traced back to Napoleon (Hayward 1973). From being mainly the responsibility of the clergy during the *ancien régime*, education was transformed into a central state activity in the Napoleonic period. Napoleon created the Imperial University, which contained within it the structure of the future Education ministry itself; this involved the division of France into 22 academies, each headed by a rector. The first *lycées* were also established by Napoleon. The legacy of central state regulation survived Napoleon. As early as 1833, the Guizot law, named after the French education minister, set down the principles of primary education for boys. The Ferry laws of 1879–86 created a system of universal primary education. This was specifically designed to instil pupils with republican citizenship values and to combat the influence of a dense network of confessional schools. From the 1880s onwards, primary schools provided the bedrock of support for the Republic. Though regulated at the national level, they were financed by municipal authorities and in practice they were open to diverse local influences (Legrand 1988).

The existence of a centrally regulated state education system was a powerful symbol of French republican culture. There was a close linkage between education and citizenship; schools aimed to inculcate the universal values of the Republic. Loyal to a particular model of republican integration and threatened by a holistic Catholicism, the founding fathers of the Third Republic viewed schools as the means to integrate young citizens into the universal, lay and modern values of French republicanism. Education was openly a form of social engineering. A national education system was valued as a means of disseminating republican ideals and transforming France's variegated provinces into loyal subjects. It was also a means for breaking the hold of traditional conservatives over the peasantry. The spread of national education through the nineteenth and twentieth centuries gradually broke down older regional barriers and succeeded in inculcating a well-defined sense of Frenchness (not least through imposing the use of French over minority languages and regional dialects). The strongest defenders of this system were to be found amongst republicans for whom centralisation was a guarantee of equality of provision.

Ideas and widely disseminated beliefs have been of primordial importance in sustaining a centralised pattern of school management. The referential framework of public service provides a particularly constraining set of ideological beliefs concerning the role of teachers, parents and consumers. The centralising forces in French education (especially the main teaching union – the SNES – and the central ministerial divisions) are sustained by a strong normative attachment to public service, equality of opportunity and national standards. Public schools have traditionally been isolated from their social, cultural and economic environments in order to satisfy criteria of natural justice and equality of opportunity and to lessen the effects of social and economic inequalities on education outcomes (Derouet 1991). State school teachers believe in their pedagogic and civic missions. The prestige and security of French schoolteachers has depended on an effective system of central control and regulation. Teachers adhere to the principle of national recruitment and control of the curriculum. Secondary teachers are public servants. They are recruited by competitive examination and are attached to an academic discipline group before being posted to a specific institution.

The Education ministry has been taken to exemplify the French state model (Ambler 1985). As an organisation with 1,300,000 employees in 1998, the French Education ministry is one of the world's largest bureaucratic structures; the weight of this bureaucratic leviathan, and the strength of the vested interests, is an additional force favouring centralisation. The civil servants of the main divisions within the Education ministry and the teaching unions (previously the FEN, now the SNES) have traditionally acted as the gatekeepers at a national level. Salaries, pay and promotions are determined by mixed parity committees, composed of trade union representatives and Education ministry officials. Educational mobility generally remains determined at the national level; and only a small number of annual transfers between schools are allowed on the basis of seniority.

This bureaucratic–professional coalition was determined to resist any moves to political or administrative decentralisation. Centralisation guaranteed equality of opportunity and national standards. The teaching unions saw themselves as guardians of republican values; more importantly, their power was tied up with a national system of professional regulation. Consumers (parents and pupils) are also attached to a system of national diplomas, a factor of social and occupational mobility. With the rapid move to mass secondary education in the 1980s and 1990s, pupils have proved to be a highly effective lobby in favour of a well-funded national education system. Even parents have been much more effective when operating nationally through parents associations rather than at the level of the individual school (Legrand 1988).

Though habits of centralisation are deeply ingrained, we should guard against oversimplified classifications. The image of a uniform educational system runs against the complexities induced by local influences, parental strategies, private provision, organisational reforms and political decentralisation. Confessional primary and secondary schools have always provided an alternative to state schools. In the 1951 Barangé law, such schools were allowed to receive a public subsidy. In the Debré law of 1959, schools receiving public subsidy were invited to sign a contract (*contrat d'association*) with the state. For all practical purposes, these schools have to conform with national educational policy, including strict adherence to the national curriculum. But they have proved popular as they offer a measure of parental choice, allowing families to escape the narrow geographical catchment area of state schools. The attempt by the Socialist government of 1981–6 to incorporate church schools into the national education system rapidly mobilised parents and Catholic associations. The 1984 Savary bill was abandoned under the pressure of mass demonstrations.

As demonstrated by Vasconcellos (1993), local influences have always mattered. Local actors lobby hard to secure new schools or prevent school closures. Through the mediation of local actors (especially mayors, firms, churches and associations), the types of local educational supply have been adapted to the characteristics of the local economy and cultural environment (Zay 1994). Communes have always funded the building and equipment of primary schools, which have in practice been open to diverse local influences (Legrand 1988). Some more precise examples of local influences will be considered in chapter 7.

As defined in chapter 1, governance partly refers to changing organisational processes and sets of ideas that call into question vertical forms of bureaucratic organisation. According to received wisdom, the French Education ministry is notoriously resistant to change. It sheds secondary responsibilities only in order to be able to concentrate on new tasks (Durand-Prinborgne 1989). Bureaucratic capture is a fundamental trait of French educational policy. Each incoming minister, armed with an ambitious reform project, is eventually captured by a close alliance of officials and trade unionists. As the former education minister Allègre (1997–2000) discovered to his cost (notably over *lycée* reform), any move which appears to threaten established positions or to water down public services invariably meets bureaucratic and professional opposition.

The portrayal of immobility is something of an exaggeration. The Education ministry has been amongst the most innovative in experimenting with various new management techniques, such as management by objectives ('projets de services') and financial decentralisation ('globalisation'). It has contributed to the effort to modernise the public sector through adopting new procedures of evaluation and contractualisation. Indeed, it has gone some way to hive off functions to semi-autonomous agencies, a model familiar in England. For example, the Jospin government created EDUFRANCE in November 1998, as a semi-autonomous agency to export French knowledge and attract foreign students to France, functions previously assumed by the ministry. Much more radical proposals were mooted within the Education ministry, with former minister Allègre favouring the creation of separate agencies to deal with competitive civil service examinations, staff recruitment, school examinations and academic inspection. Allègre was unsuccessful: the mainstream view remains that agencies are synonymous with a privatisation of educational management and a threat to the equality and neutrality of the state. The discourse of evaluation has also made great strides in French education (Fixari and Kletz 1996). There has been an increasing use of institutional audits in schools, and since 1995 the Education ministry has published league tables of school performance, classifying schools in relation to both their absolute and their 'value-added' performance (Thélot 1994). Unlike in England, there is as yet no clear linkage between the evaluation of performance and the allocation of resources.

Along with the drive to administrative decentralisation, contractualisation was the centrepiece of Allègre's project to modernise the Education ministry. The emphasis on contracts within the Education ministry forms part of the discourse of management by objectives that has penetrated the education policy community since the Jospin law of 1989. The Allègre ministry (1997–2000) experimented with two types of contract: those agreed between the ministry and the academies (the regional field services of the Education ministry); and those – limited to four pilot regions – concluded between the academies and individual schools. These public sector 'contracts' are consistent with the main traits of French style governance investigated in chapter 3. They are not legally enforceable contracts. They are more akin to mission statements that set out aims, objectives and means to achieve them rather than mutually binding pledges. Unlike the State–Region planning contracts, moreover, education contracts were concluded between different actors within the Education ministry; they did not extend to external partners such as elected regions or parents. Whatever their limitations, these contractual procedures were an organisational innovation in the context of the Education ministry. For the first time, the academies were called upon to define their own pluri-annual objectives, to set out a method for achieving these and to allocate resources for implementing goals from increasingly decentralised ('global') budgets.

Contracts are not limited to vertical channels within the Education ministry. The emergence of new educational actors has given rise to more interdependent, networked and contractual forms of decision-making at the regional level. The procedure known as the Contract of Objectives, introduced in the 1993 Training Act, was a centrally inspired attempt to involve business more closely in the definition of its training objectives. Contracts are signed between the state, the region and a particular profession, with each party agreeing to specific commitments, financial or otherwise. A training contract will typically include the regional council, the rectorate, the regional prefecture, a professional federation and other training agencies. Other education-related contractual processes included the University 2000 scheme, whereby French regions and other local authorities were called upon to contribute financially to the construction of a generation of new universities.

Though the strong model of administrative control in France has not been fundamentally overhauled, some observers argue that the reforms and regulations have created a French-style new public management (Demailly 1993). The regulatory framework of school governance in France has undergone important changes. At the territorial level, successive measures of administrative decentralisation since the 1960s have strengthened the regional level field services of the Education ministry, while the decentralisation reforms of 1983 and 1985 gave local and regional authorities important new responsibilities in secondary education (Cole 1997). The parallel movements of administrative and political decentralisation are central to understanding the new policy dynamics of educational governance.

How did this pattern of educational governance come about? The overly bureaucratic and centralised French educational structure began to crack under the pressure of delivering educational services. The pressures for some decentralisation in the sphere of secondary education were overwhelming. The familiar arguments of proximity, of adaptation to local needs and of local participation were raised in education as in other policy fields (Marcou 1992). The policy-makers of the early 1980s believed that the quality of educational services could be improved through increased school autonomy, and the involvement of the meso-level local authorities (departmental and regional councils) in educational planning. The involvement of locally elected councils in planning infrastructure (buildings and equipment) and making educational forecasts would alleviate the burden on the overloaded central state. Local and regional authorities would contribute to financing the efforts of national education policies, notably as a consequence of the decision taken in the 1989 Jospin law that 80 per cent of an age cohort should achieve the *baccalauréat*. This commitment required a large-scale expansion in the number of *lycées*; the new regional authorities would finance this expansion. Educational reforms (in 1983, 1985, 1989 and 1999) also attempted to open up schools to their external environment, notably through the creation of school projects (*projets d'établissement*), new teaching methods (team and tutorial teaching) and the involvement of parents, local authorities and local businesses on the governing boards of schools.

Educational planners believed that the benefits of organisational decentralisation could be achieved without calling into question the underlying bases of a national education system. There has been no fundamental shift of power to individual schools as has occurred in England (Fialaire 1992a; Cole 1997). Control over core functions (staff movement between academies, overall pedagogical orientation, and the distribution of financial resources to the academies) remains determined at the central level. Even the partial decentralisation of secondary education met determined resistance from the key actors of the anti-local coalition: teachers, central civil servants and powerful forces within the ruling Socialist party itself (Mény 1990; Hatzfeld 1991; Fontaine 1992; Marcou 1992). Many civil servants and most teachers were highly suspicious of any local autonomy in educational provision. The involvement of local authorities would, it was feared, be detrimental to the prevailing ethos of egalitarianism and uniform standards within the education system (Corbett and Moon 1996). Such apprehension explained the incomplete nature of the education decentralisation reforms of 1983 and 1985. Local and regional authorities were given several narrowly defined functions: new building operations, extensions and renovations to existing buildings, the supply of material equipment, provision for the daily functioning of schools and the – contested – right to produce educational forecasts. Within these narrow limits, the regions were to have responsibility for the *lycées* (upper secondary schools); the departments would control the *collèges* (lower secondary schools); and the communes would – where applicable – continue to administer the nursery and primary schools. This division of responsibilities was based on the idea that the state could abandon its secondary functions (buildings and equipment) without losing control over the education system. As we will now demonstrate, this belief was immediately challenged by assertive local and regional authorities.

Decision-makers in local French education policy networks

The top-down model of French educational management has been significantly modified in the past three decades. Structural and institutional reforms have introduced new actors in the form of the local and regional authorities and have partially reshaped the operation of established actors such as the Education ministry. There has been a slow penetration of new ideas and new actors into hitherto closed policy communities. Schools themselves have slowly become more responsive to their environments. Moves to political and administrative decentralisation since the early 1980s have made it more realistic to refer to a sub-central educational policy-making community, with a genuine margin of autonomy, within which sets of players interact. The most important of these are state officials, representatives of sub-national authorities, trade unions, parents associations and business interests. After setting out the input of these various actors into education policy-making, we conclude that a new principle of competitive interdependency accurately represents the sub-national governance of French education.

State actors

For administrative purposes, France is divided into academies (corresponding approximately to the regional sphere of intervention) and academic inspectorates (the departmental structure). Each academy is headed by a rector, who is the minister's direct representative in the provinces. The position of rector is a politico-administrative–educational hybrid. Always an educationalist, the rector is a political appointee who represents the incumbent government in the academies, and who also heads the regional field service of the Education ministry. At the juncture between politics, policy and administration, the rector is often in the firing line. The traditional friction between the French Interior and Education ministries is regularly played out at a sub-national level by the strained relationship between the rector and the regional prefect, whose authority over the territorial field services does not extend to Education, Justice and Finance. Inter-organisational tensions can also manifest themselves within the Education ministry itself: between the rectorates and the central ministry; within the rectorates themselves (where there is often discord between the rector and his permanent officials) and between the rectorates (the regional structure of the Education ministry) and the academic inspectorates (the departmental echelon). The rector derives his legitimacy from a combination of statutory powers and the ability to maintain productive relationships. Statutory powers include those of opening and closing classes, distributing centrally apportioned budgets to schools, and – since 1999 – managing staff mobility within the academy. One of their most overlooked prerogatives is that rectors alone determine how the Education ministry should be organised within their academies; the regional field services vary considerably according to the nature of local circumstances, and the preferences of individual rectors. The influence of a given rector depends increasingly on the capacity to build inter-organisational relationships, especially with the regional councils. Governing the academies effectively requires a strong rector able to define a coherent policy towards the elected region as well as towards the upper echelons of the Education ministry. The contractualisation procedure appraised above requires the rectorates to define a regional education policy, even when they would prefer not to.

Schools

Though central controls have been progressively lightened by administrative and political decentralisation since the 1960s, the degree of central regulation of school management remains high. French teachers are civil servants who are allocated to schools from a national pool. Educational mobility is determined at the national (and now, to some extent, the regional) level. Headteachers have little control over their staff, whose performance is evaluated (periodically) by subject-based inspectors. As academic advancement depends mainly upon seniority – and falls completely outside the sphere of competence of the head-teacher – there is little material incentive for individual teachers to invest their energies in the collective school environment. Indeed, there is deep suspicion of school autonomy on behalf of many teachers (and their unions) who insist on respect for national rules and regulations over and above local initiatives. Embedding the school in local communities runs against the republican ethos of the school as a neutral site whose purpose is to teach the values of the Republic. Secondary school teachers are primarily loyal to an academic discipline, rather than to an institution; their high sense of corporate, discipline-based identity also explains the deep reluctance of many teachers to engage in non-teaching activities.

Even at the micro-level, however, the direction of change is towards greater school autonomy. A series of incremental changes in the governing of French secondary schools (*lycées* and *collèges*) since 1975 has produced stronger headteachers, slightly more influential governing boards and some budgetary autonomy. The creation of schools as public corporations (*Etablissements publics locaux d'enseignement* – EPLE) in 1985 was a highly significant benchmark. Public corporations are bodies with their own character as autonomous entities in French public law. They are self-managing in areas not specifically proscribed by ministerial regulations. School plans, for example, are accepted or rejected by the school board. Headteachers now have enhanced resources at their disposal. Through the funding formula known as the overall teaching total (*dotation horaire globale*), school boards are able to apportion 10–20 per cent of school budgets to non-core curriculum activities; this gives them some leeway over what is taught in schools and in the balance between teaching and non-core activities. The obligation (under the 1989 Act) upon schools to produce a school plan (*projet d'établissement*) can enhance school autonomy in various ways – and not necessarily in ways imagined by the law-makers. Ambitious headteachers use school plans to promote rare or elite subjects (such as ancient languages) in order to attract the best pupils from beyond the normal geographical catchment area. Pressures for increased evaluation and for rigorous performance indicators have grown as schools have begun to make use of their greater autonomy than their status as public corporations implies.

Local and regional authorities

The appearance of new actors is the most tangible sign of change in French education. The French regions have emerged as the significant new policy-makers. As with local authorities in the UK, education forms by far the largest item of the regional council budgets (usually over 50 per cent). Though the 1983 and 1985 laws envisaged a secondary role for the elected regions ('buildings and equipment'), many French regions have become assertive in pursuit of their policy objectives and have attempted to tie funding to the pursuit of precise educational or economic policy objectives (Mény 1990). Producing educational goods is tied up with establishing the legitimacy of the regions as relatively new institutions. The strategies adopted by particular regions have varied, depending upon factors such as their size, the nature of the policy problem they had to face and their political identity. Far from being devoid of influence, however, the input of the regional councils has been demonstrated in spheres such as the renovation and construction of school buildings, the physical location of *lycées*, training policy, and – through the regional education forecasts (*schéma prévisionnel de formations*) procedure – the definition of educational priorities (Cole 1997). Often evoking the principle of 'who pays decides', some regional politicians have attempted to trade off agreement to build new schools against influence over what is taught therein. The principal weaknesses of the regions derive from their meagre organisational, financial and specialist resources and their inadequate functioning as democratic institutions (see chapter 3).

Many of the above remarks apply also to the departmental councils, which have similar legal responsibilities ('buildings and equipment') with respect to the *collège*. Though the political saliency of education for the departmental councils is somewhat weaker (25 per cent of the budget) they have developed sophisticated administrative services to provide demographic forecasts and deliver educational services. French communes also have an input both in relation to nursery and primary education, where they have responsibility for school buildings and main-tenance, and with respect to secondary schools and universities built upon land they own. They remain proprietors of most schools (including *lycées* and *collèges*). They can be called upon by the regional or departmental authorities to contrib-ute to the running costs of *collèges* or *lycées*. They must give their assent before any new school is opened in their territory. At a less formal level, mayors lobby effectively. Attempts to suppress a section or to close down a school are routinely met with fierce resistance from local politicians.

Professional, business and non-governmental interests

Ambler (1985) describes French education policy as neo-corporatist. Neo-corporatism refers to a close interdependent relationship between professional interest groups and the machinery of the state. Ambler diagnosed three neo-corporatist features: a mass membership trade union movement in the form of the *Fédération de l'éducation nationale* (FEN); a centralised form of bargaining and access to central policy-makers; and extensive delegated administrative powers. Powerful trade unions participated in the formulation and implementation of national education policy, especially in relation to matters of staff management (pay, promotions, transfers). The neo-corporatist character of policy-making has weakened during the past two decades. Setbacks (over church schools in 1984), declining representativeness, weakening ministerial access and conflicts of inter-est between primary and secondary teachers produced a formal split within the FEN in 1993. The most powerful contemporary schoolteachers' union – the SNES – enjoys a less cosy relationship with the Education ministry, openly preferring direct action tactics to behind closed doors accommodations. The fall of the Allègre ministry in March 2000 demonstrated the persistence of a strong capacity for collective action.

Traditionally distrustful of the national Education system as a bureaucratic monolith, business interests have become more involved in secondary education during the past two decades. At a national level, business representatives are consulted over the content of the secondary professional and technical qualifications taught in the technical schools (*lycées professionelles*). At the academy (i.e. regional) level, the nature of business participation in secondary education is three-fold. Firms can express a preference for their apprenticeship tax (*taxe d'apprentissage*) to be paid to *lycées*. In their capacity as funders for certain secondary schools, one or two representatives of companies often sit on the boards of schools. Local firms accept pupils from technical and professional schools on short-term training courses. Business has also become more closely involved with the regions, notably through the Contract of Objectives procedure discussed above.

The emergence of new actors has produced more interdependent relationships. The main actors in sub-central secondary education decision-making are the rector, the prominent regional politician (either the president of the regional council, or the regional politician in charge of the education dossier), and their respective officials. To some extent, the regional prefect performs an arbitrating role between the rector and the principal regional politician. The relationship between these actors is one of competitive interdependency. In spite of intense organisational rivalry, actors are bound to each other by a tight pattern of resource dependencies. 'Without cooperation from all sides, one could well imagine a complete blockage of the system' (interview). A regional council might decide to build a school, but the implementation of this decision depends upon the rector agreeing to provide the teaching posts, and the regional prefect consenting to place the proposed school on the 'Annual List of Operations', the financial probity of which is controlled by the field office of the Finance ministry. The rectorates determine teaching needs, but in practice they depend upon the co-operation of the regions to build schools and finance equipment. Though the 1983 and 1985 laws confirmed the prerogatives of the French state in matters of pedagogical definition (academic orientation, teaching posts and examinations), the regions themselves were given the right to make educational forecasts (*schémas régionaux des formations*) and to produce regional investment plans (*plans prévisionnels d'investissements*). The smooth functioning of the system necessitates the co-operation of the state, the regions and – increasingly – the professional branches. In most circumstances, it is in the narrow organisational interests of each partner to co-operate, quite apart from there often being a statutory duty to do so.

There has certainly been much change in French secondary education. New actors have emerged; new management practices have been introduced; new types of horizontal and vertical relationships have evolved; new ideas have circulated. In so far as it is increasingly contractual, negotiated and inter-organisational, secondary education is exemplary of the underlying trends of French-style governance.

Conclusion

As defined in chapter 1, the governance approach appears – *a priori* – more convincing in certain arenas of public action than others. The approach is most obviously persuasive in sectors where public goods are provided by private sector players. This is the case in economic development policy that involves to a varying extent both the public and private sectors. It is less obviously the case in education policy. In both countries the education system itself long resisted reform. Where change has been implemented (more convincingly in England than in France) it has been imposed in a top-down manner, rather than antici-pated through local experimentation. In both countries the education system itself long resisted attempts at externally driven change.

This illustrates specific qualities of secondary education as a policy sector. The insular preferences of the educational policy community have been often shared by public policy-makers. In France and England policy-makers traditionally sought to insulate schools from external interference, though this began to change in both countries in the 1980s. Traditionally schools promote equality of opportun-ity, socialisation and citizenship – and these goals are those promoted by the state itself. The business community in both countries has proved incapable of formulating precise demands upon the educational system. For these reasons secondary education is more resistant to pressures to reform the state than other policy sectors.

We can nonetheless identify powerful features of governance in the experience of both countries. The governance approach in secondary education points to the emergence of new ideas, actors and structures into a previously less penetra-ble policy field; the cases of England (especially) and France (to a lesser extent) both provide support in this direction. Though powerful forces contest change in both countries, there are similar problems of autonomy and challenges of governance. There have been common pressures across developed nations to improve economic performance by investing in human capital. The close linkage between education and economic performance operated by policy-makers has driven the move to mass secondary and higher education in both countries. Even if there remains much mutual distrust between business interests and the educational policy communities described above, the direction of change in both countries has been for more business involvement in educational policy formulation and the opening up of schools to their external environment. This trend is demonstrated by business-orientated educational reforms in both coun-tries – the *lycées professionelles* in France or city technology colleges in the UK. It is also illustrated by moves to more autonomous models of school governance.

Does this analysis confirm policy convergence? The argument is superficially attractive. There is far less ideological distance between the English and French models as educational reforms in both countries have undergone reverse tra-jectories. Even as the two countries have moved closer, however, they have reasserted nationally distinctive patterns of managing similar policy problems.

This difference is apparent when considering policy change in English secondary education. Thoroughgoing and radical change was imposed by central government with little or no consultation with local government, in the name of choice and efficiency. Educational governance has been genuinely transformed since the late 1980s by the introduction of an English-style new public management: management by objectives, performance indicators, quasi-markets, organisational decentralisation and central regulation. Even in this clear-cut case of English dogmatism, central government has been forced to maintain interdependent relationships with local authorities. Local education authorities have retained an important role, in many senses functionally equivalent to that of the rectorates in France (both provide demographic statistical provision, and determine the opening and closing of schools). In the English dual state tradition – one of weak territorial decentralisation of the spending ministries, including DfEE – the efficient management of schools continues to rely upon the logistical infrastructure provided by the local education authorities. But there has been a qualitative change which has weakened local authority control over education. The new educational governance no longer operates within a clear framework of local political accountability, preferring responsiveness to parents in the quasi-market to more traditional forms of local self-government.

There is also evidence of change in French education, and it is possible to discern some movement in the direction of the easing of an overbureaucratic, overcentralised system. In the French case, internal change has been driven by the diminishing capacity of an over-centralised state to provide educational services alone; by the overarching decentralisation reforms of the early 1980s which legitimised sub-national authorities as policy stakeholders; by organisational reforms within the Education ministry; and by the (limited) opening up of schools to their environments. As in other spheres of public administration, French-style governance is embodied in contractual processes and new forms of inter-organisational relationships. The pattern of centralisation has been modified, and the traditional form of neo-corporatism has weakened somewhat. In the French case also, there has evolved a new style and a new discourse in school management, where school projects, auto-evaluation and value-added performance tables are the counterpart to enhanced school autonomy. Consistent with national traditions, the French style of new public management is a top-down discourse, developed in the Education ministry and resisted elsewhere. Attempts to introduce genuine school autonomy run against the firm opposition from educational professionals and teachers – and the indifference of parents. Even local and regional authorities usually prefer not to intervene too closely in matters of educational governance. The ideology of public service and equality of opportunity in education provides a strong point of reference for most French people. The belief in education as a public service – run by public servants with security of tenure and a monopoly of professional expertise – limits moves to local governance. Even when reforms have been thoroughgoing – as in the case of England – and the direction of change is convergent, there is a strong argument that changes in educational governance are managed in ways that are consistent with national traditions.

6 Governing English cities

In the previous four chapters, we investigated how diverse political and economic pressures have modified patterns of local policy-making in England and France. In the next two chapters, we examine how local governance works in practice. While our discussion in earlier chapters sets the scene, these two chapters aim to find out what has happened on the ground. Which organisations are involved in policy-making? What are the relationships between the key decision-makers? How has the practice of policy-making changed? Has local governance produced more effective political leadership or merely a lack of co-ordination and increased confusion in decision-making?

The local context is our third unit of analysis along with national institutions and policy sectors. This chapter charts the emergence of governance-style changes in the English cities of Leeds and Southampton. Each city has a tradition, a geography, a history of leadership, a level of social capital and a stock of political resources. How do these local factors influence policy-making in the spheres of economic development and secondary education? Do decision-making processes vary between localities within countries? If so, is an understanding of local contexts a prerequisite for allowing us to make claims about the nature of institutional and policy change in each country. We seek answers to these empirical and theoretical questions in this and the next chapter.

Local policy-making in Leeds

Leeds is one of the major English cities alongside Birmingham, Manchester and Newcastle, having a population of just less than 800,000. It is decidedly a northern city and it is the administrative centre of the region of Yorkshire and Humberside. Leeds City Council dominates the local government scene. The unitary authority is the second largest in England after Birmingham. It is physically large, 213 square miles, extending far into the rural hinterland and beyond. It employs about 36,000 people, has a budget of about £500 million and is a major landowner in the city. It is a powerful player, with a dominant influence over the local political scene. The city has had a long tradition of powerful civic leadership and self-sufficient pride, with its roots in the Victorian era (Briggs 1963).

Politics in Leeds is bound up with a strong identity within the city and a sense of superiority over other Yorkshire towns such as Sheffield.

Leeds also has deeply embedded traditions of pragmatic and non-ideological politics. The city has never been dominated by one political faction – until the 1980s at least. The town has been ruled by Conservative and Liberal as well as Labour administrations, and the city's politics have not been marred by the excesses of party politics. For the past two decades, the Labour Party has been the most significant player in Leeds city politics. Labour grew in importance in the early twentieth century as in other cities. But in Leeds it was particularly dynamic, sustained by a strong working-class Irish Catholic culture in east Leeds and a tradition of Jewish radicalism. Underpinned by its strong, pragmatic traditions, the Labour Party in Leeds was able to avoid the withering away of inner city Labour Party organisations that occurred in other northern cities in the 1970s and 1980s, such as Liverpool and Manchester. Although the working class has been partly replaced by urban professionals, a pragmatic and diverse Labour tradition continues. This legacy ensures that, when Labour is in power, the council's policies are based on linkages to local constituencies rather than on the groups and fashions of the urban left. Labour politics in the city is not greatly ideological; rather it is distributional, based on the loyalty and demands of deeply entrenched sub-city Labour organisations located in the different cultures and traditions of areas, such as west, north-west and east Leeds. The council retained its pragmatic outlook and never fell out with business as did other northern cities (John and Cole 1998).

Traditions of powerful civic leadership in Leeds have facilitated the emergence of strong local leaders. From 1981 to 1996, Leeds had two key long-serving Labour leaders. The first was George Mudie (1981–89), now MP for Leeds East, who was a former NUPE union official, a very able administrator and a political operator of the highest skill. Mudie ruled Leeds with an iron hand. Aided by a small group of trusted officers, the leader decided all policy and most operational matters. George Mudie even dispensed with the post of chief executive as he largely carried out this function himself. The subsequent leader, Jon Trickett (1989–96), now MP for Hemsworth, modified this autocratic style of decision-making. But in essence he used the same means of command and control established by Mudie. In Leeds city politics, power in the organisation flows from the leader. The reasons for the concentration of power are not just personal. One factor is the large size of the authority. There needs to be a powerful figure to pull such a potentially unwieldy organisation together. Other reasons are cultural – Leeds produces strong leaders because of its hierarchical, closed and deferential political culture.

The above factors, especially the traditions of municipal intervention and hierarchical leadership and the size of the unitary council, all mark out Leeds as a site for traditional local government. The combination between an inward looking city culture and the factional nature of intra-party conflicts created a closed, hierarchical and reactionary form of city politics. Up until the late 1980s, the council did not want to work with new organisations and resisted reform. By the early 1990s, this began to change: the tradition of pragmatism, the close contacts between elites in the city centre business district, the council's links to the private sector and the vision of its leadership propelled Leeds into the world of governance and opened up its factional and organisational form of politics to new influences.

Local economic development policy in Leeds

Leeds is a compact city that has thriving financial, insurance and legal service sectors. Though these activities developed rapidly during the 1980s and 1990s, the city retains its engineering and light industrial sectors. This economic diversity and the growth of the financial and public sectors enabled the city to weather the recessions of the early 1980s and the early 1990s. Inward investment stimulated the local economy and provided new jobs at the same time as some of the traditional sources of employment in manufacturing had declined. Thus from 1981 to 1991 employment in the financial services sector grew from 27,500 to 47,700 people whereas manufacturing employment declined by 10 per cent (though about 60,000 people were still employed in this sector in 1995). In the late 1970s and early 1980s the council's planners pragmatically responded to the changes in the economy and encouraged the expansion of office space and the creation of a business district to the south of the railway station.

In keeping with traditions in Leeds, even the left-wing council leader Mudie was pragmatic towards the business community. Like other council leaders at that time, Mudie set up an economic development arm, the Leeds Development Agency, which incorporated planning and a direct economic development function. In November 1987 he created the Leeds City Development Company in partnership with the Leeds Chamber of Commerce and Industry. As in many other cities around this time, Mudie forged a growth coalition based on an alliance between the planners and the property developers and he attempted to foster a property-led regeneration boom in the deprived areas of the city. Consistent with his autocratic style, however, little effort was made to involve the wider community in these schemes. Pressure group opposition and the relative failure of these projects marked the end, for a time, of the 'top-down' strategy.

The next leader, Trickett, pursued a different agenda from Mudie. Endowed with a distinctive political style, he adopted more progressive ideas in areas such as transport, women's and green issues and stressed the importance of an integrated partnership approach to economic development. By creating a consensus among the key partners in the new partnership body, the Leeds Initiative, the leader hoped to build a problem solving network. Trickett aspired to be leader of the city, not just of Leeds City Council, a vision that favoured an inclusive vision of local political leadership.

Trickett's more inclusive leadership style spilled over into a partnership approach in local economic development. In contrast to his predecessor Mudie, who had followed a conventional 'in-house' policy, Trickett ensured that city-wide consultation took place before the city's economic development strategy was drafted. Initial consultation occurred with the universities, the Training and Enterprise Council and the Chamber of Commerce and Industry. The leader then introduced a draft plan to several groups of business people and to a meeting of the partnership body, the Leeds Initiative, all of which produced changes. A similar approach was applied to transport. Whereas the council's previous attempt to redesign a new public transport system had failed through lack of consensus in the city, Trickett and his executive director of development promoted a far more balanced approach. This was based on a two-year debate with all the potential interests about the issue of transport in the city. The resulting strategy rescued the city's transport policy and in the end allowed the city partners to support the city's proposal for a supertram (Leeds City Council 1991).

The key event affecting networks across organisations in local economic development policy in the city was the creation of the Leeds Initiative in 1990. This is an economic development partnership body composed of the key public and private decision-makers in the city.[1] The leader of the council chaired the Leeds Initiative, with the president of the chamber as the vice-chair, an arrangement that reflected the partnership's origins as a chamber/city initiative. The Initiative met in private every two months to discuss a carefully prepared agenda. Though meetings would usually ratify agreements reached elsewhere – if at all – they enabled participants to exchange ideas. Local actors were overwhelmingly of the view that the forum created trust.

The origins of the initiative illustrated the gradual shift in the relationships between the key organisations in the city. The Chamber of Commerce responded to the government's 1987 Action for Cities initiative, which called for business participation in local economic policy. In response, the chamber assembled a working group and produced a document – 'Leeds International City of the Future' – that articulated its strategic concerns about the future of Leeds. The document proposed policies based on the chamber's perception 'of a widespread feeling in the business community that matters of importance to the city's future are not being adequately addressed'. The report bemoaned the lack of co-ordination in the city and called for local government, central government and business to act in concert. Leading people in the chamber were not alone in pushing for a strategic partnership; such public–private partnerships were also being advocated by central government. The council understood that if the city was to receive central government funds, partnership-based bids would have to be put together. The Leeds Initiative was the result.

The early days of the Initiative were energetic. The leader, for a while, let go of tight council control of the policy-making process. The success of the Initiative could be measured by the number of proposals and initiatives that it spawned, though it is difficult to know how many of these schemes would have got off the ground anyway. The other indication of success in the early years involved the number of companies and organisations wanting to be members of the project working groups co-ordinated by the Leeds Initiative. There was a bandwagon effect, whereby participation produced more participation. Initiatives included the attraction of the Royal Armouries to Leeds (though this was really organised outside the Leeds Initiative).

The Leeds Initiative partnership was based on a mutually beneficial exchange between the two driving actors, the Chamber of Commerce and Leeds City Council. The chamber gained a greater role in decision-making as a result of its participation – perhaps even a monopoly of business access to decision-making. The president of the chamber had regular direct access to the leader of the council; the relationship had previously been far more distant. The success of the initiative reflected well upon the chamber and raised its reputation with larger companies as well as with local politicians. For the city, the benefits were even more obvious. When the Leeds Initiative worked best, the city council was able to maintain its leadership and legitimacy in a changing and uncertain local policy environment. Local partnerships also allowed the council to play the grants game more effectively.

The council leadership came to identify its own objectives with those of the local business community. It recognised the importance of business in sustaining local economic prosperity and was comforted in this belief by the change in political values that affected Labour politics nationally. The Leeds public–private exchange was genuine insofar as business gradually shifted its view to incorporate publicly inspired ideas, such as the importance of tackling inner city poverty and unemployment. In Leeds, closer public–private co-operation represented something of a shift from a pattern of traditional local government to one of local governance. This process was driven as much by the changing ideas of the local political leadership as by the power of business interests, central government policy and local public opinion. While traditional, hierarchical organisational politics did not disappear, city leaders cultivated new relationships with outside bodies, either formally in the Leeds Initiative or through informal contacts.

Actors in local economic development

If the main Leeds network is based on a relationship between the public and private sectors, actors from other public sector and quasi-autonomous organisations also played a role. First and foremost of these was the TEC. As a result of central government directives in 1994, the TECs were directed to adopt a local economic development role, which put them in intense conflict with the existing organisations. The TEC was perceived as an outsider on account of the fact that it had taken functions away both from the city council and the chamber. Though these disputes were hidden behind a public front of harmony, the bad feeling and lack of trust were palpable. The city and the chamber recognised the power of the TEC as the vehicle for government policy and resources, but the process of achieving agreement was difficult. Relations between the city, the chamber and the former Urban Development Corporation (UDC) were more straightforward. Invested by central government with a specific mission and set of tasks, the UDC was not a key player in the local economic development network, but relations were generally co-operative.

Even in an independent-minded city such as Leeds, local economic development strategies require close involvement with central government. Central civil servants are involved with the local elite scene for a number of reasons. Through advising ministers over planning applications, they exercise powers over local authorities and have to be consulted in the development of the local plan. Central government also had a direct presence, in so far as the Environment ministry was the paymaster for the Urban Development Corporation, as was the Department of Employment (before its absorption into the Department for Education in 1995) for the TEC. The government is the arbiter for different types of government grant, from city challenge, to the single regeneration budget and transport grants.

As observed during fieldwork, there was a consensus within the Leeds economic policy network on overall objectives, particularly economic growth. On the other hand, because of turf wars between organisations, a lack of trust between protagonists and conflicts over money, there was also intense conflict over who should control the Leeds Initiative and other local partnerships. The solidity of the Leeds economic development network was assured above all by a stable local political leadership. Jon Trickett was leader for seven years. Brian Walker, leader since 1996, is also a solid figure who has been prominent on economic development and planning matters since the early 1980s. This helped build trust and stability when many of the institutions and roles were changing. In spite of the machinations of inter-organisational competition, stable leadership has created a moderately effective and legitimate form of local governance.

Education policy in Leeds

Until its effective dismemberment in June 2000, Leeds local education authority was the third largest LEA in the country. It controlled some 43 secondary schools and 244 primary schools and administered a budget of over £300 million. Consistent with both its size and the local political culture, the education authority was traditionally considered to be highly bureaucratic and hierarchical. Within Leeds LEA, power flowed downwards from the chief education officer to the rest of the officers. Schools and their heads were very much at the bottom of this order. Before 1988, they were not involved with decisions about policy matters and not even much about implementation.

The local education authority was an independent bureaucratic empire – and in the 1970s councillors tended not to involve themselves much with details of administration. Even the chair of the education committee rarely visited the education department. This changed with the election of Labour in 1980, when the councillors gradually took over detailed control over policy. In a move of great symbolic importance, the chair of the education committee and several other councillors moved their offices into the education department. This initiative marked a radical break with the historic independence of the education officers. It demonstrated a distrust on behalf of the councillors of the education professionals in the LEA as well as the personal interest carried by former leader

George Mudie into education, something carried on by Jon Trickett. In both cases, a powerful local political leader was determined to steer the main policy decisions made in the name of the council.

The Labour council pledged to check the authoritarian management style of the education department. Distrustful of the officers, Labour politicians placed themselves at the centre of the educational machine, taking detailed decisions on matters of administration as well as policy. This challenged the traditional 'dual elite' model whereby the chair of the education committee (and sometimes the leader) liaised directly with the director of education, but did not intervene in matters of administration. Labour councillors now made a point of directing lower-level heads of section over matters of detail. Of equal importance, education also fitted neatly into the clientelistic form of politics practised by Mudie. Important budget decisions, particularly those over capital expenditure, were orientated to favour the needs of inner city schools. In a similar fashion, many decisions over conditions of employment were brokered between the councillors and the trades unions.

Central government played little direct role in local policy and its implementation. Even though the 1980s saw the gradual centralisation of the education system, central government relied on local authorities to implement reforms, initially limiting its role to that of encouraging change through its powers of approval and sanction. Even in the 1990s, the officers and members of the education department had little contact with civil servants in the DfEE. Contacts between central and local officials were either formal, in preparation for central government approval of a school closure for example, or to check information and central government policies. The only signs of changes were the contacts involved with the TVEI initiative. In terms of the decision-making network, other organisations, such as the Chamber of Commerce or the TEC, played a minor role, except in initiatives such as the Education–Business Partnership in Leeds. The main relationships were those between the education department, the councillors, the trades unions and the schools with, before 1988, the schools playing a marginal role. The importance of this last partner was to change.

Even before 1988 Leeds' management practices and relationships with schools were anachronistic. At a time when some education authorities were forging ahead with experiments with delegating budgets and involving parents and teachers, Leeds education was still run from its castle in Merrion House in a manner which alienated many school heads and governors. The landmark Education Reform Act 1988 shattered the council's dominance by handing power to the schools. This was more dramatic in Leeds than elsewhere because of the way council leaders had favoured the inner city schools and had neglected the interests of those in the relatively wealthy 'leafy' suburbs, particularly the schools in the north-east of the city which had enjoyed the beneficence of the West Riding education regime before the 1974 reorganisation. Once the council had to agree to formula funding, they had no option but to redistribute resources away from the inner city core. The legislation that allowed schools to opt out of council control gave the whip hand to those in the suburbs who could use exit as a threat. The loss of a few prominent schools could have encouraged many others to join them, thereby threatening the end of the local education community in Leeds. This was the principal fear of local politicians and council officers at the time. With this impetus, the closed world of councillor- and officer-dominated decision-making had to open up to schools. Schools became part of the governance of education in Leeds because they had the power and because Leeds' leaders wished to broker a coalition which would keep all Leeds' schools within its fold.

Mudie was slow to identify the change in the balance of power since he represented the old politics more than anyone else. His successor as leader, Jon Trickett, realised that Leeds City Council had to share power if it was going to have much of a chance to shape education policy in Leeds as a whole. In an attempt to anticipate change, Trickett set up the Schools Commission in June 1992 shortly after the Conservatives won their fourth consecutive term of office at the national level, partly in the anticipation that the government was going to push school autonomy and opting out still further over the next four years. The council charged the commission with a review of the management of secondary education, with particular reference to quality, governance, parental choice and – crucially – the distribution of resources. The Schools Commission operated at arm's length from the council, without the direct participation of education department officials. Chaired by the vice-chancellor of Leeds University, Alan Wilson, who let the commission run itself, it comprised prominent headteachers and governors, particularly those from the outer city schools. The commission produced 73 recommendations in its 1993 report, *The New Partnership*, and advocated an activity-led formula. With a new director of education, hired from outside the authority, who arrived in 1994, and an innovative chair of education, Councillor Sloan, education policy-makers enthusiastically adopted the proposed reforms. Many new reforms were introduced. The clientelistic method for distributing resources, such as repairs money for schools, was replaced by a needs-based system. The teachers, and to a lesser extent the governors, appeared for a short while to be driving education policy in Leeds. A working group dominated by headteachers, who met after the commission had reported in 1993, tried to agree a formula which would redistribute resources across Leeds.

The breath of fresh air in Leeds education policy did not, however, last long. For one thing, the commission was above all a brilliant tactical manoeuvre which made the teachers think they were deciding policy, much of which was more or less either central government policy anyway or good education practice for much of the country. For another, the hands-off stance was temporary as the implementation of the proposed reforms would have to be agreed and carried out by the local education authority. While the local authority took great pride that by December 1994 it had implemented all 73 recommendations of the commission, the proposal radically to alter the formula was too much for Leeds' politicians and there was no agreement to reform the formula in 1993. The politicians could not oversee a reduction of resources to inner city schools. This would cut into their core power base. And even though George Mudie had gone to parliament, rather unlike a typical English national representative he was deeply involved with local education policy and implementation. He helped the lobby of inner city and east Leeds schools that sought to retain the favourable distribution of resources. The decision on the formula was postponed for a year. The officers took over and formulated a less radical reform of the formula that did not take so many resources away from the inner city but managed to increase the resources to the outer schools by a £2.2 million increase in the education budget. The authority this time had managed to create a relative consensus. The outer schools were assuaged but the traditional structures of power in Leeds re-emerged unscathed.

Leeds council remained by far the dominant player throughout the period of fieldwork by its size and legitimacy. In the end such a monopolistic strategy backfired. The local education authority was called to account largely because of the low standards of performance in Leeds' schools. With comparative indicators an ever more pervasive benchmark of educational performance, Leeds was deemed by the regulatory agencies to have failed in its management of the education service, a result that showed the short-sightedness of the narrow politicised form of management in Leeds.

The final part of the story is brief. In November 1999 the Office of Standards in Education (OFSTED) completed its inspection of Leeds LEA. In February 2000 OFSTED published its report. The report found the LEA's provision to be unsatisfactory in two-thirds of areas where judgements were made, extended almost consistently across its core responsibilities. The report recommended that Leeds needed to bring about major improvements to its services to schools. OFSTED identified 33 areas where improvements needed to be made. Following publication of the OFSTED report, the council drew up proposals addressing the 33 recommendations, but also proposing wider improvement throughout the service. The proposals, contained in a provisional document called *A Framework for Excellence*, were published and submitted to the Department for Education and Employment (DfEE) in May. This was the council's provisional action plan to bring about the improvement required. On receiving the OFSTED report, Leeds City Council appointed consultants PricewaterhouseCoopers (PwC). PwC looked at a number of alternative ways of providing education support services to schools. The consultants concluded that, while the council would be able to address some of the problems, it did not have the capacity to bring about the improvements demanded by OFSTED. Since receiving the OFSTED report, the council has been in constant discussion with the DfEE and the consultants to set up a new model for delivering services. PricewaterhouseCoopers recommended to the council and the DfEE the establishment of a joint venture company which began operation in April 2001.

Educational governance in Leeds shows a mixture of radical change and continuity. The change has followed national trends, with the transfer of budgets and many decisions to the schools and the assertion of power by a group of headteachers. Neither the LEA nor the schools were able to control the effects of the competitive quasi-market introduced in the 1988 Act. Aspects of continuity were the strength of the education authority, the power of local politicians, and the weak input of parents, governors and other local pressure groups, such as the Chamber of Commerce. Even though central government is more directly involved than hitherto, education in Leeds only gradually responded to the change in the balance of power at the national level. There was strong resistance to abandoning a clientelistic mode of operation that was politically tried and tested. Though the spirit of local resistance was strong, Leeds City Council ultimately paid the price by losing control over the management of the city's schools in 2000, the penalty for resisting broader national trends and for failing to raise standards of educational performance. This reaffirmed the harsh reality of the new educational governance (one where failing schools are not tolerated even in socially deprived areas) for traditionally minded local authorities.

Local policy-making in Southampton

With a population of 190,000, Southampton is a much smaller city than Leeds. As a district authority until 1997, Southampton City Council did not have control over the important services of strategic planning and education. Lacking the prestige of a large regional capital, with only a small number of large businesses and without the powers and finance of a metropolitan council, it is much harder than in Leeds to find the powerful coalitions of public and private actors seeking to affect public decisions. While Leeds City Council covers the Leeds urban area and beyond, the tightly drawn city boundaries do not coincide with the larger economic entity of Southampton, which encompasses the local authorities of Eastleigh to the north, and, to a lesser extent, Fareham, Test Valley and the New Forest district councils. This mismatch, as well as Southampton's traditional political independence, is at the heart of the governance problem of the city.

Co-ordination and liaison difficulties also extend upwards to the county and the TEC. These bodies try to give a wider strategic perspective that relates to the large and diverse Hampshire. Overlaid above the county is the vast and even more diverse region, the south-east of England, which the government office co-ordinates. As well as being fractured administratively, Southampton is not an administrative capital like Leeds. This lack of a regional identity has prevented the emergence of a unified local government, business, central government and public sector elite. Alongside these geographic and organisational factors is the more familiar local economic policy issue of elected councils dealing with unelected organisations, such as the TECs, which threaten to supplant their functions. In addition, elected authorities have had to respond fully to the new activism from the rest of the public sector and the business community.

Party politics is characteristic of the south where a Labour tradition in the main cities is surrounded by the Conservative heartlands in much of Hampshire and the challenge of the Liberal Democrats. Thus Southampton has been controlled by Conservative, Labour and the Liberal Democrats since 1945. Labour was important in the post-war period of reconstruction, planning and building.

The Conservatives ran the city in the 1970s and early 1980s, and Labour has run it with occasional Liberal Democrat administrations since 1984.

A medium-sized, spatially amorphous city, Southampton is not a compact place such as Leeds, nor does it have a similar tradition of municipal interventionism or of public–private co-operation. A city with a weak industrial heritage, Southampton has a mixed economy with few large firms (the exceptions being Dimplex and Ford), but with a dense network of smaller and medium-sized businesses. Like many other southern cities, Southampton witnessed a rapid development of its service sector during the 1980s and 1990s (with the creation of successful consultancy and accountancy firms) and the expansion of its higher education capacity.

The prosperity of the region and the city until the early 1980s meant that the city council did not consider economic development policy to be an essential activity, though, of course, planning and transportation matters were always policy issues. During the period from 1971 to 1977, employment in the city grew at an annual rate of 8.7 per cent, mainly concentrated in the service sector (Mason and Witherick 1981: 6). This late interest in economic development contrasted with the northern cities and their traditions of local and central state intervention in the local economy. The Conservatives, who were in power until 1984, did carry out some economic development activity, such as setting up an economic development unit, and promoting developments like the Marlands shopping centre. They also began the negotiations for the redevelopment of the city centre. In comparison to what followed under Labour, however, they were not active.

When Labour was elected into office in 1984 there followed a period of activism under the charismatic leadership of Alan Whitehead. The Labour council became imbued with the development orientated spirit of the times. Involving business in all economic development activities was central to the new approach. As in the case of Mudie in Leeds, the key to Whitehead's strategy was property-led regeneration on the back of the 1980s economic boom. This partnership was based on close, self-interested collaboration between local business interests (especially local property developers) and the Southampton political leadership. The terms of the trade-off served the interests of both partners. The council would release land and grant planning permission on the basis of proposals from developers. In return – central government financial rules permitting – the council used the financial resources thereby accrued to fund other public–private projects. Many, though by no means all, of these early projects were successful. An early example was the attraction of Toys-R-Us to Southampton. A new factory was built on council-owned land, whose sale funded a multi-storey car park. In full view from the railway station and box-like in its construction, it is perhaps not an attractive inner city development, but at the time it signified a willingness to attract inward investment, acted as a catalyst for other public–private deals and showed to the business community that the council was willing to work with the private sector.

Yet Southampton, like many UK cities, does not have enough of a financial or national power base to follow through the larger schemes. UK local political leaders are not as able to mobilise national and local actors behind *grands projets* as are their French counterparts. The prime example of this was the 'people mover', an ambitious scheme to have a rapid transit system that would circle the city centre. Although derided in some quarters as a crazy idea, it had strong support from the business community, the local media and popular opinion. The chamber and even the county were wholeheartedly behind the scheme. Yet the political opposition was able to defeat the proposal as it required a private member's bill approved by parliament. The local Conservatives and the two Conservative MPs, James Hill and Christopher Chope, destroyed it as a political vendetta. The local Labour leadership was unable to access higher-level national networks in support of the project.

What occurred in Southampton – similar in some ways to George Mudie's plans in Leeds – was a growth coalition (Logan and Molotch 1987). That it was short lived reflected the nature of the 1980s boom with its spiralling property values and subsequent rapid collapse. It also showed the limited powers of UK local leaders, who have to use complex public–private deals to get projects off the ground. The virtuous circle depended on property-led economic development opportunities, so at the end of the boom years public–private project successes became less common. The Labour council appeared to have lost its cutting edge, and Southampton returned to its lower public profile and more inward-looking public self when Whitehead retired from office in 1992.

By the late 1980s the recession had started to bite hard in the south, and this affected Southampton, particularly through the loss of manufacturing employment. As in Leeds, new unemployment was compensated by an expansion of the service sector, but, unlike Leeds, it was not enough to make up for the loss of employment in other areas. This led decision-makers to propose further economic development policies, particularly after local authorities were obliged to provide a statutory economic plan in 1989. As in Leeds, both the public and private sectors became increasingly nervous about the effects of greater competition in Europe and elsewhere. Economic policy actors in the public and private sectors began to believe that the city had to become proactive if it were to survive and prosper. While this process brought actors together in a strategic partnership in Leeds, this was not to happen in Southampton. Part of the reason lay in the instability of the political leadership and the loss of Labour overall control of the council in 1994–5, but the main reason was the lack of a clear focus for the economic development network.

Actors in local economic development

Unlike in Leeds, the economic development network is hard to identify because it is not clear what area it should be based on. Though the boundaries of the city of Southampton clearly demarcate a city, the economy and commuting patterns suggest a wider area of less certain boundaries. Thus it is harder to identify the current decision-making elite in Southampton than in Leeds. The involvement of actors varies according to the issue at stake. Thus there are many development projects in Southampton, such as the expansion of the port, the consolidation of the airport, the completion of the city centre reconstruction, all of which have their own networks.

In our snapshot sociometric research of 1995, the city council – and in particular its leader, John Arnold – appeared at the centre of the Southampton economic development network (John 1998). A former chair of the council's development and strategy committee, Arnold was involved with most public decisions on local economic development affecting the city. However, he lacked the charisma of his predecessor, Whitehead. Southampton City Council is involved in most economic development activity purely by virtue of the fact that it is at the centre of the Southampton region, and because the council has involved itself in this policy-making sector since the mid-1980s.

While originally not involved in local economic development activity, outlying local authorities have become more implicated in decisions affecting Southampton. Eastleigh council to the north has been trying to build closer relationships to all the actors in the Southampton area. But there is a history of competition between Eastleigh and Southampton. As a suburb and a competing retailing centre to Southampton, Eastleigh has entered into the classic competition with the metropolitan core for facilities; thus, it gave planning permission for an out-of-town shopping and cinema multiplex, to the intense hostility of Southampton and other Labour-controlled authorities which wished to oppose such developments (Whitehead 1995). Fareham is the other important and rival local authority in the Southampton area. Situated between Portsmouth and Southampton, Fareham actively sought to impose its own local economic policy leadership. Fareham is in an ambiguous position as it can link with both the Portsmouth and the Southampton networks; it can be constructive in bringing partners together; or it can play Portsmouth off against Southampton.

In the mid-1990s, there was a series of meetings to try to form a south-west strategic partnership. These meetings brought together the vice-chancellor of Southampton University, the principal of Southampton Institute, and the chief executives and leaders of Eastleigh, Southampton and Fareham councils. These key local actors formed themselves into the 'Hilton Hotel' group. Significantly, showing a contrast with the discussions in Leeds, the TEC was not invited to participate, making the notion of the partnership narrower. Even this limited effort to create a strategic partnership was not successful. Since 1995, the discussion has moved on to forming a wider partnership including Portsmouth – though without success, as Portsmouth wishes to be at the centre of its partnerships, such as the Portsmouth and South-East Hampshire Partnership. The difficulty in building inter-authority partnerships suggests there is too much competition between the various interests involved and a lack of agreement on objectives, reflecting the diverse and fluid nature of networks in Southampton. Fragmentation reflects the disaggregated spatial nature of Southampton itself; but it also derives from the fact that the city council resists wider partnership. In spite of developing various relationships with other actors, the Labour council retained a traditional view of its role.

There is no equivalent in Southampton of the urban regime that governed economic development policy in Leeds. With weak public–private interactions, the relation of business to the local state is less strong than in Leeds. The town has too few big firms – the port, Dimplex and Ford are the largest – for the regime analogy to stand analysis. Most of the members of the Southampton Chamber of Commerce and Trade are small businesses and this hampers the outlook of the organisation.

The port of Southampton is an important player, though not central to the local economy. The port is one of the largest in the Associated British Ports conglomerate (ABP). Because of its importance in the economy, its formal powers, its extensive land holdings, and the fear that ABP could invest in another location if Southampton proved operationally or politically difficult, the port is a powerful actor. ABP takes an active interest in the economic health of the city. While the economic development activities of a city council are not very important in attracting business, the city has the negative power to give a bad image to Southampton that can affect the port's business. While ABP can move business to another port, it is locked into Southampton because of previous investment and the unique opportunities for port expansion in Dibden Bay. Traditionally isolationist, the port did not in the past develop close relationships with local state or other private sector actors. This changed somewhat in the mid-1990s, as ABP made a conscious decision to have an input into the local community, through encouraging managers to positions in the community and sponsoring local charities and events. The main reason for the change was that the port needed political friends to push through the Dibden Bay development. ABP put its proposals as a Harbour Revision order to the Department of the Environment, Transport and Regions, with the planning inquiry during 2000 and a final decision in 2001. For its part, Southampton city was careful to maintain a dialogue with the port and other business actors because it sought private sector support for some of the changes it was proposing. But there was no equivalent of the quasi-urban regime we observed in operation in Leeds.

The wider Hampshire actors were also involved with decision-making affecting Southampton, both before and after the city gained unitary status (1997). The principal Hampshire actor is Hampshire County Council, the decision-maker for transportation, and strategic planning. Up until the late 1980s Hampshire followed mainly a conservation strategy, once claiming at the height of the boom that the county was 'closed for business', a stance which has a long history, and included an attempt in 1958 to contain Southampton's urban sprawl by an unofficial green belt (Mason and Witherick 1981: 25). Long resistant to development, Hampshire County Council has also now adopted a direct economic policy function. The county first embraced local economic development after 1992 when the Conservatives lost control to a coalition of Liberal Democrats and Labour. The council set up its own economic development unit, followed by the creation of the Hampshire Business Liaison Group, a public–private partnership based on the county and funded by both the county and the TEC.

The relationship between Southampton and the county was tense. This is partly because of historic competition, the perception of the haughtiness of the county by the city, the loss of Southampton's strategic functions to the county in 1974, the different identity of Southampton both economically and politically and, most of all, the aftermath of the local government review which took Southampton and Portsmouth out of Hampshire.

The other Hampshire actor was the TEC. As in Leeds, there was perceptible conflict between the chamber and the TEC. With a weak financial base, the chamber feared its role was being undermined by the business links scheme. The local authorities were also suspicious of the TEC, as they feared it would supplant their economic development role. As elsewhere in the UK, an underlying political suspicion of the TEC complicated local relationships. The TEC was seen as an agency of Conservative, as well as central state, interests. It was mistrusted by Hampshire County Council, as well as by Southampton city. There was an open conflict between the TEC and the county over the leadership of local economic development policy. This came to a head when the TEC proposed to set up a duplicate economic information service to that provided by the council.

The creation of the Government Office of South England (GOSE) had at first a limited effect on Southampton. The existence of the regional offices brought local authority actors more into contact with regional-level civil servants, especially over issues of European funding; the European section of the government office has performed an important role in this respect. The regional director of GOSE, Gillian Ashmore, was a recognised figure. However, it was difficult to speak of civil servants as forming part of a Southampton policy network, even though they were obviously connected to it.

In our fieldwork we observed many similarities between patterns of governance in Southampton and Leeds, as well as important differences. Many of the same actors appeared in the policy networks of both cities. The leader of the council was an important player, as were the economic development and planning officers. Aside from local authority representatives, the Chamber of Commerce and the TEC were central institutions in both cities. These organisational interests were to some extent predetermined. Actors had to co-operate in projects such as 'business links'. But the character of co-operation depends upon deeper influences, such as the nature of local political leadership, the structure of local interests and the existence (or not) of a strong civic identity.

The configuration of local power in Southampton lends itself less to governance than in Leeds. The effectiveness of local networks in Leeds depended in part upon an active and vigorous local political leadership, alone able to invest a dynamic quality into otherwise static local networks. There was no comparable leadership effect in Southampton, where, except for a brief period under Alan Whitehead, leadership was unstable and inward looking. On the other hand, the civic culture of Southampton is weak. There is no tradition of strong civic co-operation and there is a lack of civic identity that could be a spur to a governing regime. The weakness of local political leadership must be seen within this context. It remains to be seen whether as a unitary authority Southampton will be able to perform a more central role as the catalyst of a broad economic development network.

Education policy in Southampton

During 1995, the period of the research, Southampton City Council did not control education policy. Southampton's schools were part of the large Hampshire education authority, though much power was decentralised to the south-west division which covered Southampton and the New Forest area. Southampton's networks and pattern of governance were in a state of transition because the city council was due to take control of education in April 1996 once it obtained unitary status. Thus it was possible to observe the emergence of a purely Southampton-based network, at the same time as many decision-makers still related upwards to the Hampshire networks.

Until 1996, Southampton schools were controlled by the Hampshire south-west divisional office of the LEA, located in Southampton and headed by a member of Hampshire's management team. The divisional office had its own staff, including a schools officer, a governors' liaison unit and inspection services. By April 1996 these activities were transferred to Southampton City Council.

In part because the institutional boundaries of educational governance were so uncertain, there emerged a cohesive network of Southampton-based school headteachers. In comparison with Leeds, there are only twelve secondary schools within Southampton city, making it a small community. Although there were differences in interest between the schools, they acted together as one on many issues. Schools in Southampton had their own secondary heads association or conference, which was independent from the rest of the schools of the county – and did not fit well into Hampshire's division organisation. Southampton schools have tended to discuss policy in their own conference. This contrasts with the pattern in Leeds, where there was no equivalent association enabling headteachers to discuss issues such as school exclusions. The governors are very active in Southampton and are more in evidence than in Leeds, perhaps reflecting the different class base of the two cities. Most councillors are governors of schools and this makes for an active Southampton-based governors network. These powerful local actors meet frequently in council meetings, on school boards, as well as within an active governors' forum which meets regularly to discuss policy issues.

Above the divisional office of Hampshire LEA was the education headquarters located in Winchester. The county's education committee was chaired by a Liberal Democrat, Tony Barron, who was not from Southampton, though his deputy Brian Dash, the Labour group leader, sat on the education committee and came from the Southampton area. Essential policy-making on matters like capital expenditure, the formula and other policies took place at the Hampshire level. This increased the sense of cohesion of the network of Southampton heads and governors, convinced of the need to lobby for a more urban focus to the formula funding, and to represent Southampton within Hampshire's management partnership.

Hampshire was better than Leeds at anticipating the change in power relationships brought about by the 1988 Act and sought to involve school heads and governors from an early date. Because of the importance of Southampton, with its networks, forums and influence, most Southampton-specific issues were dealt with at the level of the south-west division of the LEA. One such issue was that of school exclusions. Another was that of race, where the city council got involved largely as a result of the activism of a group of city councillors. A further issue was that of capital funding and the competing claims for it. Here the relationships within Southampton were competitive, with the local education authority taking a traditional role of adjudicator.

In spite of these differences in structure, the types of actors involved in policy were largely the same as in Leeds. At the level of the Hampshire LEA, the elected members and officers were the key policy-makers, though the relationships between them were very different from those in Leeds. Officers in Hampshire had much more of a role in shaping policy. More than in Leeds, headteachers and governors are involved in policy, with Southampton's headteachers being organised in a cohesive and effective manner. Trades unions were principally active at the Hampshire level, though this changed with the move to unitary status. Other actors, such as businesses, were only involved in operational issues. There is an education committee of the Southampton City Chamber of Commerce that takes an interest. There was also an education–business partnership between the LEA and the Training and Enterprise Council, though this was concerned with practical matters rather than policy. There were several governors in Southampton schools from the business world, but they performed an advisory role rather than becoming key players. They could not compete with the councillor-governors. Other minor players included the social services department of the county and the recreation department of the city.

In 1995 the Southampton policy network was starting to strengthen with the onset of unitary status. The city had already decided who was to be chair of education (and then leader), and she was also the chair of the governors' forum, June Bridle. In the run-up to unitary status, Bridle chaired a shadow education committee and a 'consultative forum of representatives'. Both bodies had started to hammer out the issues. Gradually the secondary heads in Southampton became involved, having overcome their initial resistance to dealing with the council. This reversal was partly due to the efforts of June Bridle, who was also chair of governors of Sholing Girls School, one of the most influential local secondary schools. The secondary schools also became involved because they sought to resist any change in the funding formula that might threaten their interests to the benefit of inner city primary schools. For their part, some primary school heads saw reorganisation as an opportunity to reorganise the distribution of resources to reflect Southampton's urban and multi-racial character.

As surveyed in the above relationships, educational governance in Southampton was both looser and tighter than in Leeds. It was looser because formal control over secondary schools rested with Hampshire County Council. It was tighter because of the smaller spatial basis of educational governance within Southampton, which produced much closer relationships between headteachers, governors and local politicians. Once Southampton unitary authority took over control of education in 1996, the foundations were laid for a co-operative and trusting relationship between the various actors of the educational policy community. As it moved towards unitary status, Southampton's educational policy networks appeared as relatively cohesive and close knit. Within the limits of central government regulation, educational governance in Southampton would continue to be shaped by the quality of the relationship between locally elected councillors and historically independent schools. Effective educational governance depended upon the continuing co-operation of these two groups.

Conclusion

Governance in English cities bears all the hallmarks of the massive changes that affected local government from the 1980s onwards. In each of the four networks, local authorities had to deal with the weakening of their powers and the emergence of new organisations: quangos and business groups in the sphere of economic development; more autonomous schools and independent regulatory agencies in the case of secondary education. In some respects, local authorities have been less able to shape local policy. There have, on occasion, been incoherent and unco-ordinated strategies followed by each organisation. Non-elected bodies such as the TECs initially made little effort to co-ordinate their activities with the established local authority and chamber of commerce players. In the sphere of secondary education, the creation of quasi-markets and the doctrine of parental choice have created undesirable consequences (from the LEA point of view) for longer-term educational planning. Autonomous decisions in the quasi-market of schools have had a knock-on effect upon such important issues as school exclusions, the consequences of which the LEAs must deal with. The challenge of policy co-ordination and the demand for greater democratic accountability lie at the heart of British local governance. Evidence from our cities suggests that no one decision-maker is responsible for these actions and there is no clear method of deciding how to hold decision-makers to account.

As well as the retreat of the public realm, there have emerged new forms of decision-making. The new bodies we have identified – TECs, UDCs, agencies – have coveted and cultivated relationships with the local government bodies. Local government itself has changed. It has become less hierarchical. It has sought – sometimes reluctantly – relationships and partnerships with these new decision-makers. Astute political leaders have responded to the challenges of the new governance. They have attempted to generate governance capacity by building partnerships with other local players. Jon Trickett in Leeds and Alan Whitehead in Southampton were typical of this new form of local politician. The former was striking in the way in which he overcame Leeds City Council's legacy of organisational self-sufficiency and embraced partnership and networking in education and local economic development policy. Alan Whitehead was ahead of his time in his innovation and work with the private sector, and he fully anticipated the new politics.

The new governance is not synonymous with the effacement of local government. The willingness to network and to engage in modern political discussions does not undermine the traditional power bases of local government. In many ways engaging in networked practices enhances these power blocks. Governance creates more choices as compared with more traditional government practices. Partnerships, policy innovation and public–private projects increase the capacity of the city to solve its problems, which in turn can reinforce the legitimacy and authority of the existing government bodies. Astute local political leaders know that there is a balance between losing control and also being too paranoid about giving up authority. They have been able to form partnerships and hand over a little of decision-making capability to new bodies, like the Leeds Initiative.

Local government persists. In our four English case studies, local government officers and councillors were at the heart of local policy networks. While they could not dominate and dictate as before, they had the organisational, political, informational and financial resources to lead and to persuade or cajole others to follow them. In economic development, the local authority drove partnerships in both cities. In education, the local education authority retained strong influence over many financial decisions and took the lead in debates about policy even though it listened to headteachers much more than before. In both arenas, local government retained much of its power because most public and private sector elites recognised it as the legitimate leader of the local community in spite of all the limitations of local democracy.

Local governance takes a different form in the two sectors. In economic development policy, cognate actors dominated the decision-making process in both cities: the city council, the chamber, the TEC and the government office for the region. In both cities governance depended on the quality of the relationship between these partners and upon their ability to conduct joint development projects. Policy-makers could work pragmatically with each other for easily recognisable objectives and for mutual gain. In addition, they were often required to co-operate by central government which maintained a tight control over the public purse strings. The similarities of the pattern of decision-making between Leeds and Southampton owed much to the centrally led fashions of the moment. Governance in secondary education tended to reflect the new division of power between the local education authority and the headteachers, with governors, parents and other decision-makers having growing influence.

Policy-making in Leeds and Southampton was very different. Governance works in Leeds, but brutally. Networks existed, but their members had to work at them continually to produce effective co-ordination across organisations. There was continual conflict because many of the key actors did not trust each other, making it difficult for partnerships to work effectively, as the key individuals held back from co-operating. It is hard to build governing capacity in this way. The style of decision-making reflects the history and tradition of governing Leeds, which draws on the hierarchy and power of the large city council which, until recently, had few competitors. Because of the tradition of strong party control of the council, most policies are intensely political, and only a few key officials and the leader are be able to produce a council-wide vision.

Yet Leeds is not anarchic. The conflicts occur behind closed doors and the partners agree in the end to present a public front of co-operation. This demonstrates the pragmatism of Leeds' rulers in their willingness to co-operate for the good of the city. The spirit of pragmatism reflects the power of business and the regime-like quality to their relationship with public decision-makers. The long-term coalition between the public and the private sector ensured that Leeds' rulers remained moderate in the 1980s and embraced a strategic partnership with business in the 1990s. Leeds' leaders are skilled operators; they try to balance interests in the process of governing; they try to respond to new ideas and pressures but also retain the organisational structure and power base which is effective in delivering policy and maintaining their position.

The pattern of governance in Leeds contrasts with that of Southampton. After the fall from leadership of Alan Whitehead, Southampton City Council proved unable to lead a united economic development partnership, though in education it has found it easier to build a community of decision-makers. In part the contrast is a function of geography and size. Leeds City Council is a massive organisation that dominates all partnerships. Southampton City Council is much weaker, and has to forge economic relationships with partners it does not like, such as neighbouring councils, Hampshire County Council or the Hampshire-based TEC. The poor relationships maintained between Southampton City Council and the Chamber of Commerce point to the lack of leadership and the absence of an elite culture in the city that might have fostered co-operation. Where relationships are more deeply embedded, such as in education policy, and where political networks help smooth the negotiations about policy, governance works much better. While there is a marked contrast between the effectiveness of Leeds and Southampton in economic policy, there is not so much of a difference in education. This fact reflects the nature of education as a policy sector, one that needs less active leadership and is confined to the education professionals who understand each other's language. The next chapter investigates whether these city and sectoral contrasts work in similar ways in France.

7 Governing French cities

In contrast with the proliferation of large cities in England, Germany or the Netherlands, France remained a predominantly rural and small-town nation until the mid-twentieth century. Unlike in England, the French urban hierarchy was shaped well before the process of industrialisation and mass urbanisation had begun. From the origins of the creation of France as a unified nation-state, the levers of political and economic power were heavily centralised in Paris. Outside Paris, the main cities emerged as administrative centres during the pre-revolutionary French monarchy, cities such as Bordeaux, Nantes, Rouen, Orléans, Marseilles, Montpellier, Toulouse, Lyons and Grenoble. Only a few genuine industrial cities developed in the nineteenth century, of which Lille was arguably the best example. As French industrialisation was a late and geographically specific phenomenon, most French cities have not suffered from problems of industrial decay comparable to those encountered by their British counterparts.

After a century of stagnation (1840–1940) France experienced an unprecedented demographic and economic expansion during the first 30 years of the post-war period. There was a massive shift in population from rural areas to the cities. A new wave of urbanisation in the post-war period witnessed the growth of the cities of the Paris region, the creation of new towns across France and the extension of city boundaries well beyond older urban limits.

There was an obvious time lag between the growth of cities and reforming the structures of sub-national administration to cope with change. The development of French cities during the post-war period created demands for sophisticated services and equipment in housing, culture, transport or social welfare. As we observed in chapter 3, however, the structure of local government – based around the commune and the departmental councils – remained largely untouched by urban growth. The modernisation of French cities in the 1960s and 1970s was driven by innovative and reform-minded central state actors: in the DATAR, the planning commissariat, and the Equipment ministry (Thoenig 1973; Jeannot and Peraldi 1994). The drive for urban modernisation by central government resulted in the development of new city-wide inter-communal structures that were imposed upon local actors. The urban districts were initially created in the 1950s to resolve problems of co-ordinating housing management. The urban communities of the late 1960s were implemented against the opposition of most local councils. The new town policy, which transformed the French urban land-scape in the 1960s and 1970s, completely bypassed existing local government actors altogether. The tradition of state intervention in urban development has continued to the present: City Contracts, *politique de la ville*, city communities are all examples of centrally driven urban policy initiatives.

Even at the height of top-down technocratic modernisation, however, centrally driven public policy action was subject to local mediation, as we demonstrated in chapter 3. French academic observers have argued that new processes of govern-ing cities have emerged since the late 1970s. Le Galès (1995b) diagnosed the 'rise of the large city' as a prominent feature of French local governance. Biarez (1993) referred to the growth of metropolitan centres since the end of the 1960s as an important feature of local power in France. Lorrain (1991) described the new style of urban government as being contractual and partnership-based. Ascher (1998: 58) defines urban governance as 'the ability of public authorities to formulate and implement territorially based public policies together with social and economic forces'.

These definitions all point to urban governance as representing a specific form of governance applied to the territorial space of cities. The urban governance thesis is not universally accepted. Baraize and Négrier (2000) and Borraz (1998: 19) both reject the concept as too indistinct and failing to capture variations between styles of city management. Even the most orthodox accounts accept that governing contemporary cities has become an incommensurably complex affair. In this chapter, we present findings of our research into two French cities, Lille and Rennes. Why did we choose these two cities? We chose Lille because of its comparable size, socio-economic conditions and political traditions to the northern UK city of Leeds, as well as by its distinctiveness within the French context. More representative of modern French cities is the case of Rennes, a medium-sized city at the heart of a wider urban agglomeration. While Lille appeared as a traditional manufacturing centre in decline, blighted by high levels of unemployment, Rennes owed its continual expansion during the post-war period to its tertiary vocation, its attractiveness to new industries and its role as an administrative and regional capital. While the northern city grappled initially with problems of industrial adjustment and a declining city centre population, Rennes acted as a magnet for the new middle classes produced by post-war socio-economic change. As in the case of Leeds and Southampton, these two cities provide contrasting examples to allow us to test for the existence of the new urban governance.

Local policy-making in Lille

Lille is the principal city in northern France. It is a densely populated urban agglomeration reminiscent of British northern cities, with their manufacturing traditions and problems of industrial decline. It is the administrative, political and economic capital of the Nord/Pas-de-Calais region, France's largest provincial region with 4 million inhabitants. For comparative and administrative purposes, the city of Lille is defined as corresponding to the boundaries of the Lille Urban Community (CUDL). Although it contains several distinct towns, the CUDL, an inter-communal grouping of 85 communes, comprises the greater Lille area. It is roughly equivalent in size to Leeds (a population of 1,100,000) and it is a genuine decision-making arena.

Though the commune of Lille (172,149 inhabitants in the 1999 census) is the principal town within the Lille Urban Community, it is not an integrated city such as Leeds. The former textile towns of Roubaix (97,746) and Tourcoing (93,765) retain a spirit of independence, while the new town of Villeneuve d'Ascq (65,675) is a direct competitor to Lille in terms of service provision and higher education facilities. These four major towns are flanked by numerous medium-sized towns with their own traditions of local autonomy, such as Wattrelos, Wasquehal, Hem, Croix, Lambersart and Marcq-en-Barœul. Even though Lille has increased its influence over the past two decades, it is not strong enough to impose its will unconditionally on the other players. This structure imposes a style of negotiated city governance.

As persuasively demonstrated by Paris (1993), the Nord/Pas-de-Calais region has suffered more than most from changes in the international and domestic economic environment. Traditionally a centre of heavy manufacturing industry, the long-term decline of the region's principal industries (textiles, coal mining, metallurgy and steel) accelerated sharply in the 1970s and 1980s. These general trends had an impact within the Lille metropolitan area itself, particularly in the textile towns of Roubaix and Tourcoing. The Lille Urban Community remains one of the major industrial areas in France, however, with heavy industry still accounting for more than one-quarter of local employment in 1995 (Loréal and van Staeyen 1995). In spite of the efforts of its public policy-makers, Lille continues to suffer from a serious image handicap as a declining industrial region with an inadequately trained population and a relatively weak service sector.

The political traditions of the Lille metropolitan area are diverse, with strong Socialist, Gaullist and Christian-Democratic undercurrents. During most of the post-war period, the Socialists have controlled the principal cities of the region, as well as the regional and departmental councils (Bleitrach 1980; Giblin-Delvallet 1990; Ménager et al. 1995). After disappointing electoral results during the early 1990s, the PS regained a majority of local deputies in the 1997 National Assembly election and control of the Nord/Pas-de-Calais regional council in 1998 (after a six-year Red–Green coalition interlude). The seeds of the modern French Socialist party were sown in Lille and Roubaix, the latter being the first French municipality to be captured by the Socialists in 1892. The Lille townhall was also a Socialist bastion, first captured in 1896 and led by a few historic figures of the French Socialist movement. For most of the post-war period, Lille has been managed by two powerful mayors, Augustin Laurent (1955–73) and Pierre Mauroy (1973–2001). Under Laurent's leadership, Lille was a traditional SFIO municipality, governed in alliance with the Christian-Democratic MRP. The Socialist townhall faithfully reflected the reformist aspirations of Lille's working-class electorate. The municipality saw its role as being to improve daily conditions of life in a heavily working-class city. This explained its ambitious programmes of social housing and welfare protection, and its deep hostility to local employers, to the extent that Laurent appeared 'relatively disinterested in the economic development of Lille' (Bleitrach 1980: 111). Suspicion towards business was illustrated by high corporate taxation rates and by resistance to the demands of the business community for more tertiary sector provision. The strained relations between local business and the townhall accurately reflected the poor state of labour relations in this industrial heartland city. The SFIO had strong linkages with the local trade union movement, and was anxious to remain close to its working-class constituency.

By the time that Mauroy took over from Laurent in 1973 the municipality had begun to change, but by comparison with most other French cities Lille remained a bastion of municipal socialism, where there was a sharp distinction between the spheres of economic development (the function of business and state agencies) and social affairs (a domain that the Socialist townhall jealously preserved for itself).

Economic development in Lille

At the core of urban regime theory is the existence of the politico-economic coalition (Stone 1989). While questioning the general validity of urban regime theory in the European context, we have argued elsewhere that politics in Lille in the 1980s and 1990s displayed certain regime-like features, in the form of a mutually accommodating alliance between the city's business and political elites over a sustained period (John and Cole 1998). The legacy of mutual suspicion gradually gave way to an atmosphere of closer co-operation between local political and economic elites in the first half of the 1980s. This thawing of relations had several causes. The first of these was the French left's electoral victory of 1981 and its experience of national governmental office for the first time since 1956. This had a major impact on Lille politics. The left-wing government was led by Pierre Mauroy, who retained the office of mayor of Lille in line with French traditions of *cumul des mandats*. In the opinion of a close advisor: 'Mauroy was a Socialist politician who did not trust business until 1983, but who – after his experience as Prime Minister – subsequently realised that it was essential to associate business with the local political leadership.' Mauroy had been instrumental in engineering the left's change in economic policy in 1983. He had come into contact with, and had gained respect from, the Lille business community, on account of the vigour with which, as Prime Minister, he pushed Lille's interests. The most important initiative in this respect was the Franco-British Channel Tunnel agreement, signed in Lille townhall in 1986, which Mauroy had promoted closely while still Prime Minister. The Tunnel – itself a public–private partnership on an unprecedented scale – performed a powerful symbolic role in increasing confidence amongst political and economic decision-makers

(Holliday et al. 1991). In conjunction with the events driving European integration, the Tunnel contributed to the belief that the geographical position of Lille at the centre of north-west Europe could be transformed to its advantage.

While the Tunnel was eagerly grasped as an external opportunity, the initiative to bring the high-speed train (TGV) to Lille was testament to the energies of Lille's key political and economic decision-makers. Mauroy's position as a former premier was central to his successful lobbying to secure the high-speed train's passage through the centre of Lille, against opposition from the rival city of Amiens and the national railway company, the SNCF. Mauroy was not the only actor involved; the regional prefect argued strongly in favour of such a solution in meetings with premier Chirac. The TGV link revealed the vigour of a powerful local economic development network. This lobby had a formal existence in *L'Association Gare-TGV de Lille*, a pressure group which brought together an alliance of local political and economic leaders in favour of the arrival of the TGV into Lille's city centre (Simon 1993).

The Tunnel and the TGV enjoyed broad local support. The Euralille development was less consensual, in that powerful local economic interests (as well as certain communes) were openly or covertly opposed to this Lille-based development. The proposal to build a vast office and commercial complex close to the new TGV station was launched by Mauroy shortly after the decision was announced that the TGV would pass through Lille city centre (December 1986). A feasibility study was followed by the creation of a mixed economy society (SEM) in 1988, which scheduled operations beginning in 1990. The first stages of the project (the high-speed train station; a large commercial centre and a convention centre) became operational in 1994–95, with major new office capacity progressively being released in 1995–96.

Euralille was highly ambitious. The scale of mobilisation behind the Euralille project was unprecedented in the city's history. Over the four year period from 1990 to 1994, 5,000 million francs ($1 billion) was invested, transforming Lille into the largest building site in Europe. The technical details of the project were indicative of new patterns of French local governance, notably the role of the SEMs as public–private developers. The mixed economy society SEM Euralille had several original characteristics. Its fixed capital was very high for a SEM (35 million francs). It brought together a large number of French and foreign business and financial actors: CDC, CCI, IndoSuez, BNP, NatWest, Bank of Tokyo. It also included the French state railway the SNCF – an exceptional occurrence. Moreover, a very wide range of local, national and international firms were involved as sub-contractors, charged with delivery of certain aspects of the development. Of most significance, it was a 'high-risk SEM'. The SEM itself had to agree to assume the risks inherent in the Euralille development; there were no local authority guarantees in the event of financial collapse. This was highly unusual, since local authorities usually agree to underwrite and guarantee loans contracted by mixed economy societies. The various partners would have to deal themselves with the consequences of any failure.

The partners involved in the Euralille project represented a diverse economic development coalition that would have been unimaginable several years earlier. As the President of the Lille Chamber pointed out: 'this was not a SEM with 95 per cent of the shares controlled by the local authorities, but a genuine public–private partnership'. Closer collaboration with business and the banking sector had been developed by the campaign to secure the TGV in the city centre. The participation of the Chamber of Commerce in the capital of the SEM Euralille provided symbolic local business support for the project. Finally, the status of Mauroy as former premier was of great importance in encouraging state and commercial banks to invest. The crucial role performed by Mauroy at all stages of the process leading to Euralille suggested strong parallels with the activity of French presidents at the national level: Euralille would be a testament to Mauroy's strong municipal reign, as the pyramid of the Louvre was to that of former President Mitterrand.

Further evidence of closer co-operation between local politicians and economic interests was provided by the Greater Lille Committee (*Comité Grand Lille*) created in 1994. This is a forum involving public and private sector actors, to promote greater joint co-operation between actors involved in local development. In November 1995, this committee was composed of 272 local decision-makers, drawn from the spheres of politics, culture, industry and higher education. It was created on the initiative of local industrialist Bruno Bonduelle to symbolise a new climate of co-operation and partnership. The committee has a founding charter, but no formal constitution. Rather like the Leeds Initiative it is a forum for contact, rather than a decision-making partnership. An internal document portrayed the committee as being 'a club for the joint reflection of its members and the forwarding of propositions' to promote Lille as a major European city by 2015. The Greater Lille Committee was the driving force behind Lille's ultimately unsuccessful bid to host the 2004 Olympic Games. Joint public–private energies and capital contributed to the city's capture of the French nomination for the games, and for the proposed infrastructure developments. The Lille Olympic Committee raised almost 60 million francs ($12 million) to favour the Lille campaign, mainly from private and business contributions.

The actors of economic development in Lille

Networks in Lille are more complex than those of the typical French city. Not only are there a number of organisations which one would expect to be present in French urban policy, there are far more relationships because of the large number of communes and the existence of competitive alliances within the Greater Lille area. The Lille economic development network is characterised by competing constellations of actors riven by party political factors, local interests and Lille/non-Lille coalitions. As outlined in chapter 4, a protean array of actors have an impact upon local economic development policy in French cities. In the case of Lille, these include the commune of Lille itself, the Lille Urban Community (85 communes), the Nord department, the Nord/Pas-de-Calais region, the regional prefecture (SGAR), the decentralised ministerial field services, and various other public and private actors. In addition, there exists a strong tradition of business organisation, manifested in a powerful and original regional employers structure known as the *Maison des professions*; an integrated and effective Chamber of Commerce covering Lille, Roubaix and Tourcoing; and the existence of large foreign, French and local industrial groups (Auchan, La Redoute, Trois Suisses, Chargeurs, Renault) representing a broad scope of economic activity. A range of other public, semi-public and private actors had a direct or indirect input into local economic development policy. Sociometric analysis (John 1998) has uncovered three principal types of policy actor involved in Lille economic development policy in the mid-1990s. In decreasing order of importance these involved local political, economic and state organisations. The local political leadership (the mayor Pierre Mauroy, the economic *adjoint* Bernard Roman (later on Martine Aubry) and a handful of close officials occupied a pivotal role at the centre of local networks. The influence of this core group was considerable, on condition that it respected a negotiated, bargained style of local political exchange. Amongst economic interests, the Chamber of Commerce (notably its president) appeared as the most frequent interlocutor of the local political leadership, with residual suspicion limiting formal contacts with representatives of local employers associations. The regional prefecture could be an important local partner, especially when it came to facilitating central state support in relation to Euralille or the city's Olympic bid. On other occasions (1993–5) relations between Lille's Socialist politicians and the RPR prefect were tense. The politics of economic development in Lille has involved a series of attempts to keep these unstable coalitions together. Rivalry and mutual suspicion are never far beneath the surface. But there are substantial reasons why Lille-based actors – public and private – should seek to co-operate. Economic crisis, the need for a new economic strategy, Europeanisation and greater public recognition of public–private partnerships have all played a role in uniting the communes within the CUDL and in narrowing the traditional distance between local authority and local business actors.

Education policy-making in Lille and the Nord/Pas-de-Calais region

One of the defining features of French-style governance is the indistinct character of territorial and administrative boundaries. Governance is messy. There is no tidy fit between national, regional and local spheres of public policy action that is consistent across all policy domains. Alone amongst the major French spending ministries, the Education ministry organises its field services around the regional, rather than the departmental level. The principal sub-national unit of the Education ministry is the rectorate, the regional-level field service, whose boundaries correspond approximately to those of the elected regional councils. As the state remains the most important policy actor in French education, at a formal level the pertinent arena for studying sub-national education policy-making is the region, rather than the city. In a less formal sense, there are various direct and indirect means whereby city-based actors can exercise influence over regional-level education policy choices.

Each region faces specific issues and policy challenges in secondary education, as well as distinct constellations of actors involved in determining educational priorities. The Nord/Pas-de-Calais has suffered from a heritage of poor educational standards and inadequate training. The region traditionally endured one of the lowest levels of educational achievement in France. This was measured by below average rates of success in the *baccalauréat*; by a pattern of training traditionally geared towards specific labour-intensive industrial activities (such as textiles and mining); and by the highest proportion of technical secondary schools (*lycées professionnelles*) in the country. From the mid-1980s onwards, a powerful coalition – encompassing education professionals, regional and local politicians, regional state actors and local pressure groups – was determined to reverse the educational underprovision of the region. Against a backdrop of rapid de-industrialisation, a history of underqualification and an unemployment rate well above the national average, education and adult training were believed to be essential tools for retraining a dislocated population and combating unemployment. Agreement on the ends of educational policy mitigated the effects of institutional, political and procedural rivalries.

The principal actors in sub-national education policy-making are the state field services (rectorates and academic inspectorates) and the elected regions. State and region are unequal partners, as can be demonstrated in the Nord/Pas-de-Calais region. As measured in terms of administrative personnel or budgets, there is no real comparison between the resources available to the state agencies and those of the local and regional authorities. The bulk of technical and professional resources within the sector of secondary education were concentrated within the state field agencies. The Lille academy is the largest in France after Versailles. In 1994, it employed 800 administrative staff in its regional headquarters; and over 87,000 teachers and related educational staff in its sub-divisions and schools (Lille Academy 1994a). The educational division of the Nord/Pas-de-Calais regional council counted 30 full- and part-time employees, with no control over teaching or maintenance staff. Routine contact with educational professionals (school heads, trade unions) and pressure groups (parent federations, religious orders and business interests) occurred almost exclusively at the level of the state field agencies. Local and regional authorities were far removed from the day-to-day management of schools and had little contact with members of the educational policy community.

We should not conclude that the regional council was devoid of influence. Since 1986, the Nord/Pas-de-Calais regional council has performed an important role in relation to the decentralised education sector. This has been facilitated by the enormity of the educational policy challenge facing the region, by the presence of political heavyweights within the regional council, by the size of the region (4 million inhabitants) and by the disinclination of other local authorities (essentially the two departmental councils in Nord and Pas-de-Calais) to dispute the region's leadership. As observed during fieldwork (from 1994 to 1996 and in 2000), an assertive regional council felt itself to be engaged in a competitive – and sometimes conflictual – partnership with the Lille rectorate. There was a keen sense that education was the key service upon which the regional council would be judged, that decentralisation was a fragile edifice, and that the 'proximity' argument was a just one.

As the regional councils determine ultimately whether or not to build new schools, they have a powerful bargaining resource in their dealings with the state authorities. When the building programme is as extensive as that undertaken in the Nord/Pas-de-Calais from 1989 to 1994, their bargaining position is further enhanced.[1] The Nord/Pas-de-Calais region attempted in its 1994–98 Training Plan (*schéma prévisionnel des formations*) to harmonise the location of schools, training needs and the economic priorities of the region, openly challenging the rector's right to sole authority in matters of secondary education. As it built and equipped schools, and as it spent 60 per cent of its budget on education, the regional council demanded a greater input into educational choices. This demand was publicly resisted by the rector of the Lille academy, who claimed sole authority (in the name of the public education service) to determine pedagogical choices. More detailed analysis highlighted that the regional council was able to influence educational choices – albeit on the margins – through its legal responsibility to build schools and its willingness to pay for expensive equipment (such as audio-visual and science laboratories) in specialist areas it sought to promote (Cole 1997). Though relations between the rectorate and the regional council were strained to breaking point in 1994–96, they subsequently improved as the underlying consensus in favour of raising educational standards in the Nord/Pas-de-Calais region facilitated co-operation.

French local and regional authorities have a general legislative competence that allows them to intervene across the policy spectrum. Though secondary education does not formally fall into the sphere of competence of the commune of Lille, the city fathers considered themselves to form part of this educational expansion coalition. The legal responsibilities of the Lille commune in educational affairs were fairly narrow, restricted to nursery and primary education. In addition to organising a range of extra-curriculum activities, the commune had managed a special fund (*Caisse d'école*) since 1883, in order to subsidize school meals for children from poor families (Lille Municipal Council 1993b). The city's interest in the educational debate went beyond these noble concerns. In the sphere of secondary education, channels of influence were more indirect, a by-product of the central role occupied by Mauroy within the regional Socialist Party network. On account of the close linkages between Mauroy and the PS politicians in charge of secondary education in the regional council (Percheron then Délébarre), Lille politicians were able to involve themselves closely in regional educational policy. As in the other cities surveyed, moreover, developing higher education and research capacity was perceived as an integral part of an urban economic development strategy. The commune of Lille and the urban community participated enthusiastically in the University 2000 scheme, granting

120 million francs (£12 million) to bring the Law faculty to a run-down quarter of Lille. Though there were links into the regional educational policy community, the linkage appeared on occasion tenuous. The counterpart to an affirmative regional presence was the absence of a specifically urban, city-based focus in secondary education. This stands in obvious contrast with the sphere of economic development.

As explored in these two different policy spheres, Lille is probably more characteristic of governance trends than most other French cities. No other city has had to manage such acute economic stress; responses to conditions of lasting economic crisis have mobilised local actors in both policy sectors. The management of secondary education demonstrated new forms of public sector partnership, with an assertive regional authority leaving its imprint on policy choices. Economic development revealed a broader-based coalition including public, private and voluntary sector actors. As a result of these patterns of local political and economic management, the example of Lille serves to demonstrate well the transformation of French urban politics since the early 1980s.

Local policy-making in Rennes

Rennes is situated on the eastern edge of Brittany, almost equidistant between Brest and Paris. The communal boundary of Rennes reveals a medium-sized city of 200,000 inhabitants, whose population increases to 333,000 when incorporating the Rennes Urban District, an inter-communal association of 33 communes. Prior to 1945, Rennes was a provincial capital barely touched by the industrial revolution. Its local industry consisted of a brewery, a publishing house and a dense network of small and medium-sized businesses (Le Galès 1993). Its local development was closely related to its status as the administrative capital of Brittany, dominated by the army, by the legal profession and by the regional offices of government departments. A university city since the seventeenth century, Rennes was for long the only Breton city with a university.

Rennes expanded rapidly during the post-war period, with its population doubling from 100,000 to 200,000 between 1950 and 1980. The city owed its post-war expansion to a virtuous combination of favourable state investment decisions in the 1950s and 1960s, its role as an administrative and regional capital with a strong tertiary vocation, and its attractiveness to new industries. Rennes is an important centre of public sector employment as a result of the city's university and research institutes, its large hospital serving the Brittany region and its status as a regional capital. Private sector business interests operate on a much smaller scale than in Lille. Rennes has a modest industrial sector (the car manufacturer Citroën and the publisher Ouest-France are the two main private employers), offset by a large and diversified small and medium business culture, with particular strengths in transport, food processing industries and telecommunications. Employment is higher in Rennes than in the rest of Brittany or in relation to the national average. The city's population is young, upwardly mobile and highly educated.

Rennes' political traditions have been deeply influenced by the Christian-Democratic movement and more recently by the Socialist Party. The city became one of the citadels of post-war French Christian-Democracy; in 1945, four out of seven Ille-et-Vilaine deputies belonged to the Christian-Democratic Popular Republican Movement (MRP). The post-war development of Rennes was shaped in part by the policy choices adopted by Henri Fréville, the MRP mayor from 1953 to 1977. The Fréville period laid the bases for the Rennes model, accepted in part by Fréville's successor as mayor of Rennes, Hervé. Four aspects of municipal management particularly characterised Fréville's period as mayor: the attempt to attract inward investment from public and private actors (symbolised by the establishment of the car manufacturer Citroën between 1953 and 1961); the development of Rennes University and the research sector; a novel system of land management and urban development; and the creation of the Rennes District in 1970. A powerful *notable* in his own right, Fréville was able to promote a local development strategy because it coincided with the French state's ambition to modernise Brittany (Phlipponeau 1977). Close co-operation with state officials formed part of the Rennes economic development strategy. The city's urban programmes in the 1950s and 1960s were drawn up jointly with the relevant field services of state ministries (Duchemin 1994). Successive prefects colluded with Fréville, unblocking necessary credits to facilitate development.

In municipal power since 1977, the Socialist Party in Rennes appeared initially as the inheritor of the reformist tradition which had been alive in the left wing of the MRP. Unlike in Lille, the PS was renovated in the Ille-et-Vilaine department by forces from outside of the SFIO (as well as from a radical, anti-clerical faction within the old party): these included former Unified Socialist Party (PSU) activists, members of regionalist political clubs and associative movements, left-Catholic groups and new party members influenced by the ideals of May 1968. Ideologically and politically innovative, Rennes' Socialists were heavily influenced by the 'Grenoble' model of local municipal activism, with its belief in decentralisation, its disdain for traditional *notables* and its advocacy of new forms of political participation.

Local economic development in Rennes

While central state territorial planning played a part in the economic development of Rennes, this also depended upon an innovative vision of local development adopted by local political and economic decision-makers. In his comparison of Rennes and Coventry, Le Galès (1993) identified a Rennes model of urban management and economic development. The Rennes model was predicated upon several reinforcing features: an ideological consensus between local elites to promote the city's economic development and to achieve social progress; a strong mobilisation of new social groups organised into voluntary associations with an input into policy-making; the pervasive influence of a progressive Christian-Democratic tradition, expressed through para-Catholic associations; and an innovative style of public sector management, based on long-term urban planning and municipal interventionism, an innovative social policy and an active cultural policy. The Rennes model of local governance was built upon the pre-eminence of the new middle classes and the pursuit of policies designed to satisfy these social groups.

The Fréville heritage was one of municipal intervention beyond the norms current elsewhere, of the mobilisation of local actors in pursuit of collective aims, and of synergy between economic development and related sectors. Fréville's successor Hervé remained faithful to the salient features of the Rennes model. Hervé summarised the Rennes model in terms of planning, forecasting, partnership and projects. Planning involved a tight control over land use and urban development. Forecasting took the form of annual revisions of the district's economic development plan. Partnership was a method of functioning; the city had a long history of collaboration with other partners, and had signed conventions across a range of policy spheres. Projects formed part of a global approach towards local development. An economic development strategy had to be consistent with local policies pursued in the spheres of education, culture, housing and the environment.

As first outlined in its economic development plan in 1983–84, and modified on several subsequent occasions, the city's economic development strategy was based specifically upon promoting cultural activities, attracting and using new technologies, and encouraging inter-communal co-operation. The city of Rennes claimed to be innovative in each of these areas. The Rennes municipality has been one of the most successful in presenting itself as a city of culture (Vion and Le Galès 1999). The municipal government has promoted a politically astute mix of high-brow and popular culture. While the city's opera and municipal theatre are amongst the best in France, Rennes is best known for its youth culture policy, especially the annual rock festival organised by the municipal council. Detailed consideration of the cultural achievements of the Rennes municipality lies beyond this chapter. They are testament to the cultural awakening of localities across France and to the belief that there are political benefits from satisfying the cultural aspirations of diverse local electoral clienteles. Local cultural policies have the additional advantage of demonstrating the ambition of local authorities to govern in all areas of local public policy.

Attracting new technologies was a second affirmed priority. One of Mayor Hervé's principal achievements lay in the creation of the Rennes Atalante science and technology park. Rennes Atalante demonstrated the possibilities of local economic development. The concept behind it was to create a partnership in order to promote a broader synergy between local government, the research community, the universities, public sector agencies and high technology firms (especially in the fields of information technology and telecommunications). Opened in 1984, by 1994 Rennes Atalante had created 3000 jobs (Rennes Atalante 1994a). The technical details of the Rennes Atalante science park are illustrative of the Rennes model of local economic development. This might be identified as one of controlled innovation. The physical development of the science park was carried out by a mixed economy society (the SEMAEB) dominated by public and quasi-public actors. SEMAEB was responsible for buying land, developing the buildings and reselling them to companies present on the site. Local authority guarantees minimised the risk involved for the various partners; this was not a high-risk SEM, but a traditional, local authority dominated partnership. The SEMAEB continues to manage the original Rennes Atalante site.

Inter-communal co-operation lay at the heart of the Rennes model. We observed in chapter 3 how the belief that a coherent approach to local development requires a high degree of inter-communal co-operation has gained general acceptance. This area was one where Rennes could claim to be in the avant-garde. Rennes was the first French city to adopt a completely supra-communal approach to local business taxation. Relying on provisions contained within the Joxe law of 1992, the Rennes district decided in 1992 that its 33 communes would each deliver the product of its business tax to the (inter-communal) district, with resources subsequently distributed on an equitable formula basis between all communes. By this audacious decision, the Rennes district attempted to combat one of the inequitable consequences of the business tax; those communes with the greatest social needs are in general those which are the least attractive for business investment, hence those receiving the smallest income from the business tax. This measure of controlled innovation was consistent with the spirit of past patterns of local governance in Rennes: business interests had never dictated policy. Certain local businesses complained of the increasing taxation levels this decision had provoked, notably those based on the territory of Cesson-Sevigné, a commune which previously had one of the lowest levels of business tax in France. Vigorously disputed claims were also made that no new inward business investment had occurred within the Rennes district since 1992.

These three examples all indicate an innovative style of local management. The controversy caused by the Rennes metro illustrates a more traditional model of French municipal action, one based upon directive mayoral leadership. Upon his re-election as mayor in 1989, Hervé announced his desire to build an underground railway system (known as the VAL) as a solution to the city's public transport problems. The decision was Hervé's alone. Local public opinion preferred the cheaper option of an overground tram. The local business community was almost unanimously opposed to the VAL, with business opposition organised by André Génovèse, managing director of the Citroën car plant. Such animosity was understandable: the VAL was to be financed partly by increased taxation on local businesses, in the form of a rise in the transport levy (*versement transport*). While the VAL would be confined to Rennes' city boundaries, local firms throughout the wider district would have to pay the increased transport levy. The VAL dossier troubled the consensus that had hitherto characterised governance in Rennes. Local associations affirmed their distance, as did local economic elites. Hervé's re-election in 1995 comforted the mayor of Rennes in his determination to proceed. With a public utility decree finally signed in November 1996, the last obstacle to the beginning of the construction work was removed. In insisting upon an unpopular solution against local popular and elite opinion, Hervé demonstrated that local governance in Rennes depended upon determined municipal leadership as much as anything else.

Actors of economic development in Rennes

The structure of the Rennes economic development network was far more homogeneous than in Lille. This was due to the more compact spatial organisation of the city, the domination of the city centre over the outlying communes, the strong political identity of the PS district majority, and a long tradition of inter-communal co-operation. The most visible actors of local development in Rennes included the familiar mixture of local politicians (especially the mayor Hervé and his economic *adjoint* Normand), representatives of local economic interests (in the Rennes Chamber of Commerce and the regional employers federation), and regional state officials (John 1998). The Rennes network appeared both as more political and more directive than that of Lille. As extra-polated from snap-shot interviews carried out in 1995, the governing coalition consisted of the Rennes commune and its satellites, the Rennes district, certain associations, several public sector educational institutes, and specific private interests who worked closely with the townhall, representing a minority of the local business community. Within Rennes itself, fieldwork in 1995 uncovered a resurgent right-wing coalition that challenged both Hervé and the consensual model of Rennes municipal politics. On a broader level, the district network was itself contested by a rival coalition based around the Ille-et-Vilaine departmental council (and its centrist president Pierre Méhaignerie), the core of the local business community (Citroën, Ouest-France, Légris), along with several Catholic educational institutes and interests (notably those represented on the private Ker Lann campus). These coalitions had become more adversarial and politicised during the period 1990–95, with lessening co-operation and contact between the two. We will return later to the question of how representative the 1995 picture was in the context of the post-war history of Rennes.

Education policy in Rennes and the Brittany region

The context of education policy-making in Rennes contrasts starkly with that examined in Lille. The policy dilemmas facing the northern city centred around how to tackle severe problems of educational underachievement; in 2000, the Rennes academy had one of the highest proportions of pupils obtaining the *baccalauréat* outside of Ile-de-France. Different educational contexts thus produced distinctive policy problems. Traditions of scholarship have a long pedigree in the academy of Rennes. In the predominantly rural Brittany of the nineteenth and early twentieth centuries, educational achievement was the only means of social and geographical mobility. The city of Rennes occupied a specific position within Brittany. As an expanding regional and administrative capital, Rennes provided public sector employment for the upwardly mobile children of Breton peasants. The existence of a large hinterland strengthened the vocation of Rennes as a regional capital, wherein education performed a critical economic role.

The commitment on behalf of all local actors to the maintenance of the highest educational standards formed part of an underlying consensus, which lessened the impact of political cleavages and institutional rivalries. There were three principal features of this consensus: a commitment to retaining the region's tradition of academic excellence; the promotion of education not only as a means of social mobility but also as a tool of regional economic development, and an acceptance of the specific role performed by the Catholic education sector in Brittany.

All Rennes-based local actors wished to enhance the size and quality of the education system. This aim was most obviously demonstrated in higher education, where there was a close linkage with economic development in a city with over 50,000 students. The commune of Rennes participated enthusiastically in the University 2000 scheme; indeed, the PS-run city even associated itself with the private Ker Lann campus, created by the UDF president of the Ille-et-Vilaine department, Méhaignérie. Neither the commune of Rennes, nor Rennes district (which provided school transport) had major formal responsibilities in relation to secondary education policy-making. Their main obligations were within the sphere of nursery and primary education. As in other spheres of its public activity, however, the Rennes commune produced its own educational project (*projet éducatif rennais*) which manifested political ambitions well beyond the council's minimal legal responsibilities. Since education and training were fundamental municipal objectives, the city of Rennes felt a duty to assist all schools present upon the communal territory. Solicited for support by the Brittany region and Ille-et-Vilaine department, the commune of Rennes agreed to make an ongoing financial contribution to the upkeep of the public *collèges* and *lycées* within the city and funded certain items of educational equipment. The commune also revealed itself to be a generous beneficiary of private schools, allocating 10 million francs (£1 million) for private ('contracted-in') schools in 1993. This financial effort was aimed to preserve the position of Rennes as the most dynamic academy in France outside of the Ile-de-France region.

Private education is particularly widespread in Brittany, accounting for the schooling of 40 per cent of Breton schoolchildren (Rennes Academy 1999). The presence of an unusually high proportion of school children educated in Catholic schools influenced the policy environment within which local educational choices were made. Unlike in most other regions, Catholic schools were included in forecasts of educational provision made by the Rennes rectorate and Brittany region. All significant local authorities – the Brittany region, the four departments (Ille-et-Vilaine, Morbihan, Finistère and to a lesser extent Cotes d'Armor), and the leading cities – provided generous (and on occasion illegal) financial support for the Catholic school sector (Fontaine 1990, 1992). There was a consensus in favour of this policy, shared by local and state actors alike. In so far as it accepted the policy of 'equal treatment for public and private', the Rennes rectorate aligned itself with the prevailing local political culture more openly than in most French regions, as did the PS-controlled Rennes council itself. Initially representative of a lay, anti-clerical strand of local political opinion, Edmond Hervé was elected as Socialist mayor of Rennes in 1977 only after reaching an informal compromise on the issue of private schools (Vion 1996).

Quite apart from their differences, many similar tendencies were observed in Rennes and in Lille. In both cities, the day-to-day management of schools remained the internal business of the Education ministry. Relations between school headteachers and officials in the Rennes rectorate were regular and hierarchical; those between headteachers and representatives of the region were far more episodic. In both cities educational professionals resented outside interference and in both the activism of the teaching unions was confirmed. The expertise acquired by union leaders was such that they could attain status as repositories of the collective memory of the academy; the FSU president interviewed in 1995 had been in post since 1968 (formerly as president of the FEN) and had known 12 different rectors. The teaching unions had the capacity to disrupt, and were regularly received by the rector. As in the Nord, parents groups were weak. The FCPE lacked the means to impose a dialogue, either at the level of the academic authorities, or even within individual schools.

The most significant relationship in sub-national educational governance is that between the rectorate and the elected region. At the moment of the decentralisation of secondary education (1986) the Rennes rectorate could count upon vastly superior technical and professional resources, with 400 permanent administrative staff, employing over 20,000 teachers (Rennes Academy 1994). The Rennes rectorate prided itself on being 'the best in France'. Its officials had a strong sense of organisational identity, built upon a solid record of academic success: the academy regularly had one of the highest success rates in the *baccalauréat*. The consistently high performance indicators boosted organisational confidence. Unlike in Lille, the Rennes rectorate was not openly challenged by an assertive regional authority.

At its origins, the Brittany region's education division, the DEE, consisted of two former rectorate officials and three part-timers (Fontaine 1990, 1992). The DEE gradually expanded and developed in competence; by 2000 the division consisted of over 20 people in total. Regional input into the formulation and implementation of secondary education policy gradually increased. Initially content to follow the rectorate, the Brittany region's training plans became more ambitious as it developed its technical and professional expertise. The third Regional Plan of 1992 (*Horizon 1995*) illustrated this evolution: *Horizon 1995* attempted to define training priorities by employment zone (*zone d'emploi*), and to match employment and training needs (Brittany Regional Council 1992). In the fourth Regional Plan (prepared during the fieldwork in 1995), a new programme (ARIANE) defined training needs for all young people under 26 years old, including those in secondary school. This repeated the familiar pattern whereby increased expertise, experience and resources led the regional councils to adopt a more expansive vision of their educational role. Unlike in Lille, there was no open test of force between the regional council and the rectorate and the two partners came to appreciate each other's efforts. The rectorate acknowledged that the Brittany regional council had acquired substantial technical competence in the education sector. For its part, though the regional council used the training plan procedure to define its own regional educational priorities, it never questioned the primacy of the state in pedagogical affairs.

As in Lille, what evidence there is of new patterns of educational governance in Rennes rested upon the emergence of new policy actors and the increased practice of inter-organisational co-operation. In England, one aspect of governance in secondary education is the greater involvement of non-state actors in educational management. There is much less evidence to support such analysis in the case of French education, where public service beliefs continue to isolate schools from their environments and where there is an inherent suspicion of external interference. The functional relationship with the business community is confined essentially to school placements and to the consultation of business interests over the appropriate school curriculum in the technical *lycées* (*lycées professionelles*). The relationship with the business community was rather different in Brittany and in the Nord/Pas-de-Calais. While there was a long tradition of business involvement in vocational education in the northern region, in rural Brittany there were not enough local firms to offer work placements for all students.

While remaining an outsider to the national education system *stricto sensu*, business interests have become more closely involved with the elected regions in defining their training needs. We observed in chapter 5 how the procedure known as the Contract of Objectives (*Contrat d'objectifs*), introduced in the 1993 Training Act, was an attempt to involve business more closely in the definition of its training objectives. In the first agreement of its kind, in 1995 a Contract of Objectives was signed by the president of the Brittany Building Federation, by the French state (represented by the regional prefect and the rector) and by the president of the regional council (Brittany Regional Council 1995). The contract stipulated that the Building Federation would need 3000 young people over a five-year period, which the other partners engaged themselves to train.

As demonstrated in these two policy sectors, governance in Rennes has several specific traits. It is shaped by the city's role as the capital of a region with a strong sense of identity, by its consensual post-war political traditions, by the characteristics of its socially mobile population and by its customarily strong local political leadership. There is a measure of broad political consensus within which political disputes are played out; this is demonstrated by a strong tradition of inter-communal collaboration across party lines. There were aspects of political and policy continuity between Fréville's social catholicism and Hervé's modernising socialism. In this respect, the embittered relationships between the Rennes governing coalition and urban society in the early to mid-1990s were rather unrepresentative of the broader context of the city's post-war history. On balance, Rennes appeared capable of a more integrated approach to local political management than most other French cities.

Conclusion

As uncovered in the detailed case studies of Lille and Rennes, French-style urban governance involves new forms of mobilisation of political, social and economic actors. It encompasses the development of city-wide structures (such as the Lille Urban Community and the Rennes Urban District) and identities. It attests to the emergence of ambitious city visions, as typified by the economic development projects considered in both cities. As measured by the policy dynamism of municipal teams in the spheres of economic development, culture, urban planning, transport or education, urban governance implies the development of sophisticated local public policies in all areas of city interest. City visions are outlined in complex local planning documents, such as the *projet d'agglomération* in Rennes and the *schéma directeur* in Lille. The importance of the symbols of common city purpose, such as Olympic bids, public–private forums and transnational networks, also formed part of this new governing style.

As cities have developed their governing capacity, they have strengthened their bureaucratic structures and staffs. City planners can also draw upon sophisticated policy expertise in the urban planning and place marketing agencies. As demonstrated with respect to Euralille, cities have proved adept at using old tools – such as SEMs – for new purposes, such as economically based public–private partnerships.

Cities have adapted to their changing external environment within and beyond the nation-state. Domestically, they have adjusted to the transformation of the French state. Cities have emerged with enhanced authority from the decentralisation process. The removal of prefectoral *a priori* control and the expansion of sources of local finance have liberated big-city mayors, broadening their scope of contacts, and increasing the possibilities to engage in large-scale development projects.

Adjusting to a changed external environment can also involve an increased awareness of Europe and European integration as providing new opportunities for city positioning and transnational networking. This role was most obvious in the case of Lille. The European dimension clearly underpinned the various economic development projects of the 1980s and 1990s. The vision of Lille as a city lying at the crossroads of north-western Europe, equidistant from three European capitals, Paris, London and Brussels, sustained local decision-makers. The opening of the Channel Tunnel in 1994, followed by the arrival of the high-speed train (TGV) in Lille city centre and a series of audacious public policy initiatives (Euralille, the Olympic bid), testified to elite confidence in the possibilities of regenerating the city as one of the principal metropolitan centres of north-west Europe. Local decision-makers refer to Lille as a transnational city of 1.5 million inhabitants; this is more than political hyperbole, in that several Belgian border towns have developed strong cultural and economic ties with the northern French city. Hence the symbolic importance of incorporating representatives of the Chambers of Commerce of four Belgian towns in the Greater Lille Committee. Moreover, Lille was one of the first French cities to engage in direct lobbying through opening an office in Brussels. Playing the European card is justified by the city's size and geographical location; it also helps to reinforce the cohesion between traditionally divided local elites. By contrast, local decision-makers in Rennes were acutely aware of the city's peripheral location in relation to the European centre of gravity. This emerged in the questionnaire as being the principal perceived weakness of the Breton capital. Some comfort was offered in the form of the European Union's Atlantic Arc programme; this allowed Rennes to build transnational networks with other cities and regions in countries on Europe's western fringe (in Ireland, Britain, Spain and Portugal).

Lille and Rennes displayed different features of urban governance. Lille appeared as a large and complex city, with disaggregated administrative and functional structures. It was far more difficult than in its British twin city Leeds to identify one strategic economic development network. Whereas in Leeds most matters affecting the city involved the city council, the TEC, the chamber and sometimes the government office, no such assumption was possible in Lille. There was a far more varied scope for policy actors, both public and private.

There was no long history of inter-communal or city-wide co-operation in Lille, far less of public–private partnership. The legacy of parochial divisions had been only too apparent during Arthur Notebart's presidency of the CUDL (1973–89), when rival communal and personal interests had frustrated any concerted economic development strategy (Giblin-Devallet 1990). The governance of Lille during the 1980s and 1990s challenged much received wisdom about the city. First, there were new types of co-operation between public sector actors, most visible in the management of the Lille Urban Community. From 1989 onwards, the large players tolerated the mayor of Lille Mauroy's presidency of the CUDL, in exchange for an equitable distribution of community resources between the leading towns and territorial interests present within the metropolitan area. Local actors recognised the importance of co-operating in order to promote the interests of greater Lille as a city, as opposed to its component towns. Competition with rival metropolitan centres was too intense to allow the luxury of too many internal divisions.

Second, during the course of the decade 1985–95, there were several examples of public–private co-operation. A tradition of mutual suspicion in Lille between local politicians and business elites gave way to closer co-operation throughout the 1980s and 1990s. Public–private partnership lay behind the campaign to secure the TGV for Lille, the Euralille development and the city's Olympic bid. This central finding of closer co-operation between local political and economic elites is consistent with the notion of urban governance as a process that transcends the traditional separation of public action into the political and economic spheres.

Local governance in Rennes has traditionally been more cohesive than in Lille. This is in part because, as a spatially compact medium-sized city, its administrative and functional structures are less disaggregated. Rennes has a strong tradition of inter-communal co-operation and of political compromise. Though relations between the local political leadership and the business community deteriorated sharply during the early to mid-1990s, this appeared rather untypical of the post-war political management of Rennes. Whether under Christian-Democratic or Socialist stewardship, Rennes' political leaders have boasted an original model of local governance. Rennes was one of the first French cities to adopt a global approach to local economic development as encompassing the range of activities in spheres as diverse as culture, housing, education and transport; to embrace a general philosophy of planned and co-ordinated urban development, and to associate the voluntary sector with local decision-making processes. The legacy of such past decisions is apparent in contemporary governing processes. This was demonstrated in the particularly strong emphasis on linkage between education and economic development; and the provision of cultural services designed to strengthen the image of the city as young, dynamic and prosperous. For all the importance accorded to partnerships, however, the Rennes model was a municipally driven one, based on planned local development and an active municipal presence in all areas of city interest.

From studying Lille and Rennes there is ample evidence of innovation, but also much that remains of the classic pattern of French local politics. French-style local governance does not operate in a vacuum. Its path continues to be shaped by a national tradition which stresses the legitimacy of central state intervention to guarantee public service and equal treatment across the national territory. In the two policy sectors surveyed, the French state remains very present; as the dominant actor in secondary education, and as a pervasive background presence in local economic development, ready to intervene to reward (as testified by the resources channelled by the French state in the State–Region plans) or punish as appropriate.

While there are powerful trends to urban governance, moreover, there remain strong structural barriers to the emergence of genuine city governments. Most European countries modernised their local government structures after the Second World War, but there was no fundamental change in the French case. Though we must await a definitive judgement, herein lies the potential significance of the 1999 Chevènement law which has led to the creation across France of genuine inter-communal authorities, with extensive powers in the fields of economic development and local taxation. These 'city-wide communities' offer the prospect of a long-term remedy to the chronic weakness of French local governance. The strengthening of inter-communal structures has also highlighted the democratic deficit that persists within French local governance. Though vested with tax-raising powers and precise policy attributions, the EPCI (urban communities, urban districts, city-wide communities) are not yet democratically accountable through direct elections. Structures such as the Lille Urban Community or the Rennes Urban District (renamed Rennes Metropole in 2000) continue to suffer from a manifest problem of political legitimacy (they are indirectly elected) and accountability. These questions will now be addressed in the concluding chapter.

8 Local governance in England and France

This final chapter draws together the various strands and themes running throughout *Local Governance in England and France*. We address the research questions chapter 1 poses and that we develop throughout the book. The main body of the chapter considers how patterns of contemporary local governance are influenced by national contexts, policy sectors and local environments. The book concludes by discussing the implications of these findings for political accountability and the nature of the contemporary public sphere.

Local governance revisited

In chapter 1 we highlight the core features of local governance. We identify the external causes as the internationalisation of the economy, transnational policy-making in bodies such as the EU, and international policy transfers. Internal changes involve pressures for more decentralised forms of public policy-making, new forms of private sector involvement in policy delivery, changing patterns of political participation in local politics, reforms in public service delivery based on proximity and improving quality, and new ways of co-ordinating public decision-making. While external changes provide a plausible context, internal factors have led more directly to local governance. In both countries, local governance manifested itself in blurred boundaries between public and/or private actors, organisational decentralisation, institutional fragmentation and the growth of networks and partnerships.

Central governments in both countries have recognised the complex nature of contemporary policy problems and the inadequacy of purely administrative solutions. On both sides of the channel, central government has restructured local political systems to deal with new challenges and organisational overload. This has taken forms that are consistent with national institutional and administrative traditions. Governance does not mean convergence. In England, there have been profound public sector management reforms and moves to consumer-led forms of service delivery. In France, policy overload produced increasingly bold measures of administrative decentralisation from the 1960s onwards, a movement complemented by the far-reaching political decentralisation measures of the 1980s. The result in both countries is a myriad of new actors in the local scene, whether they are central government agencies, regional directors, presidents of regional and departmental councils or city mayors, all of whom wish to share in the making and implementation of policy.

Governance is about the greater interdependency of the public and the private sectors. It involves a redefinition of what is public and what is private. New forms of urban governance are best manifested in the various and diverse types of public–private partnership that we describe in both countries. There were important variations between England and France, however. While private sector involvement in delivering services has increased in both countries, the underlying rationale differs. In England, during the Thatcher period, there was an ideologically informed preference for minimal state solutions; in France, the involvement of private actors in service delivery is more of a pragmatic response to the functional weakness of French local authorities and the power of private utility groups. Reformers in England believed in the superiority of business management methods, but the new public management has a much weaker resonance in France where the modernisation of the public sector has been undertaken as a means of defending the public service against the neo-liberal challenge (Hayward 1998).

We treat governance mainly as a dependent variable, mediated by the three independent variables of national context, sector and locality. The preceding six chapters identify and explain the move from government to governance according to country, sector and locality. The independent variables – countries, sectors, cities – are themselves influenced by broader environmental processes of change. Thus, national contexts were not static; both countries faced common external and comparable internal pressures. Change affected policy sectors: the impact of Europeanisation and internationalisation transformed the nature of local economic development; and new ideas influenced secondary education. Cities have also adapted to their changing internal and external environments; urban governance is a specific form of governance in cities. In the main body of this final chapter, we now consider how governance is mediated by the variables of country, sector and city.

National contexts

Throughout this book we have been interested in the extent to which state traditions, constitutional arrangements, bureaucratic structures and political values affect the administration of public policy. Institutional accounts of decision-making examine the importance of history, key events, legal systems, bureaucratic structures, conventions and norms (March and Olsen 1989). In essence, the new institutionalist project aims to show that the institutions of the state count (Steinmo et al. 1992; Evans et al. 1985). The habits and traditions of action have a salience far above the importance of transnational economic pressures or social structures. Arguments based upon national context implicitly challenge ideas of convergence across political systems and assume that policy change is dependent upon embedded, nationally specific, institutional structures.

In chapter 1, we interpret the comparative politics literature on English and French central–local policy-making as a good account of the 'most different systems' approach. The two nations present many obvious contrasts. To quote Wright (1996), Franco-English comparisons invariably conclude by affirming 'fundamental similarities masking essential differences'. While England and France share similar levels of economic development and both are unitary states, different principles and historical traditions govern their sub-central politics. Chapter 1 considers these traditions. Despite its shortcomings, the classic analysis captured much of the essence of English and French local politics up until the end of the 1970s, and in certain respects beyond. In important respects, reforms of the two countries' sub-central political systems have adapted rather than transformed existing patterns. The decentralisation reforms consolidated many existing practices in the French system of sub-central government. They did not fundamentally alter the organisational traits of French local government, which was marked by communal fragmentation, a weak fiscal base, organisational interdependence and external dependency; on the other hand, they did broaden the horizons and policy ambitions of local authorities. In the English case, we demonstrate in chapter 2 that the erosion of elected local government and the decline in importance of multi-functional organisations has been over-stressed (John 1994).

French academic criticisms of the governance approach often reveal their cultural blindness. Governance belongs to Anglo-Saxon liberal democracies with their belief in market values and competition, but is inconsistent with French republicanism. The institutional reading in the French context is certainly strengthened by the role of the state. French local authorities have to contend with the ideology of the state as the embodiment of universally shared values in a manner which has no equivalent in England (Birnbaum 1985). The state is superior to particularistic interests such as localities, political parties, interests or private firms. The state has a public service mission to ensure equality of treatment for all French citizens. The belief in equality and the superiority of public service over private provision act as powerful constraints, indeed structural barriers to certain UK-style developments. This belief in equal treatment under state tutelage was fully apparent when considering the sector of secondary education, but it has a more general application.

Though contractual processes have generally been interpreted as a form of French-style local governance, they can also be interpreted in a manner consistent with established French state traditions. Mabileau (1997) argues the case strongly. He contends that state actors were the most important in defining policy objectives in programmes such as City Contracts, State–Region plans and the University 2000 scheme. If anything, these procedures empowered state actors in areas from which they had traditionally been absent. In urban policy, for instance, prefects were granted the power to act (*pouvoir de substitution*) in place of local authorities in deciding the attribution of the minimum income and the allocation of social housing. In the 1988–93 Socialist government's flagship City Contract (*contrat de ville*) programme, urban policy networks were co-ordinated by state actors (Main 1991). However democratic their initial inspiration, moreover, the State–Region planning contracts have been a means of limiting the autonomy of French regions and securing central state policy objectives. These statist tendencies have been reinforced by the Jospin government. The Chevènement law of July 1999 empowered prefects, by allowing the territorial representative of the state to insist upon supra-communal forms of local taxation against the wishes of individual communes. These examples are consistent with French top-down administrative traditions whereby the state gives a lead and obliges local authorities and other partners to follow.

On the other hand, we observe in chapter 1 that 'steering at a distance' is quite consistent with broader governance developments. French-style governance is best embodied in various contractual processes that have produced unpredictable outcomes. Through its use of contracts, the French state has begun to operate in a more flexible manner in an attempt to mobilise resources beyond its control. Though the aim is to give a direction to negotiated policies, contractual procedures are inherently unstable. They involve negotiation between partners with the status of formal equals. They represent an important break with universal values of republicanism and the belief in the superiority of the state. They can produce outcomes that are variable across the national territory.

There was little contact between centre and periphery in the traditional model of English central–local relations. The British 'dual polity' suffered from dogmatic policy-making on account of a central government that pushed through policy with little consultation because it had few links with local authorities. Ashford's innovative portrayal of English local politics made little reference to political choice exercised within inter-organisational policy networks. There were some simple institutional facts behind this analysis. Local authorities enjoyed a monopoly of public sector decision-making within their domain, such as social services, housing, education and transport. With weak central–local linkages, local councils were insulated from wider local and national political power holders. There was little need to negotiate with other decision-makers or to build horizontal relationships with public and private agencies. In most cities, a 'dual elite' of local politicians and selected council officials usually controlled policy. There was little central government intervention in the day-to-day running of councils and a low involvement of local pressure groups.

This framework has changed dramatically since the 1970s. Reforms have undermined the traditional dominance of local authorities whose powers have been reduced by central government initiatives. Encroaching central government influences have been documented extensively (Stewart and Stoker 1989; John 1994). In no other western European state has central government pushed through such radical changes in the way in which services are administered, particularly the extent of privatisation, contracting and marketisation. The effect on subnational government, which, in the years after 1945, was given the task of administering vast tracts of the welfare state, has been to limit its discretion and autonomy and to transfer the control of services such as housing, education and transport to private or unelected bodies.

There is continuity and change in both countries. The importance of continuity should not be underestimated. It flows from the longevity of institutions that have established ways of processing issues and the existence of precise organisational cultures. Policy change is invariably incremental. Country specific explanations retain their strong explanatory power. The persistence of overarching national frameworks does not indicate stability, however. The governance perspective implies that change has occurred. Indeed, the direction of change is rather similar in England and in France. In both countries, institutional fragmentation has encouraged closer inter-organisational co-operation. The nature and the number of local policy actors have changed and in both countries new actors have emerged. A new style of partnership politics is evident in both cases. Moreover, substantive policy dilemmas are comparable. To varying degrees, city governments in both countries have developed inter-organisational networks as a response to the changing conditions of local governance.

In chapter 1, we pose the question of whether governance signified a trend towards policy convergence. While common pressures do not necessarily imply convergent responses, and while policy change is interpreted according to national cultures, we conclude that there has been some narrowing of previously highly distinctive institutional and ideational patterns. Even when the case for policy change is the most convincing, however, it falls short of declaring that the two countries have converged. Changes are processed in accordance with national traditions. In the French case, state actors have reinvented their roles and have even reasserted their power (Wright 1995). In England, in spite of extensive central government reforms of its finances, structures and functions during the 1980s, local government remains as the funder and main policymaker for most of the services which it administered at the end of the 1970s.

At the same time, there is no escaping the changed environment of local politics in all four cities we studied. The actors that local politicians have to operate with, the types of policies they have to formulate and the wider consequences of their decisions are vastly different from what they were in the late 1970s. In France the system is far more open and policy more unpredictable than before 1982 in particular. New decision-makers, such as departments and regions, have real power. The central state has decentralised many functions, budgets and staffs. Regional prefects are important actors, particularly in the process of drawing up the State–Region plans. New policy sectors, such as European funding, have emerged. Mayors have to build wider coalitions than they used to and politics has a more interdependent and networked character than hitherto.

Policy sectors

Policy sector approaches argue in favour of patterned relationships in the same policy sectors across comparable countries. Defined in a strong sense, a policy sector is a 'multi-levelled social structure' (Benson 1982). From this viewpoint, sectors are structures and are as identifiable (and impermeable) as institutions.

Like institutions, sectors have their own rules, customs and internal hierarchies. Each has its own power structure. There are obvious similarities between approaches based on policy sectors, and those preferring the metaphors of policy subsystems: whirlpools or triangles of actors which dominate decision-making in sectors like agriculture or energy (see Jordan 1990 for a review).

The basic presuppositions of such approaches have been challenged. Many writers believe that the stable policy-making subsystems which dominated the politics of sectors like agriculture and energy have now weakened. Instead of closed policy communities, there are now more diffuse issue networks of actors (Heclo 1978). There are more participants in decision-making; policy issues are more complex; and there are more links between policy sectors, such as the environment and agriculture. The idea that a particular sector creates a form of politics seems less credible when types of policy-making increasingly merge into each other.

By selecting two conceptually distinct policy sectors – economic development and secondary education – we accept that policy sector provides an important conceptual tool for differentiating distinct arenas of public policy. Detailed examination of local economic development and sub-national secondary education in England and France effectively demonstrate that the types of actor vary somewhat according to policy sector in both countries. Whilst economic development mobilises a broad coalition of actors from the public, private and voluntary sectors, secondary education remains prone to professional and bureaucratic influences.

Economic development is hard to define. One definition is that of any public or private action which is thought to improve the economy of a local area (Campbell 1990). As such it covers a wide range of policies and economic projects are often hybrids between activities such as education, housing, transport, tourism and European liaison. The economic development networks we uncovered in our French and English cities were far removed from the social closure model described by writers on British policy networks (Rhodes 1988). They bridged diverse interests and mobilised participants from various backgrounds. Economic development networks demonstrate some similar features across France and England. In both countries, and in all four cities, there was a triad of actors who are involved in economic development: they comprised local politicians, representatives of local economic interests and regional state officials. The similarity in the types of actors reflected the common problems each country faced in economic development.

Because economic development cross-cuts into different kinds of issues and because it is hard to prohibit any authority from becoming involved in it, many agencies are involved. The agencies concerned with economic development were comparable (but not identical) on both sides of the Channel. In England and in France there are several ministries at central government level with an economic development function. There are departments concerned with planning and urban development, education, training and economic competitiveness. Each ministry has local field or special purpose agencies. Second, most locally elected bodies wish to play a role in economic development. These range from small municipalities worried about inward investment and local employment, to larger authorities with planning functions that take a more strategic view. The increased involvement of economic actors was a central feature of city governance as uncovered in chapters 6 and 7. Business city interests manifested themselves most cogently in larger cities where governing processes were more complex and where the stakes of international metropolitan competition were higher. Economic, social and political elites need to have a wide perspective on governing affairs so as to be able to rise above the inevitable conflicts that emerge in city spaces. In all cases, business involvement was far more important in economic development than in secondary education.

There are important qualifications to the conclusion of increased business influence. There are structural limitations to business involvement in European cities. The strength of the state in England and France ensures that public sector actors, either from local planning and transportation agencies or from the decentralised bureaux of the central state, tend to monopolise decisions on land use, transportation and urban development. The role of the central state is solidified through its control of local taxation and expenditure in England and by extensive central subsidies in both France and England. European business is far less autonomous and powerful than its American counterpart.

The involvement of economic actors in urban governance was affected by national contexts and city environments. National institutional variations were important. Thus, the French Chambers of Commerce were para-statal rather than purely private sector organisations. Though they were the genuine representatives of small and medium-sized local businesses, the privileged tax status of the chambers was resented by other business lobbies, organised in employer associations and amongst individual firms. French business appeared to be more divided than in England. City environments were arguably even more important than national contexts, insofar as larger cities demonstrated more complex patterns of governance than medium-sized ones.

Secondary education has particular qualities that distinguish it from economic development. The role of professional policy communities in particular sets secondary education apart. While economic development officers play an important role in their sphere, they do not wield expert power in closed networks in the way that education professionals do or have traditionally done. Education is a heavily regulated core state activity where national differences have traditionally been pronounced. No other arena of public policy is so redolent of national state traditions and institutional heritages. Secondary education networks were classically structured by the very different state traditions in the two countries. The French republican model, built upon the Revolution and a bitter church–state conflict, was propagated through a centralised, uniform and lay state education system. As education was linked to the process of nation-state building, uniformity and citizenship in a far more explicit manner than in England, the French state remains the principal player in secondary education policy-making. In England, the delivery of education services was a core feature of the dual state tradition, whereby local government implemented welfare state services.

Though educational relationships continue to have different dynamics in the two countries, there was a comparable evolution. Secondary education is not immune from the pressures of economic competition and new ideas. The governance approach in education implies the emergence of new ideas, actors and structures into a previously closed policy field; examples from England and France provided some support in this direction. There was also some evidence of policy transfer between the two countries. In England the Conservative government's reforms – especially the introduction of a national curriculum – appeared to borrow from a more directive French-style of management (Duclaud-Williams 1993). Reciprocally, reforms to the pattern of school management in France in the 1980s borrowed from the perceived English experience (Legrand and Solaux 1992) in areas such as pupil-centred learning and enhanced school autonomy.

The assertion of the importance of sectoral distinctions does not underplay policy change. Both economic development and secondary education were transforming from highly institutionalised structures to more open, more flexible but less transparent ones. This was manifestly the case in economic development where comparable actors featured in economic development networks in both countries. To a lesser extent, it was also the case for secondary education. In England the formerly tight educational decision-making networks have been superseded by looser ones, composed of headteachers, chairs of boards of school governors and officials in the local education authority. In France, state-centred bureaucratic networks have – to some degree – been prised open to accommodate new actors in the sub-national regional and local authorities. The changing educational relationships were of similar dimensions in both French cities.

The temporal dimension is extremely important when comparing policy sectors. If a comparable study had looked at secondary education and economic development in 1975, it would have discovered many more institutional differences in both sectors. Education was much more centralised in France and local government dominated the English system more unequivocally. By the mid-1990s local government actors had become more important in France, but less influential the other side of the Channel. In 1975 economic development was largely state driven in France, and a local planning matter in England. In economic development policy at the end of the twentieth century there was a broader range of actors in France, and a similar collection of them in England. In part these similarities derive from the growth of economic policy-making as a sector since the 1970s: structural economic change, competition between cities, and central and local policy initiatives have encouraged new forms of co-operation between political and economic actors. The operation of policy sectors thus depends upon country contexts and local environments. Education appears more revealing of national state traditions and political cultures than economic development, which is more open to external influences.

Local contexts and effects

Each locality is shaped by a range of historical, socio-economic, cultural and political influences. City networks reflect variations between localities, as expressed in their specific local, political, cultural and institutional heritages. Local economic policy networks reflect the outlook of local elites, and may vary according to different patterns of business ownership, traditions of municipal intervention and the particularism of state field officials. Local education networks may be structured by factors such as socio-economic conditions, local religious alignments or the dynamism of local politicians or officials.

As chapters 6 and 7 reveal, patterns of local governance in Lille, Leeds, Rennes and Southampton were shaped by particular socio-economic, historical and cultural contexts. Each city had its own culture and its own particular ways of understanding the external world. The politics of place are important. This explains why there is no single model of local development; the Rennes model, for instance, depended upon a high degree of public sector intervention as well as upon a close consensus between elites on the virtues of local development that was lacking in Lille prior to the 1980s. The urban regime that came to dominate politics in Leeds emerged because of a type of business city interest that simply did not exist in Southampton. Sociological variables produce different types of public policy so that the provision of cultural services to a sophisticated middle-class electorate can have a tough economic rationale in one city, but not in another.

The urban governance perspective helped explain increased co-operation between political, economic and social actors based on mutual self-interest in an era of internationalisation, European integration and intense inter-urban competition. To an extent, all cities aspired to become entrepreneurial cities, with strong political leadership and co-ordinated administrative structures, with a powerful city vision, and with an ability to build local and regional partnerships and to cultivate good vertical links to regional, national and European levels. Not all cities were capable of this. Our four cities were differentiated by several criteria that influenced their ability to act as entrepreneurial cities. We consider that spatial organisation, city size, styles of political leadership, the nature of the policy sector and the national context form the principal criteria on which to base comparative judgements.

The first dimension of comparison related to the spatial organisation of cities. Two of our four cities (Lille and Southampton) were distinguished by their disaggregated political and administrative boundaries. In Lille, the complex local government structure, where power is divided between 85 communes and a powerful, but contested, urban community, as well as departmental and regional bodies, created a pattern of bargained governance. No single political leader could completely dominate metropolitan governance in Lille; Mauroy's influence depended upon building coalitions and promoting bipartisan consensus across organisations. In Southampton, local government boundaries were equally disaggregated (between Southampton City and Hampshire County Councils). In the southern UK city, however, there was no equivalent strong local political leadership; nor did political parties provide cohesive linkage between the different organisations involved in city governance. In contrast, our other cities, Leeds and Rennes, had more compact administrative and political structures. The concise spatial organisation of Leeds, where the city council dominated decision-making, and its strong traditions of single party control encouraged the formation of a hierarchical and exclusionary decision-making system, based on tight, politically driven, policy networks. Leeds City Council was able to negotiate with local business interests from a position of strength. Rennes was an equally compact and almost equally spatially unified city, with the commune of Rennes controlling its outlying districts and relying on strong party control to implement policies such as tax harmonisation across the urban district. Indeed, in terms of local government relationships, the pairing of cities works better between Southampton and Lille, and between Leeds and Rennes. In other respects, however, the essential distinction is between the larger and smaller cities.

The contrast between large and medium-sized cities provides a second dimension of comparison. The metropolitan character of large cities and their exposure to international and European economic forces opened them up to new forms of urban governance, as chapters 6 and 7 investigate. Policy-makers in Lille were driven by the belief that, in a context of internationalised economic exchanges, only cities of at least 1 million inhabitants are visible and viable. Hence they made efforts to promote a metropolitan-wide identity and strengthen ties with the business community. Elites voiced similar justifications for closer public–private co-operation in Leeds. The particular form of urban governance uncovered in Lille and Leeds – the formation of long-term coalitions between local politicians and businesses – bore certain similarities to the 'urban regimes' of American cities (John and Cole 1998). In Leeds, local collaboration with business had longer roots that had become manifest in the Leeds Initiative; in Lille, the hostility between the business community and the Socialist-dominated local authorities lessened after the great economic crisis of the 1980s. Both sides realised the importance of closer co-operation. While business interests also participated in politics in our other two cities, these relationships were much weaker. In Southampton, the business community was too weakly organised; in Rennes, a history of smooth co-operation between the Rennes townhall and local economic elites had been fractured by the mayor's ambitions and costly redevelopment proposals. While there was much co-operation between local councils and urban society in all four cities, the larger cases demonstrated more complex forms of governance than the medium-sized cities. Smaller cities are less exposed to external influences; larger cities are governed on the basis of more complex coalitions.

A third dimension of comparison related to the style of local political leadership. Political leaders appeared at the centre of networks in both countries (John 1998; John and Cole 1999). In each of our four cities the leader or mayor played a critical role, to a greater or lesser degree, in bringing together the other actors. In the French case, city mayors were central in structuring relationships. In Lille and in Rennes they were locked into powerful national networks and dominated or neutralised their local parties. In Lille, the power of the mayor was demonstrated by Mauroy's ability to mobilise public and private actors around large infrastructure projects, such as the TGV, Euralille, and the city's Olympic bid. In Rennes, the power of the mayor was demonstrated by Hervé's determination to persist with the VAL project in spite of local business opposition. French mayors appeared to have been liberated by the impact of the decentralisation reforms of the 1980s, which consolidated and strengthened their influence over local policy-making and broadened their scope of contacts, notably with representatives of urban society. English local leaders also performed an important role, especially by promoting large dynamic projects attracting generous local and central funding. In Leeds the leader of the council appeared in a very powerful position at the centre of local networks. English local leaders were less solidly implanted than their French counterparts. There were weaker patterns of central–local linkage, but stronger traditions of party control and a more collective management of local councils. Nonetheless, in both countries, visionary local political leadership could make a difference. Economic development projects such as Euralille in Lille or the Royal Armouries in Leeds depended on visionary leadership to give direction to the operation of urban networks and the new style of partnership politics. The mobilising qualities of local political leaders within networks proved crucial; where local political leadership was weak (Southampton), or contested (Rennes), networks stagnated. Where leadership was directive (Leeds) or genuinely negotiated (Lille), networks prospered. The networks in Leeds and Lille had high capacity, partly through the vision of the political leadership, whereas in Rennes and Southampton actors were less able to mobilise and to achieve their goals.

A fourth dimension for comparing cities related to sectoral differences. Though they differ markedly between the two nation-states, secondary education networks are quite similar within French and English localities. In spite of the contrasting character of the cities in each country, the administration of education concerns the same broad issues and is governed by identical legal frameworks. Local effects are difficult to measure in relation to secondary education on account of incongruous administrative structures; in neither country do the boundaries for the administration of education (the county in the English non-metropolitan areas, the academy in France) necessarily correspond with natural urban areas. This contrasts with economic development, where city administrations, the local bodies that are co-determinous with urban areas, tend to take the lead in local economic policy networks. In economic development the nature of the locality impinges far more upon the structure and functioning of local networks. There is a greater opportunity for local leaderships to bring about change. Local elite cultures are more differentiated. Above all, the performance of local economies can produce differences in the economic networks across cities.

City-based actors figured prominently in economic development networks in all four cities; secondary education networks were far less amenable to the particularities of cities (John 1998; John and Cole 2000). In France, secondary education networks involved regional state structures and elected regional authorities; city-based actors were of lesser importance, though complex local environments mediated the effects of nationally determined policies. City-based local government actors were much closer to the heart of sub-central secondary education decision-making in England; the local education authorities remained essential actors in both cities and prominent local politicians invested considerable political prestige in matters of education. In both cities, however, as elsewhere in England, the traditional local government actors were the principal losers of the Conservatives' education reforms; individual schools were promoted at the expense of local authorities, whose power was also checked by central government. City-specific interest became less important.

A final dimension related to country contrasts. While city networks varied according to sector, they were also influenced by national contexts. Though many similar trends could be identified in England and France, there were important differences. Cities were much larger in England, but there were more actors in France. There were more tiers of government and a wider variety of actors involved in the French case. The division of sub-national authorities into three or four layers with overlapping responsibilities created the potential for confusion. The complex structure of the central state and its omnipresence in French localities created many points of intersection between state officials and local representatives. There was potentially more of a problem of co-ordination and management of the different interests involved. This was illustrated in our big cities by the difference between the tight strategic network in operation in Leeds and the large, open, shifting network in Lille, with its myriad coalitions based on communal rivalries. Other national differences impacting upon city governance included the role of *cumul des mandats* and the effect of interlocking central–local networks. French local leaders retained a far greater visibility and legitimacy than their English counterparts.

Thus our cities were differentiated by contrasts between policy sectors, the nature of local political leadership, larger and smaller cities, their spatial dimension and administrative organisations and national contexts.

Countries, sectors and cities: concluding remarks

The implications of these results for our argument are complex. Our eight case studies all combined a national context, a policy sector and a city environment. In seeking to infer the relative importance of institutions, sectors and cities, the research concluded that they were interdependent. Rather than discovering that only national contexts are important or that variations occur principally according to sector or city, we observe that country, sector and city contexts all influenced and mediated the process of local governance. Our eight case studies produced eight separate versions of local governance, each with cognate and distinctive features. It was logically impossible hierarchically to differentiate between them. The conclusion to draw is that there is no necessary tendency towards either cross-national similarity based on common policy problems or divergence due to institutional variation. The dilemma of whether institutions, sectors or cities matter cannot be authoritatively resolved. It depends on how they interact with each other, and such contingencies depend on the variety of wider political and economic forces at work.

Local governance and the public sphere

The comparative approach shows how governance takes various forms according to country, sector and locality. There is no uniform pattern. There was a massive variety of political arrangements and practices across and between local political systems in the first place; flexibility, networks and fragmentation compound these variations. In this sense our four cities all display contrasting approaches to co-operation which reflect the nature of their towns, their political cultures, their levels of social capital and the balance of costs and benefits of co-operation. Politics has changed. Both political systems have adapted to create new forms of political relationships. The form of governance is shaped by these national, policy and city contexts. As developed in chapter 1 and applied throughout subsequent chapters, the move from government to governance is more pronounced in England than in France, in economic development rather than in secondary education and in larger rather than smaller cities.

Advocates often present governance as a better form of politics. There are strong normative underpinnings to governance, especially when it expresses a preference for minimal state solutions (Osborne and Gaebler 1992). Rather than assuming there is a global paradigm of new forms of public sector management, we seek to avoid both simplistic notions of convergence and a commitment to integration as a desirable outcome. While local governance can imply an opening up of politics, it also raises serious problems of political accountability.

Governance poses new dilemmas of political control and review. These are acute in relation to styles of public sector management, the proliferation of non-elected public agencies and the internal functioning of policy networks themselves. The blurring of public and private boundaries lies at the heart of the governance idea. With the growth of 'contracting out' in both countries, private or hybrid actors – firms and mixed economy societies – can be vested with precise public service missions. In both countries, the reformers have identified deficiencies of classical bureaucratic service delivery forms and have attempted to remedy them. In England, there has been a preference for the minimal state; in France, public management reforms have been aimed to create a 'better state'.

Since the 1960s, England and France have experienced a steady stream of administrative reforms that seek to improve organisational performance. In England, new interpretations of accountability emerged under the impact of the Thatcher governments. From being defined as a problem of the public sphere, accountability became reinterpreted as one aspect of the new public management. Given a push by the Thatcher administration, English public sector actors (including local authorities) adopted many private sector techniques and objectives, such as quasi-markets, competitive tendering, contracting out and devolved management (Lowndes 1997). Conservative governments insisted upon the accountability of service deliverers to consumers and the adoption of 'good' governance practices within organisations, such as performance indicators and a focus on the user or consumer. Such a shift was manifest in the local sphere where major changes such as compulsory competitive tendering and consumer 'choice' were imposed on English local government in the 1980s.

There was no real French equivalent of the new public management. Shorn of the ideological New Right underpinnings of the Thatcher programme, however, many similar prescriptions emerged. French governments from that of Rocard (1988–91) onwards pledged to modernise the public sector and to introduce organisational reforms. Changing organisational practices were introduced through new contractual relationships between public sector organisations, greater administrative decentralisation, enhanced budgetary autonomy, the increased use of performance indicators and a more commercial outlook for public service agencies. As we observe in chapter 5, the Education ministry, which for many is the exemplar of an inward-looking administration, has been amongst the most innovative in experimenting with various modern management techniques. While the precise solutions were nationally distinctive, policy-makers in England and France both recognised the need to adapt top-heavy bureaucratic administrations to perform more flexible tasks and to engage fully in inter-organisational relationships.

An increasingly opaque institutional environment has created comparable concerns of accountability in both countries. One consequence of the 'hollowing out' of the state in England has been the rapid growth of non-elected public agencies (alternatively known as EGOs (extra-governmental organisations) or quangos (quasi-autonomous non-governmental organisations)) performing executive functions in spheres such as housing, education, prisons and health. There is clearly an accountability gap or deficit in these organisations that are responsible for the administration of much public policy and public expenditure. Established by acts of parliament, these agencies do not fit into normal understandings of political accountability. In 1996, there existed 5750 such bodies (de Beer 1997), accounting for half of the public expenditure of elected local government. In an apparent breach of the doctrine of individual ministerial responsibility, ministers have refused to answer questions in select committee enquiries relating to the operations of such agencies, as opposed to the general policy underpinning their administration (Dowding 1995b: 155). Non-elected public agencies enjoy a large measure of independence from parliamentary scrutiny; hiving off public functions to EGOs thus minimises the inconvenience of political accountability. The process of appointments to these organisations has been a non-transparent one: the nomination of the chief executives is in the gift of the incumbent government, allowing for accusations of patronage. Moreover, the distribution of functions between these and other public sector bodies is confused and arcane, as chapter 4 demonstrates with the case of the Training and Enterprise Councils.

In France, there has been a less remarked upon, but equally remarkable growth in non-elected public agencies. There now exist almost 20,000 non-elected inter-communal bodies in France, organised under eight different types of inter-communal agreement (Ascher 1998; Marcou 2000).[1] These inter-communal associations escape serious public scrutiny, especially since decentralisation has loosened the strict financial controls previously exercised by state tutelage authorities. There is an obvious problem of political accountability of these bodies, which often have budgets that dwarf those of the municipal councils (including that of the leading commune in a city). The process whereby representatives are selected to serve on the urban communities or urban districts is highly clientelistic. As members are indirectly elected after municipal elections, they are in fact selected by mayors, who each have a quota of places. Though they can claim a weak political legitimacy, these bodies have important budgets and functions; the consensus opinion is that technical experts exercise a preponderant influence within these bodies with few democratic safeguards.

The case of the Lille urban community (CUDL) illustrates the point. In legal terms, the CUDL is an extension of the communal structure, with decisions taken by the majority of the assembly, composed of representatives of the 85 communes. The CUDL has the size, technical expertise and budget to be a major actor in any development project. Its budget of 6 billion francs (in 1995) compared favourably with those of the three most important directly elected sub-national authorities: the commune of Lille (4 billion), the Nord/Pas-de-Calais region (4 billion) and the Nord departmental council (8 billion). It has service delivery responsibilities in the spheres of social housing, firefighting, transport, water, sewerage and highways. It is by far the largest employer of service personnel of any Lille organisation, with 3000 agents in 1996. The technical and professional expertise of CUDL officials – often emanating from the same technical corps as their counterparts in the national ministries – surpassed that of officials in the Lille municipal council and the Nord/Pas-de-Calais region. But they were not subject to any direct democratic control. We identified the emergence of city-wide political structures as an important feature of urban governance in chapter 7. The direct election of these city-wide authorities – one of the recommendations of the Mauroy Commission into local government reform – would enhance urban governance capacity and improve their political accountability.

The emergence of policy networks was identified as a critical feature of governance. In an increasingly interdependent world, decision-makers need to set up a dialogue with each other. To overcome the difficulties of co-operation, regular contact is the basis for the trust needed when an actor fears that he or she will lose out by making agreements. When they function effectively, networks allow the pooling of resources in favour of positive sum benefits; members of a network can become conscious of being policy stakeholders, with co-ownership of local public policies. Without networks, there would have been no Royal Armouries, no SRB bids, possibly no Euralille (though Hervé got his metro even without the support of the business community). There is also a sense in which networks open up closed political systems, by introducing fresh ideas, by promoting policy learning and because new actors infuse decision-making processes with renewed energy. For organisations with a heavy sense of the past and an inward-looking mentality, like Leeds City Council, competition and relationships with other organisations can loosen the past burden of internecine conflicts.

Whatever the advantages in terms of governance capacity, in both systems networking also signified secretive patterns of decision-making. Rather than lying between markets and hierarchies, networks functioned behind closed doors. Networks signified forms of private government, shielded from the limelight of public accountability. Whether or not decisions were preceded by public debate – which was more likely the case in England than in France – they were likely to be taken in closed relationships of restricted visibility. The problem was posed in rather different terms in the two countries: the concern for accountability in England stemmed from a belief expressed by many actors that far-reaching reforms had destroyed a previously straightforward accountability relationship. The concern for co-ordination in France reflected the disaggregation of what was previously claimed (excessively) to be a highly co-ordinated system, based around prefectoral oversight of local authorities and limited local autonomy.

Herein lies a paradox. If partnerships are to be a source of ideas for projects and a basis for co-operation rather than a symbolic cover for policies already decided elsewhere, they must be independent. Partnerships are a good forum for resolving conflict, building trust and instilling a sense of process. In certain cases – such as with the Leeds Initiative – partnerships can have the quality of autonomous political institutions, which establish their own organisational rules and governing norms. But this entails some independence from the political process, as well as an acceptance by the organisations involved that participants need to go along with the consensus built up during the meetings. This occurred with the Leeds Initiative. Although the agenda was very carefully prepared by the city's officers and many decisions were referred back to the council and other organisations between meetings, the Initiative meetings themselves created new projects which had to be followed up and reported back to the Initiative. For a period the Leeds Initiative itself appeared to be driving policy as much as the council's policy led the partnership. The blurring of responsibility and the various sources of initiative in governance relationships makes accountability harder to operate. Moreover, by stressing a consensual governing mode, partnerships elude real political problems. In fact, some participants of partnerships, particularly those from the private sector, argue that they need to be flexible and unaccountable to work.

The implications for democratic accountability are potentially serious. If the old politics was based on narrow collusion between local political and state elites (in France) or on a closed community of councillors and officers (in England), the new centres of decision-making responsibility are arguably even more difficult to identify. When there are different types of actors operating at various territorial tiers across contrasting policy sectors in a fast-changing and protean environment, policy itself becomes looser, evolutionary and contingent. The implications for democracy of the role of the private sector and of shifting networks are large. Though there are benefits of such a loose structure, there needs to be a better-thought-out relationship between the role of private sector actors and their links to public power, as it is articulated at different territorial levels.

Political leadership is central to the new governance. Political leaders have forged new coalitions. They have engaged in closer relationships with private and voluntary sector actors. To some extent, these developments have occurred in both countries, but the institutional design of French local government appears in most respects to allow for a more harmonious linkage of political accountability and the harnessing of governance capacity. In our two French cities, we did not discover the hollow core of unco-ordinated relationships we found in Southampton and to an extent in Leeds. Here the enhancing of the power of the elected leader was crucial in giving a new form of co-ordination in a more complex multi-agency pattern. Thus the leading mayors in Lille and Rennes were able to push for new visions and new projects in local economic development policy. They were able to build innovative coalitions of central and regional state, local public and private sector actors in a bid to prepare their cities for a more active European and international role. The absence of far-sighted and visible political leadership in the English case was striking throughout the comparison.

The case of Lille illustrates neatly the dilemmas of political leadership. One of the most interesting aspects of economic development in Lille was its combination of old and new styles of political governance. Economic development projects in Lille depended in part on a series of coalitions – public–private, intercommunal and local–state – but none of these coalitions would have materialised without the energy of the mayor, Mauroy, whose activism gave policy-making a coherence, identity and legitimacy wholly lacking in the UK case. Although there was little consultation before the Euralille development, there was no doubt who was responsible for it. Voters had a direct chance to pass judgement on Mauroy's efforts to redevelop Lille in the 1995 municipal elections – and they backed him. Thus in spite of the complexity of new governing relationships, it is still the mayor, with new powers and a new role, who is able to bring some coherence to a more uncertain and shifting world. Ironically, Ashford's (1982) conception is reversed. England now has flexible governance and extensive interpenetration of centre and locality; in France, strong local political leadership ensures that there is a sense of direction in the new mode of urban governance. Rather than England being overrationalised, it is overflexible, overpragmatic and ever shifting, whereas French mayors cling onto a belief in an integrated strategy. Whereas France probably needs more democratic safeguards against personal power, UK local governance certainly needs more powerful but accountable figures to pull the shifting framework together.

Notes

Chapter 1

1 We studied eight local policy networks: the economic development policy network in Leeds; the economic development policy network in Lille; the economic development policy network in Southampton; the economic development policy network in Rennes; the secondary education policy network in Leeds; the secondary education policy network for Lille; the secondary education policy network for Southampton; and the secondary education policy network for Rennes.

Chapter 2

1 The exact figure is difficult to determine with any degree of certainty. The 1971 law on fusing communes brought down the number of communes from around 38,000 to around 36,000, but the figure has gradually crept up: in 1998, there were 36,518 (INSEE 1999).

Chapter 4

1 These include legal provisions that individual communes must ensure that their local plans (*Plans d'occupation des sols* – POS) are consistent with the objectives outlined in the structure plans (*schémas directeurs*). Structure plans are drawn up by inter-communal syndicates in consultation with the state, the regional and departmental councils and the consular chambers. In theory all other tools of urban policy must be consistent with the structure plan.

Chapter 5

1 We draw a distinction here between a centralised model of secondary school management and more flexible patterns of local primary and nursery school management. Primary schools, which are built and financed by municipal councils, have always been embedded in local communities. Until the creation of the *collège* by the Haby law in 1976, most children only attended primary schools until the school-leaving age of 16. *Lycées* catered for an academically gifted minority. Even in the case of primary schools rooted in their local communities, however, we would emphasise the comparative importance of central regulation, especially in relation to curriculum and citizenship issues.

Chapter 6

1 Membership included the top officers and leading members of the council; the president, directors and director-general of the chamber; the chair and chief executive of the

TEC; the vice-chancellor of Leeds University; the principal and a professor of Leeds Metropolitan University; the regional director of the government office for Yorkshire and Humberside; the director of the theatre; the managing director of the *Yorkshire Post*; the chairman and chief executive of the UDC (until April 1995); the chief constable of West Yorkshire Police; and a representative from the regional TUC.

Chapter 7

1 A vast programme of school buildings was undertaken by the Nord/Pas-de-Calais regional council, more ambitious than in any other region outside of Ile-de-France. The regional council had to plan for an unprecedented increase in the numbers of pupils attending *lycées*: from 75,000 in 1986, to 110,000 in 1991. In the course of the Nord/Pas-de-Calais region's five-year investment plan of 1989–94 the region committed itself to 48 major infrastructure operations, of which 19 involved building new *lycées*, and 29 involved modernising, extending or renovating existing buildings. The bulk of these operations were completed by 1994 (DFIS 1995). By 2000, the proportion of the 16–18 age cohort attending *lycées* was just below the national average, as were success rates in the *baccalauréat*.

Chapter 8

1 These are the single-purpose syndicates (SIVU), the multi-purpose syndicates (SIVOM), the urban districts, the urban communities, town communities, city-wide communities, communities of communes and the *pays*. A distinction is normally drawn between inter-communal syndicates (SIVU and SIVOM), where communes delegate specific functions to joint boards; and the *établissements publics de coopération intercommunale* (EPCI), bodies recognised with an autonomous identity in French public law.

Bibliography

Agence d'Urbanisme de la Métropole Lilloise (1991) *Lille: devenir une métropole internationale*, Lille: 35.

Agence d'Urbanisme de la Métropole Lilloise (1993a) *La Stratégie Lille-TGV*, Lille: 27.

Agence d'Urbanisme de la Métropole Lilloise (1993b) *Schéma Directeur de Développement et d'Urbanisme de la métropole lilloise: avant-projet*, Lille: 216.

Allen, F. (1996) *Atlanta Rising*, Atlanta: Longstreet.

Alter, C. and Hage, J. (1993) *Organisations Working Together*, London: Sage.

Ambler, J. (1985) 'Neo-corporatism and the politics of French education', *West European Politics*, 8, 3: 23–42.

Ambler, J. (1995) 'Conflict and consensus in French education', paper presented to the ECPR Bordeaux joint sessions, April–May: 27.

Andrew, C. and Goldsmith, M. (1998) 'From local government to local governance – and beyond?', *International Political Science Review*, 19, 2: 101–17.

Antony, D. and Bourgeois, M. (1995) *Le Préfet de région et les services de l'état*, Besançon: Franche-Comté regional prefecture: 90.

Archambault, E. (1997) *The Non-profit Sector in France*, Manchester: Manchester University Press.

Archer, M.S. (1979) *Social Origins of Educational Systems*, London: Sage.

Ascher, F. (1994) 'Le partenariat public–privé dans le (re)développement: le cas de la France', in W. Heinz (ed.) *Partenariats public–privé dans l'aménagement urbain*, Paris: L'Harmattan, 197–247.

Ascher, F. (1998) *La République contre la ville: essai sur l'avenir de la France urbaine*, Paris: Editions de l'Aube.

Ashford, D. (1982) *British Dogmatism and French Pragmatism: Central–local Policy Making in the Welfare State*, London: Allen and Unwin.

Ashford, D. (1990) 'Decentralising France: how the socialists discovered pluralism', *West European Politics*, 13, 4.

Association des Maires de France (1989) 'Le guide du nouveau maire', *Départements et Communes*, 37, 50: 1–75.

Auby, J.-F. (1987) *Le Commissaire de la République*, Paris: PUF.

AUDIAR (1993) *Rennes, ville universitaire*, Rennes: AUDIAR.

AUDIAR (1994) *Le District de Rennes: un territoire, des hommes*, Rennes: AUDIAR.

Audit Commission (1989) *Urban Regeneration and Economic Development*, London: HMSO.

Aurousseau, J. (1993) 'Stratégie de l'état dans la région Nord/Pas-de-Calais', *Latitude 59–62I*, la lettre du préfet de la Région Nord/Pas-de-Calais, March: 16.

Axelrod, R. (1984) *The Evolution of Cooperation*, New York: Basic.

Axford, N. and Pinch, S. (1994) 'Growth coalitions and local economic development strategy in southern England', *Political Geography*, 13, 4: 344–60.

Bagnasco, A. and Le Galès, P. (eds) (1997) *Villes en Europe*, Paris: La Découverte.

Ball, S.J. (1994) *Education Reform: A Critical and Post-structural Approach*, Buckingham: Open University Press.

Ball, W. and Solomos, J. (eds) (1990) *Race and Local Politics*, London: Macmillan.

Balme, R. (1996) *Les Politiques du néo-régionalisme*, Paris: Economica.

Balme, R. and Bonnet, L. (1995) 'From regional to sectoral policies: the contractual relations between the state and the regions in France', in J. Loughlin and S. Mazey (eds) *The End of the French Unitary State: Ten Years of Regionalization in France, 1982–1992*, London: Frank Cass.

Balme, R., Faure, A. and Mabileau, A. (eds) (1999) *Les Nouvelles Politiques Locales: Dynamiques de l'action publique*, Paris: Presses de Science Po.

Baraize, F. and Négrier, E. (2000) 'Communautés d'agglomération et développement durable', paper presented to the colloquium on 'Décentralisation et développement durable', University of Reims, 10–11 May: 14.

Barber, M. (1996) *The National Curriculum: A Study in Policy*, Keele: Keele University Press.

Barges, R. (1990) 'La décentralisation du système éducatif dans le Nord/Pas-de-Calais', in Y. Mény (ed.) *Les Politiques décentralisées de l'éducation: analyse de quatre expériences régionales*, unpublished report for the French Ministry of the Interior.

Bassett, K. and Harloe, M. (1990) 'Swindon: the rise and decline of a growth coalition', in M. Harloe, C. Pickvance and J. Urry (eds) *Place, Policy and Politics: Do Localities Matter?*, London: Unwin Hyman.

Bastien, F. and Neveu, E. (eds) (1999) *Espaces publics mosaïques*, Rennes: Presses Universitaires de Rennes.

Batley, R. and Stoker, G. (1991) *Local Government in Europe*, Basingstoke: Macmillan.

Becet, J.-M. (1982) 'Le maire, statut et pouvoirs', *Pouvoirs*, 24: 135–58.

Becquart-Leclercq, J. (1976) *Paradoxes du pouvoir local*, Paris: Presses de la FNSP.

Belleret, R. (1998) 'Les priorités des présidents des vingt-deux régions métropolitaines', *Le Monde*, 30 April 1998.

Benko, G. (1994) 'Réseaux productifs et régulations politiques: dix ans de réflexions économiques sur les villes', *Les Annales de la Recherche Urbaine*, 64: 80–5.

Benko, G. and Lipietz, A. (eds) (1992) *Les Régions qui gagnent, districts et réseaux: les nouveaux paradigmes de la géographie économique*, Paris: PUF.

Bennett, C. (1991) 'What is policy convergence and what causes it?', *British Journal of Political Science*, 21: 215–33.

Bennett, R. (ed.) (1990) *Decentralisation, Local Government and Markets: Towards a Post-Welfare Agenda*, Oxford: Clarendon.

Bennett, R., Wicks, P. and McCoshan, A. (1994) *Local Empowerment and Business Services in Britain*, London: University of London Press.

Benoit-Guilbot, O. (1991) 'Les acteurs locaux du développement économique local: y a-t-il un effet localité', *Sociologie du Travail*, 4: 453–9.

Benson, J.K. (1982) 'A framework for policy analysis', in D. Rogers (ed.) *Interorganizational Coordination*, Iowa: Iowa University Press, 137–76.

Bernard, P. (1992) 'La fonction préfectorale au cœur de la mutation de notre société', *Revue Administrative*, 45, 2: 101–6.

Bernstein, R.-J. (ed.) (1985) *Habermas and Modernity*, Oxford: Blackwells.

Biarez, S. (1989) *Le Pouvoir local*, Paris: Economica.

Biarez, S. (1990) 'Le discours sur la métropole en France, nouvelle communication et nouveaux rapports dans le cadre de la décentralisation', *Revue International des Sciences Administratives*, 4: 739–66.

Biarez, S. (1993) 'Recomposition territoriale et urbaine en Europe', *Sciences de la Société*, 30: 103–22.

Biarez, S. (1996) 'Repenser la sphère locale selon l'espace public', paper presented to the French Political Science Association (AFSP) conference, Aix-en-Provence: 20.

Biarez, S. and Nevers, J.-Y. (eds) (1994) *Gouvernement local et politiques urbaines*, Grenoble: CERAT.

Birch, A.H. (1964) *Representative and Responsible Government*, London: Allen and Unwin.

Birnbaum, P. (1985) 'La fin de l'état?', *Revue Française de Science Politique*, 35, 6: 981–99.

Bishop, B. (1991) *The City in Western Europe: Toward the Ideal European City*, Leeds: Leeds City Council.

Bizet, J.-F. (1993) 'Les SEM et la nouvelle conception de l'aménagement', *Droit Administratif*, 20 September: 594–601.

Bleitrach, D. (ed.) (1980) *Classe ouvrière et social-démocratie: Lille et Marseille*, Paris: Editions Sociales.

Bloch, A. (1992) *The Turnover of Local Councillors*, York: Joseph Rowntree Foundation.

Bloch, A. and John, P. (1991) *Attitudes to Local Government: A Survey of Electors*, York: Joseph Rowntree Foundation.

Blondiaux, L., Marcou, G. and Rangeon, F. (eds) (1999) *La Démocratie locale: représentation, participation, espace public*, Paris: PUF.

Blowers, A. (1980) *The Limits of Power: The Politics of Local Planning Policy*, Oxford: Pergamon.

Bœuf, J.-L. (1997) 'Quinze ans de décentralisation', *Problèmes Politiques et Sociaux*, 787, July 11: 87.

Bonacich, P. (1987) 'Power and centrality: a family of measures', *American Sociological Review*, 52, 1: 170–1, 182.

Borraz, O. (1994) 'Le gouvernement des villes: une analyse comparée dans deux villes suisses et deux villes françaises', PhD thesis, Paris: IEP.

Borraz, O. (1998) *Gouverner une ville: Besançon, 1959–1989*, Rennes: Presses Universitaires de Rennes.

Boursin, J.-L. (1981) *L'Administration de l'éducation nationale*, Paris: PUF.

Boyer, A. (1998) 'L'état en région', *Administration*, 179: 17–73.

Boyne, G. and Ashworth, R. (1997) 'Party competition in English local government: an empirical analysis of English councils 1974–1994', *Policy and Politics*, 25, 2: 129–42.

Bréhier, T. (1994) 'Le conseil général, pierre angulaire de la politique française', *Le Monde*, 19 March.

Breuillard, M. (1993) 'Dynamics and room for manoeuvre in governance: the Channel Tunnel decision in France and Britain', in J. Kooiman, *Modern Governance*, London: Sage, 131–43.

Breuillard, M. (2000) *'Local government' et centralisation en Angleterre*, Paris: L'Harmattan.

Briggs, A. (1963) *Victorian Cities*, Harmondsworth: Penguin.

Brittany Regional Council (1992) *Schéma régional des formations: horizon 95*, Rennes.

Brittany Regional Council (1994) *Le Guide-éco 1995*, Rennes.

Brittany Regional Council (1995) *Contrat d'objectifs régional*, Rennes.

Broadfoot, P., Osborn, M., Gilly, M. and Paillet, A. (1985) 'Changing patterns of educational accountability in England and France', *Comparative Education*, 21, 3: 273–86.

Brown, W.P. (1990) 'Organized interests and their issue niches: a search for pluralism in a policy domain', *Journal of Politics*, 52, 2: 477–509.

Bruyelle, P. (1976) *Lille et sa communauté urbaine*, Paris: Documentation française.

Bruyelle, P. (1991) *La Communauté urbaine de Lille*, Paris: Documentation française.

Bulpitt, J. (1983) *Territory and Power in the United Kingdom*, Manchester: Manchester University Press.

Burgel, G. (1992) 'Comment peut-on être inter-communal?', *Pouvoirs Locaux*, 14: 55–7.

Burnham, J. (1998) 'Contrasts and contradictions in French regional policy', paper presented to the Association for the Study of Modern and Contemporary France conference, Bradford, 3–5 September.

Burnham, J. (2000) 'Public–private partnerships at the local level in France', paper presented to the PSA conference on Current Issues in British and French Public Administrative Reform, CIRSA, London, 20 September: 12.

Caillose, J. (1994) *Intercommunalités*, Rennes: Presses Universitaires de Rennes.

Caillose, J. and Le Galès, P. (1995) *Les SEML dans la gouvernance urbaine*, Toulouse, PIRVILLE research report.

Campbell, M. (ed.) (1990) *Local Economic Policy*, London: Cassell.

Canter-Kohn, R. (1991) 'Unité et multiplicité du réseau', *Pour*, 132: 131–8.

Carboni, F. (1991) *Rennes: métropole de l'ouest*, Rennes: Chamber of Commerce.

Castells, M. (1991) *The Informational City*, London: Edward Arnold.

Castells, M. and Godard, F. (1974) *Monopolville*, Paris: Mouton.

Cerny, P. (1997) 'Communication', in R.A.W. Rhodes, 'The new governance: governing without government', *Political Studies*, 45: 1–2.

Chaban-Delmas, J. and Monory, R. (1994) 'Poursuivre la décentralisation: réflexions sur le bilan et les perspectives de la décentralisation', Commission du Livre Blanc, Paris: Editions Pouvoirs Locaux.

Chamber of Commerce of Lille-Roubaix-Tourcoing (1991) *Les Grands Projets de la métropole lilloise*, Lille.

Chamber of Commerce of Lille-Roubaix-Tourcoing (1994) *Chiffres clés de l'agglomération*, Lille.

Chartres, J. and Honeyman, K. (eds) (1993) *Leeds City Business*, Leeds: Leeds University Press.

Chatrie, I. and Uhaldeborde, J.-M. (1995) *Partenariat public–privé et développement territorial*, Paris: Le Monde editions.

Chirache, S. (1990) 'L'école s'ouvre à l'entreprise', *Projet*, 223: 51–9.

Chirot, F. (1994) 'Rennes réconcilie la ville et la campagne', *Le Monde*, 20–21 February.

Clarke, M. and Stewart, J. (1994) 'The local authority and the new community governance', *Local Government Studies*, 20: 163–76.

Coing, H. (1977) *Des Patronats locaux et le défi urbain*, Paris: Editions du CRU.

Coing, H., de Lara, P. and Montano, I. (1989) *Privatisation et régulation des services urbains: une étude comparative*, Paris: LATTS.

Cole, A. (1997) 'Governing the academies: sub-central secondary education policy making in France', *West European Politics*, 20, 2: 137–56.

Cole, A. (1998) *French Politics and Society*, Hemel Hempstead: Prentice Hall.

Cole, A. (1999) 'The Service Public under Stress', *West European Policies*, 22, 4: 166–84.

Cole, A. and Drake, H. (2000) 'The Europeanisation of French polity? Continuity, change and adaptation', *Journal of European Public Policy*, 7, 1: 26–43.

Cole, A. and John, P. (1995a) 'Les réseaux locaux de politique publique, le cas de la métropole lilloise', in *Les Cahiers du CRAPS*, 21: 7–22.

Cole, A. and John, P. (1995b) 'Local policy networks in Britain and France: policy coordination in fragmented political sub-systems', *West European Politics*, 18, 4: 88–108.

Cole, A. and John, P. (1995c) 'Les réseaux décisionnels locaux en France et en Grande Bretagne', in P. Le Galès and M. Thatcher, *Les Réseaux de politiques publiques*, Paris: L'Harmattan, 211–27.

Collier, P. (1994) 'A new educational ethos? The great non-debate', in G. Raymond (ed.) *France during the Socialist Years*, Aldershot: Dartmouth, 200–21.

Cooke, P. and Morgan, K. (1998) *The Associational Economy*, Oxford: Oxford University Press.

Corbett, A. and Moon, B. (eds) (1996) *Education in France: Continuity and Change in the Mitterrand Years, 1981–1995*, London: Routledge.

Crossley, M. and Villiamy, G. (1984) 'Case-study research methods and comparative education', *Comparative Education*, 20, 2: 193–209.

Crozier, M. (1963) *Le Phénomène bureaucratique*, Paris: Seuil.

Crozier, M. (1992) 'La décentralisation est-elle une réforme de l'état?', *Pouvoirs Locaux*, 12: 130–4.

Crozier, M. (1994) 'L'analyse des systèmes bureaucratiques', *Pensée Politique*, 2: 158–77.

Crozier, M. and Friedberg, E. (1977) *L'Acteur et le système*, Paris: Seuil.

Crozier, M. and Thoenig, J.-C. (1975) 'La régulation des systèmes organisées complexes', *Revue Française de Sociologie*, 16: 1, 3–32.

Dahl, R. (1961) *Who Governs?* New Haven: Yale University Press.

de Beer, P. (1997) 'Le Livre vert des travaillistes', *Le Monde*, 30 July.

de Courson, J. (1994) *Le Projet de ville*, Paris: Syros.

de Forges, J.-M. (1989) *Les Institutions administratives françaises*, Paris: PUF.

Dearlove, J. (1973) *The Politics of Policy in Local Government*, Cambridge: Cambridge University Press.

Dearlove, J. (1979) *The Reorganisation of British Local Government: Old Orthodoxies and a Political Perspective*, Cambridge: Cambridge University Press.

Degenne, A. and Forsé, M. (1994) *Les Réseaux sociaux*, Paris: Economica.

Delcamp, A. (1992) 'La décentralisation française et l'Europe', *Pouvoirs*, 60: 149–60.

Delcamp, A. (1997) 'Le modèle français de libre administration face aux autres modèles européens', *Annuaire des Collectivités Locales*: 73–99.

Delévaux, C. and Gomez, R. (1991) 'Partenariat et réseaux', *Pour*, 132: 69–74.

Demailly, L. (1993) 'L'évolution actuelle des méthodes de mobilisation et d'encadrement des enseignants', *Savoir*, 5, 1: 24–46.

Demailly, L. (1999) 'Enjeux d'evaluation et régulation du système scolaire français', communication to the Office Social du Changement (OSC) Conference, Institut d'Etudes Politiques, Paris, 31 May.

Derouet, J.-L. (1991) 'Décentralisation et droits des usagers', *Savoir*, 3, 4: 619–41.

Deroy-Pineau, F. (1991) 'Réseaux sociaux et mobilisation de ressources', *Pour*, 132: 119–29.

DFIS (1995) 'Bilan du deuxième plan', internal note, Nord/Pas-de-Calais regional council.

Dion, S. (1986) *La Politisation des mairies*, Paris: Economica.

Dogan, M. and Kazancigil, A. (1997) *Comparing Nations: Concepts, Strategies, Substance*, Oxford: Blackwells.

Dogan, M. and Pelassy, D. (1990) *How to Compare Nations: Strategies in Comparative Politics*, New Jersey: Chatham House.

Douai, E. (1995) 'Les différents formes de partenariat public–privé en France', in I. Chatrie and J.-M. Uhaldeborde, *Partenariat public-privé et développement territorial*, Paris: Le Monde editions.

Douence, J.C. (ed.) (1988) *L'Action économique locale, décentralisation ou récentralisation*, Paris: Economica.

Douence, J.C. (1992) 'L'action économique locale', *Droit Administratif*, 20: 68–76.

Dowding, K. (1995a) 'Model or metaphor? A critical review of the policy network approach', *Political Studies*, 43, 1: 136–58.

Dowding, K. (1995b) *The Civil Service*, London: Routledge.

Drewe, P. and Hébrand, J. (1995) 'Le Nord de la France, région frontalière européenne: un laboratoire de l'intégration européenne', *Franse Nederlanden*, 20: 161–77.

DRIRE (1994) *Contrat du Plan 94/99: montants financiers*, Douai: DRIRE.

Duchemin, J. (1994) *L'Urbanisation progressive de la ville de Rennes*, University of Rennes, DESS thesis: 2.

Duclaud-Williams, R. (1993) 'The governance of education in Britain and France', in J. Kooiman (ed.) *Modern Governance*, London: Sage, 235–48.

Duclaud-Williams, R. (1994) 'The challenge to the state: the case of decentralisation in French education', *Manchester Papers in Politics*, 4: 2–41.

Duclaud-Williams, R. (1995) 'Educational adaptation and educational autonomy: a comparative study of the impact of economic change on educational policy in England and France', paper presented to the ECPR Bordeaux conference, April: 33.

Dunleavy, P. (1980) *Urban Political Analysis*, London: Macmillan.

Dunleavy, P. (1981) *The Politics of Mass Housing in Britain*, Oxford: Oxford University Press.

Dupoirier, E. (1998a) *Régions, la croisée des chemins*, Paris: Presses de Sciences Po.

Dupoirier, E. (1998b) 'L'offre identitaire des régions françaises et la construction des identités régionales', *Revue Internationale de Politique Comparée*, 5, 1: 21–34.

Dupuy, F. and Thoenig, J.-C. (1983) *Sociologie de l'administration française*, Paris: Armand Colin.

Dupuy, F. and Thoenig, J.-C. (1985) *L'Administration en miéttes*, Paris: Fayard.

Duran, P. (1999) *Penser l'action publique*, Paris: LGDJ.

Duran, P. and Hérault, B. (1992) 'L'administration à la découverte du politique: l'équipement en décentralisation', *Droit Administratif*, 20: 5–25.

Duran, P. and Thoenig, J.-C. (1996) 'L'état et la gestion publique territoriale', *Revue Française de Science Politique*, 45, 4: 580–622.

Durand, G. (1995) 'L'avenir des sociétés d'économie mixte locales', *Revue d'Economie Financière*, 289–98.

Durand-Prinborgne, C. (1989) 'La déconcentration', paper presented to the Institut Français des Sciences Administratives colloque, *L'Administration de l'éducation nationale*, Paris, 3–4 March: 11.

Durand-Prinborgne, C. (1990) 'De l'instruction au système éducatif', *Les Cahiers Français*, 249: 1–8.

Durand-Prinborgne, C. (1993) 'Acteurs, processus, leurs interrelations: état des lieux', *Savoir*, 5, 4: 593–620.

Dyson, K. (1980) *The State Tradition in Western Europe*, Oxford: Martin Robertson.

Eatwell, R. (ed.) (1996) *European Political Cultures: Conflict or Convergence*, London: Routledge.

Education – Economie (1993) 'Dossier: l'academie de Lille', 18: 23–33.

El Guedj, F. (1992) 'Lille-métropole: la maison commune?', *Pouvoirs Locaux*, 14: 110–17.

Elkin, S. (1987) *City and Regime in the American Republic*, Chicago: University of Chicago Press.

Etzioni, A. (ed.) (1969) *The Semi-Professions and their Organisation: Teachers, Nurses and Social Workers*, New York: The Free Press.

Evans, P., Rueschmeyer, D. and Skocpol, T. (eds) (1985) *Bringing the State Back In*, Cambridge: Cambridge University Press.

Famery, K. (1992) 'Les paradoxes du réseau: mode d'intervention ou mode d'analyse?', *Pour*, 134: 107–13.

Faure, A. (1991) 'Pouvoir local en France: le management mayoral à l'assaut du clientèlisme', *Politiques et Management Public*, 9, 3: 116–32.

Faure, A. (1994) 'Les élus locaux face à l'épreuve de la décentralisation', *Revue Française de Science Politique*, 44, 3: 462–79.

Ferré-Lemaire, I. (1996) *Maitriser l'urbanisme 1: la loi et le sol*, Paris: Editions de l'Atelier.

Fialaire J. (1992a) 'L'évolution récente des compétences décisionnels du recteur d'académie', *Savoir*, 4, 1: 55–78.

Fialaire, J. (1992b) 'Bilan de la décentralisation dans les lycées et collèges', *Savoir*, 4, 2: 216–22.

Fialaire, J. (1995) 'Le processus de réforme de l'enseignement en Grande-Bretagne depuis 1988', *Savoir*, 7, 3: 467–84.

Fixari, D. and Kletz, F. (1996) 'Pilotage d'établissement scolaire: auto-évaluation et évaluation', *Politiques et Management Public*, 14, 2: 71–103.

Flament, C. (1992) 'La figure paradoxale du réseau', *Pour*, 134: 91–5.

Fontaine, J. (1989) 'Rennes: mandat electif et gestion du personnel', *Economie et Humanisme*, 305: 57–66.

Fontaine, J. (1990) 'La décentralisation du système éducatif des collèges et des lycées dans l'académie de Rennes', in Y. Mény (ed.) *Les Politiques décentralisées de l'éducation: analyse de quatre expériences régionales*, GRAL-CNRS report for the French Ministry of the Interior.

Fontaine, J. (1992) 'Une région, des lycées, un rectorat: l'incidence politique de la décentralisation en Bretagne', *Savoir*, 4, 4: 669–91.

Fontaine, J. (1996) 'Evaluation des politiques publiques et sciences sociales utiles', *Politix*, 36: 51–71.

Fontaine, J. and Le Bart, C. (eds) (1994) *Le Métier de l'élu local*, Paris: L'Harmattan.

Fontaine, J. and Warin, P. (2000) 'Retour des évaluations: les politiques publiques territorialisées entre affichage et incertitude de leur régionalisation', *Pole-Sud*, 12: 1–12.

Fournier, B. (1995) 'La formation professionelle gérée par les conseils régionaux: d'une décentralisation à l'autre', *Premières Synthèses*, 55, 100: 1–8.

French Interior Ministry (1990) *Taxe professionnelle et intercommunalité: dix exemples*, Paris.

French Industry Ministry (1995) 'Spécial guide régions', *Industries*, 4, February.

Friedberg, E. (1974) 'Administration en entreprises', in M. Crozier (ed.) *Où va l'administration française?* Paris: Edition d'Organisation.

Friedberg, E. (1993) *Le Pouvoir et le règle*, Paris: Seuil.

Friend, J.K., Power, J.M. and Yewlett, C.J.L. (1974) *Public Planning: The Intercorporate Dimension*, London: Tavistock.

Gabey, F. (1993) 'Métropole lilloise, l'Europe à très grande vitesse', *Urbanisme*, 263: 28–54.

Gachelin, C. (1992) 'Métropolisation: dynamiques de métropolisation, hypothèses pour la métropole lilloise', Lille: Agence d'Urbanisme de la Métropole lilloise: 17.

Gambetta, D. (1988) 'Can we trust trust?', in D. Gambetta, *Trust Making and Breaking Cooperative Relations*, Oxford: Basil Blackwell.

Game, C. and Leach, S. (1995) *The Role of Parties in Local Democracy*, Commission for Local Democracy Research Report No. 11. London: Municipal Journal.

Garnier, M. (1999) 'Trois indicateurs de performance des lycées', Paris: National Education Ministry.

Garraud, P. (1989) *Profession homme politique: la carrière politique des maires urbains*, Paris: L'Harmattan.

Garraud, P. (1990) 'Le maire urbain français: un entrepreneur politique', *Institut de Ciencies Politiques i Socials de Barcelona*, 10: 3–31.

Gaudin, J.-P. (1995) 'Politiques urbaines et négociations territoriales: quelle légitimité pour les réseaux de politiques publiques?', *Revue Française de Science Politique*, 45, 1: 31–56.

Gaudin, J.-P. (1996) 'Les politiques publiques entre arênes professionelles et dispositions citoyennes', paper presented to the French Political Science Association (AFSP) conference, Aix-en-Provence: 17.

Gaudin, J.-P. (1998) 'La gouvernance moderne hier et aujourd'hui: quelques éclairages à partir des politiques publiques française', *Revue Internationale des Sciences Sociales*, 155: 51–60.

Gaudin, J.-P. (1999) *Gouverner par contrat: l'action publique en question*, Paris: Presses de Sciences Po.

Gaxie, D. (ed.) (1997) *Luttes d'institutions: enjeux et contradictions de l'administration territoriale*, Paris: L'Harmattan.

Gerbaux, F. and Muller, P. (1992) 'Les interventions économiques locales', *Pouvoirs*, 60: 99–114.

GESI (1988) *Rennes, capitale régionale*, Rennes: AUDIAR.

Gilbert, G. and Guengant, A. (1992) 'L'émiettement communal et la fiscalité', *Pouvoirs*, 60: 85–98.

Giblin-Delvallet, B. (1990) *La Région, territoires politiques: le Nord/Pas-de-Calais*, Paris: Fayard.

Goldsmith, M. (1990) 'Local autonomy: theory and practice', paper presented to the ECPR Joint Sessions, Bochum, Germany, 2–7 April: 32.

Goldsmith, M. (1993) 'The Europeanisation of local government', *Urban Studies*, 30, 4–5: 683–99.

Goldsmith. M. (1997) 'Changing patterns of local government', *ECPR News*, 9, 1: 6–7.

Grant, W. (1993) *Business and Politics in Britain*, Basingstoke: Macmillan.

Green, C. (1981) *Power and Party in an English City*, London: Allen and Unwin.

Green, H. and Booth, P. (1996) 'Urban policy, administration and land-use planning in Lille: implementing the contrat de ville in Lille', *European Urban and Regional Studies*, 3, 1: 19–31.

Grémion, P. (1976) *Le Pouvoir péripherique: bureaucrates et notables dans le système public français*, Paris: Seuil.

Grémion, C. (1989) 'Les décentralisateurs déstablisés', *Pouvoirs*, 49: 81–92.

Grémion, C. (1991) 'Décentralisation an X', *French Politics and Society*, 9, 3–4: 32–42.

Grémion, C. (1992) 'Région, département, commune: le faux débat', *Pouvoirs*, 60: 55–65.

Griffith, J. (1966) *Central Departments and Local Authorities*, London: Allen and Unwin.

Guengant, A. (1989) *Les Nouveaux Couts d'urbanisation*, Rennes: AUDIAR.

Guengant, A. (1990) 'La réforme communale: solution ou enlisement?', *Chroniques de la SEDEIS*, 11: 380–5.

Gugliemi, G.J. (1994) *Introduction au droit des services publics*, Paris: Librairie Générale du Droit et de la Jurisprudence.

Guigou, J.-L. (2000) 'Développement des territoires et institutions: un lien de plus en plus étroit', paper presented to the colloquium on *Décentralisation et développement durable*, University of Reims, 10–11 May: 6.

Guini, V. (1990) 'Les collectivités locales entrent à l'école', *Projet*, 223: 42–50.

Gyford, J. and James, M. (1983) *National Parties and Local Politics*, London: Allen and Unwin.

Gyford, J. (1983) *The New Urban Left: Origins, Style and Strategy*, London: University College London.

Gyford, J. (1984) *Local Politics in Britain*, London: Croom Helm.

Gyford, J. (1985) *The Politics of Local Socialism*, London: Allen and Unwin.

Gyford, J. (1991) *Citizens, Consumers and Councils*, Basingstoke: Macmillan.

Gyford, J. and James, M. (1983) *National Parties and Local Politics*, London: Allen and Unwin.

Hall, P. (1986) *Governing the Economy: The Politics of State Intervention in Britain and France*, Cambridge: Polity.

Halls, W.D. (1976) *Education, Culture and Politics in Modern France*, Oxford: Pergamon Press.

Harding, A. (1989) 'Central control in British urban economic development programs', *Political Quarterly*, Supplement, 21–38.

Harding, A. (1991) 'The rise of urban growth coalitions UK style?', *Environment and Planning C: Government and Policy*, 9: 3.

Harding, A. (1994a) 'Urban regimes and growth machines: toward a cross-national research agenda?', *Urban Affairs Quarterly*, 29: 356–82.

Harding, A. (1994b) 'Analysing European trends in urban policy: is there a role for the "new community power"', paper presented to the ESRC local governance programme workshop on community power and participation, LSE, 19–20 December.

Harding, A. (1995) 'European city regimes? Inter-urban competition in the new Europe', paper presented to the ESRC local governance conference, University of Exeter, 19–20 September: 50.

Harding, A. (1998) 'American urban political economy, urban theory and UK research', paper presented to the UK Political Studies Association conference, University of Keele: 11.

Harloe, M., Pickvance, C.G. and Urry, J. (eds) (1990) *Place, Policy and Politics: Do Localities Matter?* London: Unwin Hyman.

Hassenteufal, P. (1995) 'Do policy networks matter? Lifting descriptif et analyse de l'état en interaction', in P. Le Galès and M. Thatcher (eds) *Les Réseaux de politiques publiques*, Paris: L'Harmattan, 91–107.

Hatzfeld, H. (1991) 'La décentralisation du système éducatif: les régions à l'épreuve', *Politiques et Management Public*, 9, 4: 23–49.

Hayward, J. (1973) *The One and Indivisble French Republic*, London: Weidenfeld and Nicholson.

Hayward, J. (1982) 'Mobilising private interests in the service of public ambitions: the salient element in the dual French policy style', in J. Richardson (ed.) *Policy Styles in Western Europe*, London: Allen and Unwin, 111–40.

Hayward, J. (1998) 'Moins d'état ou mieux d'état: the French response to the neo-liberal challenge', in M. Maclean (ed.) *The Mitterrand Years: Legacy and Evaluation*, London: Macmillan, 23–35.

Heclo, H. (1978) 'Issue networks and the executive establishment', in A. King (ed.) *The New American Political System*, Washington DC: American Enterprise Institute.

Heclo, H. and Wildavsky, A. (1974) *The Private Government of Public Money*, London: Macmillan.

Heinz, W. (1994) *Partenariats public–privé dans l'aménagement urbain*, Paris: L'Harmattan.

Helin, J.-C. (1992) 'Le préfet, les élus et le juge', *Les Petites Affiches*, 151: 12–16.

Herrant, T. (1991) 'La caisse des dépôts et la dette locale', *Revue d'Economie Financière*, a special issue on 'La caisse des dépôts et consignations: 175 ans', November 1991: 267–85.

Hervé, E. (1995) *Rennes, solidaire et citoyenne: projet municipal 1995/2001*, Rennes: Rennes Municipal Council.

Hill, D., Smith, B.O. and Spinks, J. (1990) *Local Management of Schools*, London: Paul Chapman.

Hirst, P. and Thompson, G. (1999) *Globalisation in Question*, Cambridge: Polity.

Hoeffel, D. (ed.) (1996) *La Décentralisation en France*, Paris: LGDJ.

Holliday, I., Marcou, G. and Vickerman, R. (1991) *The Channel Tunnel*, London: Pinter.

Hood, C. and Jackson, M. (1991) *Administrative Argument*, Aldershot: Dartmouth.

Hooghe, L. (1996) *Cohesion Policy and European Integration: Building Multi-Level Governance*, Oxford: Oxford University Press.

Ille-et-Vilaine departmental council (1995) *L'Aménagement du territoire en Ille-et-Vilaine*.

Im, T. (1993) *L'Administration de l'état face à la décentralisation: l'évolution du système d'action des préfectures*, Institute of Political Studies, Paris: PhD thesis.

Imbert, J. (1992) 'L'administration de l'éducation nationale (historique)', in Institut Français des Sciences Administratives, *L'Administration de l'éducation nationale*, Paris: Economica, 9–25.

Imrie, R. and Thomas, H. (1993) *British Urban Policy and the Urban Development Corporations*, London: Chapman.

INSEE (1999) *Tableau de l'économie française, 1999–2000*, Paris: Documentation Française.

James, P. (1980) *The Reorganization of Secondary Education: A Study of Local Policy Making*, Windsor: NFER.

Jeannot, G. and Peraldi, M. (1991) *L'Envers des métiers: compétences politiques et pratiques professionelles dans les directions départementales de l'équipement*, Paris: Equipment Ministry.

Jeffery, C. (2000) 'Sub-national mobilization and European integration: does it make any difference?', *Journal of Common Market Studies*, 38, 1: 1–23.

Jessop, B. (1998) 'L'essor de la gouvernance et ses risques d'échec: le cas du développement économique', *Revue Internationale des Sciences Sociales*, 155: 31–49.

Jessop, B. (2000) 'Governance failure', in G. Stoker (ed.) *The New Politics of British Local Governance*, Basingstoke: Macmillan, 11–32.

Jobert, B. and Muller, P. (1987) *L'état en action: politiques publiques et corporatisme*, Paris: PUF.

John, P. (1994) 'Central–local relations in the 1980s and 1990s: toward a policy learning approach', *Local Government Studies*, 20, 3: 412–36.

John, P. (1996) 'Centralisation, decentralisation and the European Union: the dynamics of triadic relationships', *Public Administration*, 74: 293–313.

John, P. (1998) 'Urban economic policy networks in Britain and France: a sociometric approach', *Environment and Planning C: Government and Policy*, 16: 307–22.

John, P. (2001) *Local Governance in Europe*, London: Sage.

John, P. and Cole, A. (1998a) 'Urban regimes in Leeds and Lille', *Urban Affairs Review*, 33, 3: 382–404.

John, P. and Cole, A. (1998b) 'A very different political animal', *Municipal Journal*, 13 March: 22–3.

John, P. and Cole, A. (1999) 'Political leadership in the new urban governance: Britain and France compared', *Local Government Studies*, 25, 4: 98–115.

John, P. and Cole, A. (2000) 'When do countries, sectors and localities matter?', *Comparative Political Studies*, 33, 2: 248–68.

John, P., Ward, H., Dowding, K. and Page, E. (2001) 'The UK pork barrel: competitive funding regimes and the political targeting of urban program schemes', forthcoming *Policy and Politics*.

Johnson, H. and Riley, K. (1995) 'The impact of quangos on new government agencies in education', *Parliamentary Affairs*, 48, 2: 284–96.

Jones, G. and Travers, T. (1994) *Attitudes to Local Government in Westminster and Whitehall*, Commission for Local Democracy Report, No. 5 (London: Municipal Journal).

Jordan, G. (1990) 'Sub-governments, policy communities and networks', *Journal of Theoretical Politics*, 2, 3: 319–38.

Jouve, B. (1995) 'Réseaux et communautés politiques', in P. Le Galès and M. Thatcher (eds) *Les Réseaux de politique publique: débats autour des 'policy networks'*, Paris: L'Harmattan, 121–40.

Jouve, B. and Lefèvre, C. (1999) 'De la gouvernance urbaine au gouvernement des villes? Permanence ou recomposition des cadres de l'action publique en Europe', *Revue Française de Science Politique*, 49, 6: 835–53.

Judge, H. (1990) 'Educational reform for Britain in the 1990s', *Revue Française de Civilisation Britannique*, 6, 1: 35–50.

Keating, M. (1993) 'The politics of economic development: political change and local development policies in the US, Britain and France', *Urban Affairs Quarterly*, 28: 73–96.

Keating, M. (1998) *The New Regionalism in Western Europe: Territorial Restructuring and Political Change*, Cheltenham: Edward Elgar.

Keating, M. and Loughlin, J. (1997) (eds) *The Political Economy of Regionalism*, London: Frank Cass.

Kenis, P. and Schneider, V. (1991) 'Policy networks and policy analysis: scrutinizing a new analytical toolbox', in B. Marin and R. Mayntz (eds) *Policy Networks*, Frankfurt: Campus.

Kenyon, T. (1995) 'Conservative education policy: its ideological contradictions', paper presented to the ECPR joint sessions, Bordeaux: 20.

Kesselman, M. (1967) *The Ambiguous Consensus*, New York: Knopf.

Kessler, M.-C. (1986) *Les Grands Corps de l'état*, Paris: Presses de la FNSP.

Kitschelt, H. (1999) *Continuity and Change in Contemporary Capitalism*, Cambridge: Cambridge University Press.

Klijn, E.-H. (1996) 'Analysing and managing policy processes in complex networks', *Administration and Society*, 28: 90–119.

Knapp, A. (1994) *Gaullism since de Gaulle*, Aldershot: Dartmouth.

Knoke, D. and Kuklinsky, J. (1982) *Network Analysis*, Beverley Hills: Sage.

Kohler-Koch, B. and Eising, R. (eds) (1999) *The Transformation of Governance in the European Union*, London: Routledge.

Kooiman, J. (ed.) (1993) *Modern Governance*, London: Sage.

Koza, M. and Thoenig, J.-C. (1995) 'Les écoles françaises et américaines de la théorie des organisations', *Revue Francaise de Gestion*, 1–2: 5–14.

Lacorne, D. (1980) *Les Notables Rouges: la construction municipale de l'union de la gauche*, Paris: Presses de la FNSP.

Lafaye, C. (1996) *La Sociologie des organisations*, Paris: Nathan.

Laffin, M. (1986) *Professionalism and Policy: The Role of the Professions in the Central–Local Government Relationship*, Aldershot: Gower.

Lagorce, Y. (1995) 'Premier chiffrage de l'effet Euralille sur le détail local', *Journal du Textile*: 14–32.

Lagroye, J. (1973) *Société et politique: Jacques Chaban-Delmas à Bordeaux*, Paris: Pédone.

Lagroye, J. and Wright, V. (eds) (1979) *Local Government in Britain and France*, London: Allen and Unwin.

Lansley, S., Goss, S. and Wolmar, C. (1989) *Councils in Conflict*, Basingstoke: Macmillan.

Lash, S. and Urry, J. (1994) *Economies of Signs and Space*, London: Sage.

Lawton, D. (1992) *Education and Politics for the 1990s: Conflict or Consensus?* London: Falmer Press.

Le Bart, C. (1992) *La Rhétorique du maire entrepreneur*, Paris: Pédone.

Le Cacheux, J. and Tourjansky, L. (1993) 'The French decentralisation ten years on: local government finances', *Local Government Studies*, 18, 4: 28–38.

Le Galès, P. (1992). 'New directions in decentralisation and urban policy in France: the search for a post-decentralisation state', *Environment and Planning C: Government and Policy*, 10: 19–36.

Le Galès, P. (1993) *Politique urbaine et développement local*, Paris: L'Harmattan.

Le Galès, P. (1995a) 'Les réseaux d'action publique entre outil passe-partout et théorie de moyenne portée', in P. Le Galès and M. Thatcher (eds) *Les Réseaux de politique publique débats autour des 'policy networks'*, Paris: L'Harmattan, 13–28.

Le Galès, P. (1995b) 'Du gouvernement local à la gouvernance urbaine', *Revue Française de Science Politique*, 45, 1: 57–95.

Le Galès, P. (1996) 'Régulation, gouvernance et territoire', paper presented to the French Political Science Association (AFSP) congress, Aix-en-Provence: 2–30.

Le Galès, P. (1999) 'Le desserrement du verrou de l'état', *Revue Internationale de Politique Comparée*, 6, 3: 627–52.

Le Galès, P. (ed.) (2000) *Cities in Contemporary Europe*, Cambridge: Cambridge University Press.

Le Galès, P. and John, P. (1997) 'Is the grass greener on the other side? What went wrong with French regions, and the implications for England', *Policy and Politics*, 25, 1: 51–60.

Le Galès, P. and Lequesne, C. (eds) (1998) *Regions in Europe*, London: Routledge.

Le Galès, P. and Mawson, J. (1995) 'Contracts versus competitive bidding: rationalizing urban policy programmes in England and France', *Journal of European Public Policy*, 2: 205–41.

Le Galès, P. and Thatcher, M. (eds) (1995) *Les Réseaux de politique publique, débats autour des 'policy networks'*, Paris: L'Harmattan.

Le Métropolitain (1998) 'La Communauté urbaine a trente ans', *Le Métropolitain*, 29, June.

Leach, S., Stewart, J. and Walsh, K. (1994) *The Changing Management of Local Government*, Basingstoke: Macmillan.

Leeds City Council (1991) *Leeds Transport Strategy*, Leeds: Leeds City Council.

Leeds City Council (1994) *Leeds Transport Package 1995/96*, Leeds: Leeds City Council.

Legrand, A. (1994) *Le Système E: l'école de réformes en projets*, Paris: Editions Denoel.

Legrand, A. and Solaux, G. (1992) 'Rénovation pédagogique des lycées: continuité ou rupture?', *L'Orientation Scolaire et Professionnelle*, 21, 2: 135–48.

Legrand, L. (1988) *Les Politiques de l'éducation*, Paris: PUF.

Lempereur, P. (1995) 'La direction régionale de l'équipement du Nord/Pas-de-Calais', *Diagonales*: 1–15.

Lequin, Y.-C. (1995) 'Monsieur le Préfet', *La Pensée*, 302: 67–85.

Levine, M. (1994) 'The transformation of urban politics in France', *Urban Affairs Quarterly*, 29, 3: 383–410.

Lewis, H.D. (1985) *The French Education System*, London: Croom Helm.

Lijphart, A. (1975) 'The comparable cases strategy in comparative research', *Comparative Political Studies*, 8: 158–77.

Lille Academy (1994a) *Rectorat, 1994–95*.

Lille Academy (1994b) *Inspection Académique du Nord, 1994*.

Lille Municipal Council (1993a) *Le Développement économique*, unpublished manuscript: 25.

Lille Municipal Council (1993b) *Service Education-Enseignement: Caisse des Ecoles*, unpublished manuscript: 23.

Lille Urban Community (1995a) *Convention d'application du contrat de plan état/region, 1994/1998*, Lille.

Lille Urban Community (1995b) *La Communauté urbaine de Lille, métropole lilloise internationale*, Lille.

Lille Urban Community (1995c) *Contrat d'agglomération*, Lille.

Lille Urban Community (1995d) *La Métropole en actions*, Lille.

Lille Urban Community (1998) *1968–1998, Lille metropole: la métropole rassemblée*, Paris: Fayard.

Linotte, D. (1990) 'L'administration de l'enseignement en France', *Annuaire Européen d'Administration Publique*, 13: 125–34.

Logan, J. and Mototch, H. (1987) *Urban Fortunes: The Political Economy of Place*, Berkeley: University of California Press.

Loréal, A. and Van Staeyen, J. (1995) 'Lille entre ville industrielle française et métropole européenne diversifiée', *Franse Nederlanden*, 20: 1–10.

Lorrain, D. (1989) *Les Mairies urbaines et leurs personnels*, Paris: Documentation Française.

Lorrain, D. (1991) 'De l'administration républicaine au gouvernement urbain', *Sociologie du Travail*, 4: 461–84.

Lorrain, D. (1993) 'Après la décentralisation: l'action publique flexible', *Sociologie du Travail*, 3, 285–307.

Lorrain, D. and Preteceille, E. (1990) 'Les grandes villes face à l'évolution des politiques publiques', *Annuaire des Collectivités Locales*: 5–22.

Lorrain, D. and Stoker, G. (eds) (1995) *La Privatisation des services urbains en Europe*, Paris: La Découverte.

Loughlin, J. and Keating, M. (eds) (1997) *The Political Economy of Regionalism*, London: Frank Cass.

Loughlin, J. and Mazey, S. (eds) (1995) *The End of the French Unitary State? Ten Years of Regionalization in France*, London: Frank Cass.

Lovering, J. (1995) 'Creating discourses rather than jobs: the crisis in the cities and the transition fantasies of intellectuals and policy-makers', in P. Healey, S. Cameron, S. Davoudi, S. Graham and A. Madani-Pour, *Managing Cities*, Chichester: Wiley.

Lowi, T. (1964) 'American business, public policy, case studies and political theory', *World Politics*, 16, 4: 677–715.

Lowndes, V. (1997) 'Change in public service management: new institutions and new managerial regimes', *Frontières*, 9: 51–82.

Mabileau, A. (1989) 'Les héritiers des notables', *Pouvoirs*, 49: 93–103.

Mabileau, A. (1991) *Le Système local en France*, Paris: Montchrestien.

Mabileau, A. (1995) 'De la monarchie municipale à la française', *Pouvoirs*, 73: 7–17.

Mabileau, A. (1997) 'Les génies invisibles du local: faux-semblants et dynamiques de la décentralisation', *Revue Française de Science Politique*, 47, 3–4: 340–76.

Mabileau, A. et al. (1989) *Local Politics and Participation in Britain and France*, Cambridge: Cambridge University Press.

McCool, D. (1989) 'Subgovernments and the impact of policy fragmentation and accommodation', *Policy Studies Review*, 8, 2: 264–87.

McCool, D. (1990) 'Subgovernments as determinants of political viability', *Political Science Quarterly*, 105, 2: 269–93.

Machin, H. (1976) *The Prefect in the French Administration*, London: Croom Helm.

Magluilo, B. (1980) *Les Chambres de Commerce et de l'Industrie*, Paris: PUF.

Magnusson, W. (1986) 'Bourgeois theories of local government', *Political Studies*, 3, 1: 1–18.

Maillot, J.-L. (1993) 'Une nouvelle donne pour le schéma directeur?', *Les Petites Affiches*, 15 February, 20: 4–7.

Main, B. (1991) 'Quels réseaux dans la ville', *Pour*, 132: 175–8.

Maloney, W., Smith, G. and Stoker, G. (1998) 'Civic engagement, social capital and cities', paper presented at American Political Science Association Annual Conference, Boston.

March, J. and Olsen, J. (1989) *Rediscovering Institutions*, New York: The Free Press.

Marchand, M.-J. (1991) 'Les lycées, les régions: an 111', *Politiques et Management Public*, 9, 1: 47–66.

Marcou, G. (1990) 'Regional development, local intervention and national policies in France: new tendencies', in R. Bennett, *Decentralisation, Local Government and Markets: Towards a Post-Welfare Agenda*, Oxford: Clarendon, 265–81.

Marcou, G. (1992) 'Les collectivités territoriales et l'éducation nationale', *Savoir*, 4, 2: 189–215.

Marcou, G. (1999) 'La gouvernance et la ville', paper presented to the FREVILLE colloquium on Gouvernance locale, Lille, 27 February.

Marcou, G. (2000) 'La loi Chevènement et les communautés d'agglomération', paper presented to the colloquium on Décentralisation et développement durable, University of Reims, 10–11 May: 10.

Marcou, G., Costa, J.-P. and Durand-Prinborgne, C. (eds) (1992) *La Décision dans l'éducation nationale*, Lille: Presses Universitaires de Lille.

Marcou, G., Kistenmarcher, H. and Clev, H.-G. (1994) *L'Aménagement du territoire en France et en Allemagne*, Paris: Documentation Française.

Marcou, G., Vickerman, R. and Luchaire, Y. (eds) (1992) *Le Tunnel sous la Manche: entre états et marchés*, Lille: Presses Universitaires de Lille.

Marin, B. and Mayntz, R. (1991a) 'Studying policy networks', in B. Marin and R. Mayntz (eds) *Policy Networks*, Frankfurt: Campus.

Marin, B. and Mayntz, R. (eds) (1991b) *Policy Networks*, Frankfurt: Campus.

Marks, G. (1993) 'Structural policy and multi-level governance in the EC', in A. Cafruny and G. Rosenthal, *The State of the European Community*, Harlow: Longman, 391–410.

Marsh, D. (1995) 'Explaining Thatcherite policies: beyond unidimensional explanation', *Political Studies*, 43: 595–613.

Marsh, D. (ed.) (1998) *Comparing Policy Networks*, Buckingham: Open University Press.

Marsh, D. and Rhodes, R.A.W. (eds) (1992) *Policy Networks in British Government*, Oxford: Clarendon.

Mason, C. and Witherick, M.E. (1981) 'Growth and change in the Southampton area: an overview', in C. Mason and M.E. Witherick, *Dimensions of Change in a Growth Area*, Aldershot: Gower.

Mauroy, P. et al. (1988) 'Déclaration des maires de Lille, Roubaix, Tourcoing et Villeneuve d'Ascq: réussir le développement equilibré de notre métropole autour de l'arrivée des TGV européens', Lille Urban Community, 18 November.

Mawson, J. (1995) 'The re-emergence of the regional agenda in the English regions: new patterns of urban and regional governance?', *Local Economy*, 19: 300–26.

Mawson, J. and Spencer, K. (1997) 'The government offices for the English regions: towards regional governance?', *Policy and Politics*, 25, 1: 71–84.

Mayntz, R. (1993) 'Governing failures and the problem of governability: Some comments on a theoretical paradigm', in J. Kooiman (ed.) *Modern Governance*, London: Sage, 9–20.

Mazey, S. (1995) 'French regions and the European Union', in J. Loughlin and S. Mazey (eds) *The End of the French Unitary State: Ten Years of Regionalization in France, 1982–1992*, London: Frank Cass.

Mazières, B. (1996) 'Pierre Mauroy dopé par son rêve olympique', *L'Express*, 22 February.

Ménager, B. and Wallon-Leducq, C.-M. (eds) (1993) *Atlas électoral Nord/Pas-de-Calais, 1973– 1992*, Lille: Presses Universitaires de Lille.

Ménager, B., Sirinelli, J.-F. and Vavasseur-Desperriers, J. (eds) (1995) *Cent Ans de socialisme septentrional*, Lille: Université Charles de Gaulle, Lille: 111.

Mény, Y. (ed.) (1990) *Les Politiques décentralisées de l'éducation: analyse de quatre expériences régionales*, GRAL-CNRS report for the French Ministry of the Interior.

Mény, Y. (1992) 'La République des fiefs', *Pouvoirs*, 60: 17–24.

Mény, Y. (1993a) 'Le cumul des mandats ou l'impossible séparation des pouvoirs', *Pouvoirs*, 64: 129–36.

Mény, Y. (ed.) (1993b) *Le Mimétisme et le rejet*, Paris: L'Harmattan.

Mény, Y. and Wright, V. (1987) *Centre–Periphery Relations in Western Europe*, London: Allen and Unwin.

Mills, L. (1994) 'Economic development, the environment and Europe: areas of innovation in UK local government', *Local Government Policy Making*, 20: 3–10.

Mitchell, J.-C. (1996) 'Des sociétés d'économie mixte locales à capitaux publics minoritaires: utopie, évolution ou révolution?', *Revue Française des Finances Publiques*, 55: 117–29.

Molotch, H. (1979) 'The city as a growth machine: towards a political economy of place', *American Journal of Sociology*, 82: 309–30.

Moon, B. (1990) 'Challenging the idea of centralised control: the reform of the French curriculum in a European context', *British Journal of Sociology*, 41, 3: 423–44.

Moreau, J. (1989) 'Les structures supra- et infra-citadines', *Pouvoirs Locaux*, 1: 78–83.

Morgensztern, F. (1991) 'Les réseaux locals d'insertion, cet obscur objet du désir', *Pour*, 132: 109–17.

Morvan, Y. and Marchand, M.-J. (1994) *L'Intervention économique des régions*, Paris: Montchrestien.

Muller, P. (1990a) *Les Politiques publiques*, Paris: PUF.

Muller, P. (1990b) 'Les politiques publiques entre secteurs et territoires', *Politiques et Management Public*, 8, 3: 19–33.

Muller, P. (1992) 'Entre le local et l'Europe: la crise du modèle français des politiques publiques', *Revue Française de Science Politique*, 42: 275–97.

Muller, P. and Sorel, Y. (1998) *L'Analyse des politiques publiques*, Paris: Montchrestien.

National Education Ministry, France (1999) 'Circulaire de rentrée, 1999', *Bulletin Officiel de l'Education Nationale*, 1, 7 January.

Nay, O. (1997) *La Région, une institution: la représentation, le pouvoir et la régle dans l'éspace régional*, Paris: L'Harmattan.

Négrier, E. (1999) 'The changing role of French local government', *West European Politics*, 22, 4: 120–40.

Négrier, E. and Jouve, B. (1998) *Qui Gouvernent les régions d'Europe? Echanges politiques et mobilisations régionales*, Paris: L'Harmattan.

Nemery, J.-C. (2000) 'Aménagement du territoire et décentralisation territoriale', paper presented to the colloquium on *Décentralisation et développement durable*, University of Reims, 10–11 May: 9.

Newman, P. (1994) 'Urban regime theory and comparative urban politics', paper presented to the IFRESI colloquium on *Villes, entreprises et société à l'aube du 21ème siècle*, Lille.

Newman, P. (1995) 'The politics of urban redevelopment in London and Paris', *Planning Practice and Research*, 10: 15–23.

Newton, K. (1976) *Second City Politics*, Oxford: Oxford University Press.

Newton, K. and Karran, T. (1985) *The Politics of Local Expenditure*, London: Macmillan.

Nord/Pas-de-Calais Regional Council (1994a) *Bilan d'exécution du Contrat de plan état/région Nord/Pas-de-Calais, 1989–1993*, Lille.

Nord/Pas-de-Calais Regional Council (1994b) *Contrat de plan état/région, 1994–1998*, Lille.

Nord/Pas-de-Calais Regional Council (1994c) 'Schéma régional des formations: document d'orientation', mimeographed document presented to the Regional Assembly, 16 December.

Nord/Pas-de-Calais Regional Prefecture (1990) '30 mesures pour entreprendre', Lille.

Nord/Pas-de-Calais Regional Prefecture (1994) 'DRIRE: Direction régionale de l'industrie, de la recherche et de l'environnement', Lille.

Nouvion, A.-P. (1992) *L'Institution des Chambres de commerce: pouvoirs et contrepoids*, Paris: LGDJ.

Novarina, G. (1990) 'Communauté de communes, fédérations de régions: quelle coopération locale?', *Pouvoirs Locaux*, 4: 34–41.

Novarina, G. (1994) 'De l'urbain à la ville: les transformations des politiques d'urbanisme dans les grandes agglomérations. L'exemple de Grenoble (1965–1990)', in S. Biarez and J.-Y. Nevers, *Gouvernement local et politiques urbaines*, Grenoble: CERAT, 47–66.

OECD (1996) *Reviews of National Policies for Education: France*, Paris: OECD.

OFSTED (1998) 'Background briefing on OFSTED', http://www.ofsted.gov.uk/indexa.htm

Osborne, D. and Gaebler, T. (1992) *Reinventing Government*, Reading MA: Addison-Wesley.

Padioleau, J.-G. (1982) *L'Etat au concret*, Paris: PUF.

Padioleau, J.-G. (1991) 'L'action publique moderniste', *Politiques et Management Public*, 9, 3: 133–43.

Page, E. (1991) *Localism and Centralism in Europe*, Oxford: Oxford University Press.

Page, E. and Goldsmith, M. (1987) *Central and Local Government Relations*, Beverly Hills: Sage.

Paris Chamber of Commerce (1992) 'Collectivités locales et Chambres de commerce et d'industrie: compétences économiques respectives', Paris.

Paris, D. (1993) *La Mutation inachévé: mutation économique et changement spatial dans le Nord/Pas-de-Calais*, Paris: L'Harmattan.

Paris, D. (ed.) (1997) *Nord/Pas-de-Calais: changement régional et dynamique des territoires*, Lille: ORHA.

Parkinson, M., Bianchini, F., Dawson, J., Evans, R. and Harding, A. (1992) *Urban Change and the Function of Cities in Europe: A Report to the European Commission of the European Communities*, Liverpool: Liverpool John Moores University.

Peck, J. and Tickell, A. (1995) 'Business goes local: dissecting the "business agenda" in Manchester', *International Journal of Urban and Regional Research*, 19, 1: 55–78.

Pecqueur, B. (1989) *Le Projet de développement local*, Paris: Syros.

Pekonen, K. (1991) 'Governance and the problem of representation in public administration', paper presented to the ECPR joint sessions, Essex, 22–28 March: 24.

Pellegrini, E. (1995) 'Schémas directeurs: révisions, changements de visions', *Cahiers de L'IAURIF*, 108: 15–31.

Penven, A. (1998) *Territoires rebelles: intégration et ségrégation dans l'agglomération rennaise*, Paris: Anthropos.

Peterson, P. (1981) *City Limits*, Chicago: University of Chicago Press.

Petit, G. (1990) 'Lille et Leeds: entente cordiale, passée, présente et à venir', *Les Cahiers CNFPT*, 30: 52–6.

Phlipponneau, M. (1977) *Changer la vie, changer la ville*, Rennes: Breiz.

Phlipponeau, M. (1995) *Le Val à Rennes*, Spezet: Nature et Bretagne.

Pierre, J. (ed.) (2000) *Debating Governance*, Oxford: Oxford University Press.

Pierson, P. (2000) 'Increasing returns, path dependence, and the study of politics', *American Political Science Review*, 9, 2: 251–67.

Pivet, Y. (1993) 'Les sociétés d'économie mixte locales', *Droit Administratif*, 20 September: 587–94.

Planque, B. (1991) 'Note sur la notion de réseau d'innovation', *Revue d'Economie Régionale et Urbaine*, 3–4: 295–320.

Pollitt, C., Birchall, J. and Putman, K. (1998) *Decentralising Public Service Management*, Basingstoke: Macmillan.

Pontier, J.-M. (1998) *Les Contrats de plan entre l'état et les régions*, Paris: PUF.

Powell, W.W. and DiMaggio, P.J. (1991) *The New Institutionalism in Organizational Analysis*, Chicago and London: University of Chicago Press.

Pratchett, L. (ed.) (2000) *Renewing Local Democracy? The Modernisation Agenda in British Local Government*, London: Frank Cass.

Priet, F. (1992) 'La décentralisation de l'urbanisme', *Annuaire des Collectivités Territoriales*, Paris: Documentation Française, 87–107.

Prost, A. (1992a) 'La fin des professeurs', *L'Histoire*, 158: 78–82.

Prost, A. (1992b) *Education, société et politiques: une histoire de l'enseignement en France de 1945 à nos jours*, Paris: Seuil.

Przeworski, A. and Teune, H. (1982) *The Logic of Comparative Social Inquiry*, Malabar FL: Krieger Publishing Co.

Quin, C. (1995) 'Le partenariat public–privé: un outil utile de gestion des infrastructures et des transports collectifs', in I. Chatrie and J.-M. Uhaldeborde, *Partenariat public–privé et développement territorial*, Paris: Le Monde editions, 164–79.

Raab, C. (1992) 'Taking networks seriously: education policy in Britain', *European Journal of Political Research*, 21: 69–90.

Raab, C. (1995) 'Education policies and ideas in Britain', paper presented to the ECPR joint sessions, Bordeaux: 14.

Rallings, C. and Thrasher (1997) *Local Elections in Britain*, London: Routledge.

Ranson, S. (1985) 'Contradictions in the government of educational change', *Political Studies*, 33: 56–72.

Ranson, S. (1992) *The Role of Local Government in Education*, Harlow: Longmans.

Ranson, S. (1999) 'The new management and governance of education', in G. Stoker (ed.) *The New Management of British Local Governance*, Basingstoke: Macmillan, 97–111.

Ranson, S. and Tomlinson, J. (eds) (1994) *School Cooperation: New Forms of Local Governance*, Harlow, Longman.

Rao, N. (1990) *Educational Change and Local Government*, York: Joseph Rowntree Foundation.

Regan, D.E. (1977) *Local Government and Education*, London: Allen and Unwin.

Renaudin, M. (1990) *Les Problèmes d'équilibre dans la métropole lilloise*, DESS thesis, Institute of Political Studies, Paris.

Rennes Academy (1994) 'Annuaire, 1994/95'.

Rennes Academy (1996) 'Orientations académiques: douze objectifs pour l'an 2000'.

Rennes Academy (1999) 'Projet d'Academie: contractualisation', Rennes, 26 October.

Rennes Atalante (1994a) 'Spécial 10e anniversaire', *Rennes Atalante Info*: 31.

Rennes Atalante (1994b) *1984, 1994*, Rennes: Rennes Atalante.
Rennes Chamber of Commerce (1990–6) *Rapports d'activité*, Rennes.
Rennes Chamber of Commerce (1993) *Rennes: dossier de ville*, Rennes.
Rennes Chamber of Commerce (1995) *Chiffres-clefs*, 35, Rennes.
Rennes District (1989) 'Définition du projet d'agglomération et relations avec les procédures actuelles', Rennes: Rennes District.
Rennes District (1992) 'La taxe professionnelle à taux unique au District urbain de l'agglomération rennaise', Rennes: Rennes District.
Rennes District (1993) *Projet pour l'agglomération rennaise*, Rennes: Rennes District.
Rennes District (1994a) *Plan d'action économique du district*, Rennes: Rennes District.
Rennes District (1994b) *Schéma directeur*, Rennes: Rennes District.
Rennes District (1995) *Notre espace 2010: exposition du projet de schéma directeur de Rennes District*, Rennes: Rennes District.
Rennes District, Rennes Municipal Council, CODESPAR (1989) *Plan de développement du pays de Rennes, 1989–93: projet de rapport final*, Rennes: Rennes District.
Rennes Municipal Council (1991a) *Les Relations financières entre la ville de Rennes et les associations*.
Rennes Municipal Council (1991b) *Le Projet urbain de Rennes*.
Rennes Municipal Council (1994a) *1994, Rennes en chiffres*.
Rennes Municipal Council (1994b) *Le Projet éducatif*.
Rhodes, R.A.W. (1986) *The National World of Local Government*, London: Unwin Hyman.
Rhodes, R.A.W. (1988) *Beyond Westminster and Whitehall*, London: Unwin Hyman.
Rhodes, R.A.W. (1990) 'Policy networks: a British perspective', *Journal of Theoretical Politics*, 2, 2: 293–317.
Rhodes, R.A.W. (1996) 'The new governance: governing without government', *Political Studies*, 44, 4: 652–67.
Rhodes, R.A.W. (1997) *Understanding Governance: Policy Networks, Governance, Reflexivity and Accountability*, Buckingham: Open University Press.
Rhodes, R.A.W. and Dunleavy, P. (1995) *Prime Minister, Cabinet and Core Executive*, London: Macmillan.
Richardson, J. (ed.) (1982) *Policy Styles in Western Europe*, London: Allen and Unwin.
Richardson, J. (1996) 'Actor-based models of national and EU policy making', in H. Kassim and A. Menon, *The European Union and National Industrial Policy*, London: Routledge, 27–51.
Richardson, J. and Jordan, G. (1979) *Governing Under Pressure*, Oxford: Martin Robertson.
Ritraine, E. (1986) *L'Espirit des lieux*, Paris: CNRS.
Roberts, P. and Whitney, D. (1993) 'The new partnership: inter-agency cooperation and urban policy in Leeds', in R. Imrie and H. Thomas (eds) *British Urban Policy and the Urban Development Corporations*, London: Paul Chapman.
Robinson, P. (1981) *Perspectives on the Sociology of Education*, London: Routledge and Kegan Paul.
Rogers, V. (1998) 'Devolution and economic development in France, *Policy and Politics*, 26, 4: 417–27.
Rolin, F. (1990) 'Risques et chances: la décentralisation et les associations', *Territoires*, October: 23–31.
Rondin, J. (1986) *Le Sacre de notables*, Paris: Fayard.
Rosenbaum, A. (1998) 'Gouvernance et décentralisation. Leçons de l'expérience', *Revue Française d'Administration Publique*, 88: 507–16.
Sabatier, P.A. and Jenkins-Smith, H.C. (1993) *Policy Learning and Change*, Boulder CO: Westview Press.

Sadran, P. (1992) *Le Système administratif français*, Paris: Montchrestien.

Saez, G., Leresche, J.-P., and Bassand, M. (eds) (1997) *Gouvernance métropolitaine et transfrontalière: action publique territoriale*, Paris: L'Harmattan.

Saran, R. (1973) *Policy Making in Secondary Education: A Case Study*, Oxford: Oxford University Press.

Sartori, G. (1991) 'Comparing and miscomparing', *Journal of Theoretical Politics*, 3, 3: 243–57.

Sassen, S. (1994) *Cities in a World Economy*, Thousand Oaks CA: Pine Forge.

Saunders, P. (1980) *Urban Politics: A Sociological Interpretation*, Harmondsworth: Penguin.

Savitch, H. (1988) *Post-Industrial Cities*, Princeton: Princeton University Press.

Sawicki, F. (1993) *La Structuration du parti socialiste: milieux partisans et production d'identités*, University of Paris, 1, PhD thesis.

Sawyer, M. (1993) 'The economy of Leeds in the 1990s', in J. Chartres and K. Honeyman (eds) *Leeds City Business*, Leeds: Leeds University Press,

Schmidt, V. (1990) *Democratising France*, Cambridge: Cambridge University Press.

Schrameck, O. (1992) 'Education et décentralisation: l'équilibre fragile du partenariat', *Droit Administratif*, 20: 85–94.

Schulz, P.Y. (1994) 'De la nature juridique des Chambres de commerce et d'industrie: continuité et évolution', *Revue du Droit Public*, 5: 1481–1505.

Scott, A. (ed.) (1998) *The Limits of Globalization: Cases and Arguments*, London: Routledge.

Scott, J. (1991) *Social Network Analysis*, London: Sage.

SEM Euralille (1994) *L'Histoire d'Euralille*, Lille: Euralille.

Sharpe, L.J. (1978) 'Reforming the grass roots: an alternative analysis', in A.H. Halsey (ed.) *Policy and Politics*, London: Macmillan.

Sharpe, L.J. (ed.) (1993) *The Rise of Meso-government in Europe*, London: Sage.

Simon, J. (1992) 'La décentralisation du système éducatif – six ans après', *Savoir*, 4, 2: 223–37.

Simon, M. (1993) *Un Jour, un train: la saga d'Euralille*, Lille: La Voix du Nord.

Smith, A. (1995) *L'Europe politique au miroir du local; les fonds structurels et les zones rurales en France, en Espagne et au Royaume Uni*, Paris: L'Harmattan.

Smith, A. (1997) 'Studying multi-level governance: examples from French translations of the structural funds', *Public Administration*, 75, 4: 711–29.

Smith, A. (1999) 'Public policy analysis in contemporary France: academic approaches, questions and debates', *Public Administration*, 77, 1: 111–31.

Souchon-Zahn, M.-F. (1991) 'Les nouveaux maires des petites communes: quelques éléments d'évolution (1971–1989)', *Revue Française de Science Politique*, 41, 2: 197–234.

Southampton City and Hampshire County Council (1992) *Southampton Transportation Strategy*, Southampton: Southampton City Council.

Steinmo, S., Thelen, K. and Longstreth, F. (1992) *Structuring Politics: Historical Institutionalism in Comparative Analysis*, Cambridge: Cambridge University Press.

Stevens, J.-F. (1989) *Lille: Eurocité*, Lille: Nord/Pas-de-Calais Regional Prefecture.

Stewart, J. and Stoker, G. (eds) (1989) *The Future of Local Government*, London: Macmillan.

Stewart, M. (1994) 'Between Whitehall and town hall: the realignment of urban regeneration policy in England', *Policy and Politics*, 22: 133–45.

Stoker, G. (1995) 'Intergovernmental relations', *Public Administration*, 73: 101–22.

Stoker, G. (1998a) 'Cinq propositions pour une théorie de la gouvernance', *Revue Internationale des Sciences Sociales*, 155: 19–49.

Stoker, G. (ed.) (1991) *The Politics of Local Government*, London: Macmillan.

Stoker, G. (1997) 'The Economic and Social Research Council local governance programme: an overview', *Frontières*, 9: 5–36.

Stoker, G. (1998b) 'Theory and urban politics', *International Political Science Review*, 19, 2: 119–29.

Stoker, G. (ed.) (2000) *The New Politics of British Local Governance*, Basingstoke: Macmillan.

Stoker, G. and Mossberger, K. (1994) 'Urban regime theory in comparative perspective', *Environment and Planning C: Government and Policy*, 12: 195–212.

Stoker, G. and Rhodes, R.A.W. (eds) (1999) *The New Management of British Local Governance*, Basingstoke: Macmillan.

Stoker, G. and Wilson, D. J. (1991) 'The lost world of British pressure groups', *Public Policy and Administration*, 6, 2: 285–302.

Stoker, G. and Young, S. (1993) *Cities in the 1990s*, London: Longmans.

Stone, C. (1989) *Regime Politics, Governing Atlanta, 1946–1988*, Lawrence: University Press of Kansas.

Sueur, G. (1971) *Lille, Roubaix-Tourcoing: métropole en miettes*, Paris: Stock.

Téqueneau, P. (1991) 'Les territoires après la décentralisation: le dessous des cartes', *Hérodote*, 62, 3: 44–63.

Teune, H. (1990) 'Comparing countries: lessons learned', in E. Oyen (ed.) *Comparative Methodology: Theory and Practice in International Social Research*, London: Sage.

Thatcher, M. (1995) 'Les Réseaux de politique publique: bilan d'un sceptique' in P. Le Galès and M. Thatcher (eds) *Les Réseaux de politique publique: débats autour des 'policy networks'*, Paris: L'Harmattan, 229–48.

Thélot, C. (1994) 'L'évaluation du système éducatif français', *Revue Française de Pédagogie*, 107: 5–28.

Thoenig, J.-C. (1973) *L'Ere des technocrates*, Paris: Editions de l'Organisation.

Thoenig, J.-C. (1996) 'Les grands corps', *Pouvoirs*, 79: 107–20.

Thoenig, J.-C. (2000) 'Quelle legitimité pour les nouvelles structures territoriales?', paper presented to the colloquium on *Décentralisation et Développement Durable*, University of Reims, 10–11 May: 10.

Thomas, I. (1994) 'The relationship between local authorities and TECs in metropolitan areas', *Local Government Studies*, 20: 257–305.

Thomas, O. (1999) 'Eléments d'analyse du gouvernement des villes françaises: entre gouvernance opérationnelle et gestion stratégique oligarchique', *Revue d'Economie Régionale et Urbaine*, 4: 691–708.

Tilly, C. (1984) 'Les origines du répertoire de l'action collective contemporaine en France et en Grande-Bretagne', *Xxe Siècle*, 4: 89–108.

TMO Ouest (1994) *Rennes District: poles d'appui*, Rennes: TMO.

Toulemonde, B. (1993) 'Education nationale: peut faire mieux encore', *Savoir*, 5, 4: 575–93.

Toulemonde, B. (1994) *Petit Histoire d'un grand ministère*, Paris: Seuil.

Toulemonde, B. (1999) 'L'enseignement et la cohésion sociale', in S. Decreton (ed.) *Service Public et lien social*, Paris: L'Harmattan, 79–99.

Tourjansky-Cabart, L. (1996) *Le Développement économique local*, Paris: PUF.

Travers, T. (1985) *The Politics of Local Government Finance*, London: Allen and Unwin.

Travers, T. (1989) 'The threat to the autonomy of local government', in C. Crouch and D. Marquand (eds) *The New Centralism*, Oxford: Basil Blackwell.

Tudesq, A.-J. (1983) 'De la monarchie à la république: le maire, petit ou grand notable?', *Pouvoirs*, 24: 5–18.

Tulard, J., Drago, R. and Cluzel, J. (1995) 'Le cumul des mandats législatifs', *Revue des Sciences Morales et Politiques*, 2: 133–58.

Useem, M. (1984) *The Inner Circle: Large Corporations and the Rise of Business Political Activity in the UK*, New York: St Martin.

van Deth, J. (ed.) (1998) *Comparative Politics: The Problem of Equivalence*, London: Routledge.

van Waarden, F. (1992) 'Dimensions and types of policy network', *European Journal of Political Research*, 21, 2: 29–52.

Vasconcellos, M. (1993) *Le Système éducatif*, Paris: La Découverte.

Verdier, D. (1995) 'The politics of public aid to private industry', *Comparative Political Studies*, 28: 3–42.

Vervaeke, M. and Lefebvre, B. (1996) 'Local housing market and the social reorganization of space: the case of the Lille conurbanation', *International Journal of Urban and Regional Research*, 20, 2: 255–69.

Vevers, S. (1998) 'French devolution', *Guardian Education*, 12 May.

Viaud, F. and Peridy, N. (1992) *Fonctions métropolitaines de Rennes et de Nantes*, Rennes: Chamber of Commerce.

Vion, A. (1996) 'Retour sur le terrain: la préparation des élections municipales de 1995 par l'équipe d'Edmond Hervé, maire de Rennes', *Sociétés Contemporaines*, 24: 95–122.

Vion, A. and Le Galès, P. (1999) 'Politique culturelle et gouvernance urbaine: l'exemple de Rennes', *Politiques et Management Public*, 16, 1: 1–34.

Viveret, P. (1977) *Pour une nouvelle culture politique*, Paris: Seuil.

Viveret, P. and Rosanvallon, P. (1976) *L'Age de l'autogestion*, Paris: Seuil.

Walsh, S. (1995) *Public Services and Market Mechanisms*, Basingstoke: Macmillan.

Wasserman, S. and Faust, K. (1994) *Social Network Analysis*, Cambridge: Cambridge University Press.

Wasserman, S. and Galaskiewicz, J. (1994) *Advances in Social Network Analysis*, London: Sage.

Waters, S. (1998) 'Chambers of commerce and local development in France: problems and constraints', *Environment and Planning C: Government and Policy*, 16: 605–23.

Webman, J. (1980) 'Centralization and implementation. Urban renewal in Great Britain and France', *Comparative Politics*: 127–48.

Werrebrouck, J.-C. (1994) 'Les chemins d'une efficacité nouvelle du système éducatif français', *Savoir*, 6, 4: 739–69.

Whitehead, A. (1995) 'Rational actors and irrational structures', paper presented to PSA Conference, York, April.

Wilson, P. (1995) 'Embracing locality in economic development', *Urban Studies*, 32: 645–58.

Worms, J-P. (1966) 'Le préfet et ses notables', *Sociologie de Travail*, 3: 249–75.

Wozniak, F. (1995) 'Euralille: succès ou échec?', *La Gazette*, 8–9 December.

Wright, M. (1988) 'Policy community, policy network and comparative industrial policies', *Political Studies*, 36: 593–612.

Wright, V. (ed.) (1994) *Privatisation in Western Europe: Pressures, Problems and Paradoxes*, London: Pinter.

Wright, V. (1995) 'Reshaping the state: the implications for public administration', *West European Politics*, 18, 2: 102–33.

Wright, V. (1996) 'Public administration in post-war Britain and France: fundamental similarities masking essential differences', unpublished manuscript.

Wright, V. and Cassese, S. (eds) (1996) *La Recomposition de l'état en Europe*, Paris: La Découverte.

Wunder, B. (1995) 'Le modèle napoléonien d'administration: aperçu comparatif', in B. Wunder (ed.) *Les Influences du modèle napoléonien d'administration sur l'organisation administrative des autres pays*, Brussels: International Institute of Administrative Sciences.

Young, K. and Rao, N. (1997) *Local Government since 1945*, Oxford: Blackwell.

Young, S. (1996) *Promoting Participation and Community-Based Partnerships in the Context of Local Agenda 21: A Report for Practitioners*, Manchester: University of Manchester Press.

Zay, D. (1994) 'Etablissements et partenariats', *Savoir* 6, 1: 33–44.

Index

Lightning Source UK Ltd.
Milton Keynes UK
UKOW041227121012

200499UK00001B/40/A